Dear Jean
and Fred —

D0501582

Christmas.

auc.

A Cape Cod Journal

ERMA J. FISK

A Cape Cod Journal

Foreword by Bob Hale

Illustrations by Louise Russell

W · W · NORTON & COMPANY · NEW YORK · LONDON

Printed in the United States of America.

The text of this book is composed in Garamond #3,
with display type set in Cochin Italic. Composition and
manufacturing by The Maple-Vail Book Manufacturing Group.

First Edition

Library of Congress Cataloging-in-Publication Data
Fisk, Erma J.
A Cape Cod journal / Erma J. Fisk.
p.   cm.
1. Fisk, Erma J.   2. Cape Cod (Mass.)—Biography.   3. Bird
watchers—Massachusetts—Cape Cod—Biography.   4. Authors,
American—20th century—Biography.   5. Life change events in old
age—Massachusetts—Cape Cod.   I. Title.
CT275.F5643A3   1990
974.4'92043'092—dc20
[B]   89–72147

ISBN 0-393-02858-5

W. W. Norton & Company, Inc. 500 Fifth Avenue, New York, N. Y. 10110
W. W. Norton & Company Ltd., 10 Coptic Street, London WC1A 1PU

1 2 3 4 5 6 7 8 9 0

Foreword

Rarely in a journal does a writer so truthfully depict herself as Jonnie (Erma) Fisk does in *Peacocks of Baboquivari, Parrots' Wood,* and now *Cape Cod Journal.* She never hides her purposes: to raise our consciousness about the environment and our awareness of the birds she knew so well while she explores herself through the process of writing. Because truthfulness and frankness, about herself and others, were both her most endearing and her prickliest attributes, what we get when we read her books is unadulterated Jonnie, red-cheeked, hair always slightly windblown even indoors, bright eyes glistening behind round glasses, eyes that, when she trusted you, let you look deep inside. And it was inside where the vulnerable woman lived, the one who never truly got over losing her Brad, never stopped missing him not even when she was the laughing focus of a festive gathering.

I wasn't sure I liked her the first time we met, she was so positive in her pronouncements. It didn't take long for me to learn that she was resolute because she was right, well almost always right. When she wasn't, her laugh was louder than anyone else's. But it wasn't her rightness that won me, it was rumination. You never knew when something remembered from long ago, or some thought she'd been pondering, would come out, a thought that inevitably gave new depth to or cast new light on the moment.

What she does in her books is poke around in the closets of her life, muttering, remembering, reflecting, sorting, throwing some things away, treasuring others anew. As she talks to herself she shares the richness of a long life, and years of aloneness, the thrill of adventure, a spirit that kept her putting one foot ahead of the other knowing that a door would open up ahead. She makes us think about our own closets, filled with trivia and treasures.

One of my treasures is a tiny slip of paper on which is the message," Jonnie Fisk called—she'll be at home tomorrow a.m. 255-0719." Before I had a chance to return the call, her editor telephoned to say Jonnie had slept away from us early that morning. For her another door had opened.

She was mystified by the impact she had on so many people. She couldn't understand, she said, why she who had more questions than answers could help others. Her questions, and her wonderfully abrupt, meditative, comical, or heart-breaking ways of asking them is the answer. She wasn't afraid to put into words what most of us fret about or fear, or miss or want, or regret, or feel proudest of. In that she was as remarkable as she insisted each of us is.

In *Cape Cod Journal* as in the earlier books, she is truly present, sputtering, baking bread, burning toast, watching ducks on the pond, rescuing injured eagles. She believed we live on in the memories of those who knew us. She made sure in her journals none of us would ever forget Jonnie Fisk, and through them she continues urging us to "put one foot ahead of the other" and so move toward open doors and our own new adventures.

Bob Hale

A Cape Cod Journal

1982

I have washed the kitchen floor after Labor Day guests. Their towels and sheets are hung out to dry in the sun and wind of a blue and gold day. That's Step A. Vacuuming, book replacing, assessment of left over food will come in their turns. Just because I hesitantly type "writer" as my occupation on the forms that medical, insurance, government offices demand doesn't mean I sit in front of a word processor from eight until twelve every morning. (I don't even *have* a word processor.) "Retired" is probably the technical designation for my status, but it is wholly inaccurate for the life I lead. Like everyone else I have to sweep up broken potato chips, spilled peanuts, deal with the jars of jams and mayonnaise that have been left on counters, wonder when I am going to eat those dibs and dabs helpful hands stashed in the fridge after meals. Not all of them are suitable for soup. (I have a kettle of that left over too.)

If I type "housewife" on those forms it sounds as if I do nothing but the above. If I type "writer" it sounds as if I spend my time writing—or at least looking out my window thinking about writing. If I type "retired" I envision an elderly woman doing needlepoint, half-heartedly listening to television. What I am is a restless woman hating her age. A gimpy hip, my years, the flood of eager grad students entering the field I've worked in the last twenty years, most with the ability to do things I no longer can do. So I savagely attack my kitchen floor, cheerfully launder after visitors who come to keep me alive with tales of what they are doing; of their successes, fantasies, love affairs, families, failures—the life I have left behind me.

At the moment, my energy vented, I sit contentedly at the big table by my south window that serves for meals, sewing machine binges, mail and manuscript sorting—the repository for whatever is important at the moment. Instead of dealing with an untidy collection of bills and mail—and those tax forms soon due, last time I forgot them—I am looking out at a hillside that slopes through trees and brush to one of the salt ponds that give Cape Cod its special character. These ponds connect, each one differently, to the many-coved, wide reaches of Pleasant Bay with its sand bars exposed or lurking at low tide. The Bay, in turn, is confined by a long barrier beach that separates its quieter waters from the surf and storms and currents of the great Atlantic Ocean shining in the distance. When the wind is right I can hear combers pounding on the easternmost shore of our continent. Sun glitters from pine needles and the dark green leaves of oaks. Flowers—I'd better water them—are bright under the bird feeders, where birds dart in and out. I don't want to be in a rain forest, a desert, a busy foreign city on the friendly advice of the brochures that clog

my mailbox. I am entirely happy (at the moment anyway) to
be right here.

In May I had sent a manuscript to the New York publishing
house of W. W. Norton at the suggestion of a friend, one of
their authors. This was my first book, unplanned but solid in
my hands, a journal of a winter spent on a remote Arizona
mountain ranch. I wrote it the following summer, when a
group of ornithologists were using my home as a base; in and
out with sleeping sacks and sandy feet; disorderly, charming,
merry about the dinner table in candlelight, rushing off at
dawn leaving dishes on the counters, wet clothes on the floor.
Never bringing enough groceries, scattering socks and record
sheets, involving me in their studies and love affairs. In between
their descents the pages of my foetus manuscript had shaped,
grown, absorbing all my energies. I finished them the next
winter at a biological station that didn't offer enough work to
keep me busy, living again those extraordinary months of
mountain solitude, nostalgic. The experience had thrashed about
inside me as compulsively as a human embryo, I had to put it
into words.

Until my pages might be accepted by a publisher I had felt
I had to hide them, so I told no one of my absorption. How
many people write books, scribbling on pads in the subway,
at work, in bed at midnight? How many of these get published? My friends would have thought me daft. My daughter
said later she had realized from my letters that I was preoccu-
pied and had to hope it wasn't a love affair—at my age!—
although if that was what I needed she would accept it. She
had been relieved to learn it was only a book.

Originally I had sent the manuscript to a publisher friend

of a friend. He had returned it to me for revision, with caustic remarks about its untidiness. Unfortunately, while I was happily cleaning up and revising its pages, he died. His firm was small, it closed. Again at the suggestion of a friend I sent the improved and tidier version to a second publisher. It was accepted by return mail with a contract and a fulsome three-page letter. Some weeks later they were returned to me "ready for the printer," but to my angry dismay the shape and words had been altered unacceptably. After months of heated wrangling I broke our contract. Nervously. I didn't know if you could break a contract, but I judge they had had too many of my outraged letters written at midnight.

I restored the original text, again happily revising, typing, again nostalgic. When this was finished I considered taking the bundle to the town dump, but a local author and friend, Bob Finch, kindly read it, made suggestions, recommended it to his editor at W. W. Norton.

Any neophyte author knows the anxiety of the weeks of waiting that ensue when you mail off a manuscript. You haunt your post office, you pace your living room, the nearby roads. At dusk you wish hopefully, as in childhood, on the first star pricking the pale sky. You wake in the night, blaspheming, helpless. You gnaw your fingernails and wonder if you will live long enough to receive a response. You go about your business and social life, but anxiety churns just under the surface. The ringing of the telephone panics you.

By August my self-control was shredded. Screwing up my courage (I didn't want to annoy them) I wrote to this uncommunicative firm. Silence. Timidly, after a period I telephoned. A pleasant-voiced woman told me that my letter had been read, but not yet the manuscript. However, she thought she knew the shelf on which it lay and would call it to her editor's attention. They had enjoyed my letter, she comforted me.

Not too long after—well, it was a matter of weeks, I had no fingernails left, autumn rain and fog had blotted out any stars, and in discouragement I was aware that these wishes would be no more productive than my childish ones that had begged for a pony—W. W. Norton called. A male voice said the manuscript had been read, enjoyed, and would shortly be presented in their editorial meeting. (I expect this had a more formal name but I was too excited to note it.) Then again, silence. Encouraged, I had gone happily about my business.

My business at the moment is on Nantucket, where I am making a study of the birds that migrate this time of year, making a landfall on this small island before they head south over the Atlantic. I am living alone on Edith Andrew's inland farm (if any place on Nantucket can be called inland) to compare the species I take in my mist nets with those she and her students are getting at a coastal station, improbably named Mothball Pines. I need my fingernails to extract small, indignant birds from the fine nylon of the nets. Grown impatient of waiting and waiting, again I screw up courage and on a rainy day address the following to the Senior Editor title of that telephone voice:

You suggested I call you Tuesdays, when your firm has its editorial meetings, to learn of the decision on my manuscript, so I have called. You said you personally had liked it and your readers had also liked it. It had been given to a second set of readers, I should call you another Tuesday. Two Tuesdays later you reported the second set had also liked the manuscript, you were now giving it to a third set. Does this go on until some one *doesn't* like it? And then what happens?

I'm not being impertinent, this seems a reasonable curiosity. I will continue to call, though I may say you are hard to lay a finger on. Your switchboard operator regrets—you are in, she says, but evidently not in your office. Yes, I know that if you try you can't reach me either. I am down in the lower field taking warblers and catbirds from my bird nets. As I told you, I am on a study of migrating birds that move south along the Atlantic coast on their way to winter quarters, a project I work on every autumn. Nantucket is a haven for inexperienced young birds that drift or become blown from the mainland. They feed in the sparse vegetation for a day or two, move on. What I catch in my nets is a daily, exciting gamble. What you find in your mail must be much the same.

This letter won't do any good. It may even be stupid of me to send, but at least is soothes my frustration!

Three weeks after mailing that letter I am dead asleep at 3 P.M. catching up on too many dawns out at the nets, too many late nights writing reports. The telephone rings. In a fog which changes quickly from physical to emotional I recognize the voice of W. W. Norton.

"I am happy to tell you," it says, and the voice is warm, "that your manuscript, 'The Peacocks of Baboquivari,' was accepted at our editorial meeting this morning. I am sorry you were not present to hear what was said about it."

I gurgle.

"We like it," the voice continues, "for the following reasons. . . ." There are five, but I am not confused, too hysterical to note any except that they had liked the way I wrote, my choice of words, my . . . I stopped registering. He will be returning the manuscript, the voice says, with a few suggestions, a contract, and various instructions.

When he hangs up I shake my head, trying to clear it. I have vivid dreams but this cannot be one, the telephone is clicking at me, I had set the receiver down askew. I run to the bathroom to bathe my face in cold water. Is this really me in the mirror? I look for an aura. No—just a huge smile. I need a haircut.

October 1982

There was frost in the night. Mist eddies across the pond, still colorless in early morning light; drifting, obscuring boats still out in their owners' hope of one more sail before winter closes in. The marsh grass is flaxen.

Late in the morning I get a call from W. W. Norton. A pleasant editorial assistant, young from her voice, says she is sending me a questionnaire, could I please return it promptly? She makes me feel right in the pipeline. I hesitate to tell her my promised contract has not yet arrived. (This doesn't trouble me, the Norton voices generate trust.) And, she bids, would I please enclose my life history? In fifty words. I laugh all day at that impossibility.

November 1982

The Day Before Thanksgiving

At last! The manuscript of my "Peacocks" came back from Norton this morning. I clutched the package to my bosom, beamed at our postmistress, raced home. After all this time! How was I to know that Norton was working on it! Not a word in more than a month, not a voice on the telephone.

"Back to you," writes that unknown man. "You will find my comments on the yellow flags. You need not accept my suggestions, but if you do, please indicate that you have made the changes."

What a Happy Thanksgiving for me! Never mind that pie I was going to construct for my family from a Hallowe'en pumpkin, this is far more important. Let them eat ice cream.

In the package also is a book by John Hay, an author whom I know here on the Cape and am in awe of. I am to consider its typeface. I admire the jacket, the binding color. Arizona Blue for mine, I'll ask. Gluttonously on my pages I read the yellow squares of paper—"flags"—affixed to margins and slowly learn to decipher what is scrawled on them. They are supposed to be critical, constructive, but I take a complimentary couple off to put under my pillow. If I knew what this editor looked like I would dream of him. Maybe I can invent him from his voice. I have no suggestions on type and the jacket as he asks— that's *his* job! I'll ask, though, please may my illustrator's name be in bold print on the title page, not hidden away? I am having such fun with her.

The Day After Thanksgiving

The couple I housed for a wedding down the lane have departed. Thanksgiving Dinner was at my son's home so I don't have to struggle with a left over turkey. I have sharpened my pencils, filled the bird feeders so chickadees will keep me company, pulled out my country music records. You don't have to think while listening to country music, just tap your feet.

My desk corner is cozy. Outside the low, wide window are still a few late flowers in the garden, scarlet berries chipmunks haven't yet nibbled on the low cotoneaster edging the terrace. Squirrels chitter in frustration from branches where the transparent hanging globe of a big bird feeder patterned with reflections defeats them. Beyond the garden a bird sips and splashes in a shallow pool I dug, edged with rocks and plants. Afternoons the sun pours in this wide west window glowing gold, then flame, rose, saffron, lemon behind the trees. Leaves still linger on the oaks, their coppers harmonizing with a thick carpet of pine needles below. At night stars, the swelling moon, fog catch in branches. There is always something to watch, that feeds my spirit as sentences form under my fingers (or I pay bills).

Inside, my phonograph, serviceable for twenty years, and the desk with its lamp, telephone, pencil mug are at my elbow; the clock and date calendar I forget to watch. Special small photographs of Arizona, New York, Maine are pinned to my wall. My back is firmly turned to the untidy correspondence box that lives on a wooden file cabinet, an extension of this desk. Out of sight, out of mind.

Mostly I live in this corner, but when there are papers to spread out, shuffle (stupidly mix up), I work at my dining table. The wall of windows there looks down a hillside to the pond, where, in season, sailboats dance in the breeze, a lone fisherman passes in winter.

Today is gray, late November, wind pulling across the sky, scattering oak leaves, whistling in corners. The baseboard heat under this typewriter shelf toasts my toes. Everything I want is within reach.

I am starting work on the familiar pages of "The Peacocks of Baboquivari." The editorial notes on attention-calling "flags" are instructive even if I can't yet decipher his writing, even when I don't understand his reasoning, why he doesn't like a paragraph or sequence. Men think differently. His accompanying letter says I may overrule his suggestions, but maybe if he explained them I wouldn't have to. I will summon up my courage, call the 800 number he gave me, ask questions. I write off in a corner, it's often lonely (in spite of chickadees and ballads). I'd like to talk with him. His Yesses and Nos, in answer to doubts I had scribbled in margins, his Please

Clarify's, and Who Is Talking Here are companionable. I look for the philosophical parts his letter speaks of but haven't yet recognized a one. What fun this all is!

December 1982

I study again the editorial flags on my manuscript pages. Norton suggests—that man never demands flat out, he is enormously diplomatic—that I omit a chapter, replacing it with "I went away for a few weeks." Shades of that colorless university press I broke my contract with! Any reader is going to ask Why? Where? What? All those misadventures—being caught in a desert flood miles from anywhere, landing frightened, unnecessarily, in a hospital; choking on the acacia pollen of California. . . . I feel these sequences add background, so I'm not just a crone climbing about a desert mountain muttering about cats. But he is an editor, I must respect him. Probably

I am too close to the trees to see the forest. Maybe I can slide some of what I want into the letter to my brother; he gave me my station wagon, he deserves a few pages. I will write that tactful man, trying to be tactful myself, ask if he will look at my tightened, revised pages with a more tolerant eye.

I worry about this book being dull, in the middle. I worry about this book altogether, but it is Norton's money.

Today comes a letter telling me of the death of Justin, the closest of Brad's friends. A group of us summered in neighboring cottages on Lake Erie. In those days the telephone was a black box on the wall of our kitchens, ringing a different number for each. Ours was 13, Justin's 11. If one wife was absent the other would answer, take the message, report which husband was bringing guests for dinner, which usually meant a frantic dash for tunafish or ham to the only small market nearby. Every evening we gathered, the men stretched in deck chairs, drink in hand, putting a curtain between them and the work of their day while we women came and went, preparing dinner, bringing it to a big wooden table under the trees. Justin knew me at my untidiest—painting the kitchen of our rented ramshackle cottage, brooming spider webs from the porches, hollering at the children when I was angry. He drank a lot and after a few bourbons liked to tease me, a glint in his eyes; arrange a caress, knowing Brad would excuse him. He was amused by my primness, enjoyed watching me at my domestic pursuits. His own wife was social, political, not a housewife.

Hearing last summer that he was terminally ill the happiness of those summers flooded over me, I flew to his city to see

24

him. A pretty young nurse—of course, he would accept no other—led me to the living room. He waved her away, rose slowly from his chair by himself, put his arms around me.

"I want to kiss you while I'm sober," he said, "so you won't be thinking it's the bourbon." Holding hands we caught up on the years we had been apart.

"You've never remarried?" he asked finally, studying me. "In all this time? You're still a handsome woman."

I shook my head. "What did I have to offer a man after Brad?"

"You've never even had an affair?" He shook his head in disbelief, then laughed. "I guess I should know—I tried to catch you often enough." He had, too, even before Patty died. "You always fobbed me off. Why?" He was really curious. He let go my hand, poured himself a drink from the bottle that was killing him, offered me one. I shook my head again.

"I don't know. I was like a tree hollowed by lightning, burned dry. After a while, slowly, my roots came up from underground, but at a distance—a new tree, in new soil. It needed a lot of attention to thrive. I worked with men much of the time, but that's all they were—colleagues. I didn't think of them in other ways. You had given up on me?" I teased him. "I no longer felt attractive."

"Celibate for twenty-five years," he mused. "Incredible. I should never have taken that position in France."

When the nurse returned, beckoned me, he rose from his chair, again with difficulty, bent and kissed me full on the mouth with a feeling time had distilled to a crystal purity.

"I love you, my dear. I've always loved you, just the way you are. I'm glad I never broke through your defences." He kissed me again, gently. "Don't cry. I'm not in pain. And now

I can see you, have you here in this room. I will have you for company. Thank you for coming." His eyes followed me through the doorway.

Holding the letter that tells of his death I hear his warm voice, hear his warm laugh, feel his mouth warm on mine; see all of us laughing so long ago, so carelessly happy together on the shore of that lake.

Late this afternoon—it was six o'clock—W. W. Norton called me. What was that voice doing in its office at that hour, two days before Christmas? It interrupted me in the midst of concocting a Christmas eggnog; my counter, apron, and hands were sticky. Brad annually used a recipe that was a family tradition, but I couldn't find it so I had been inventing. I'm not much at mathematics, I kept forgetting how many cups and quarts of eggs, milk, cream, three liquors I'd added and stirred, so I had been testing along the way. A fair bit of testing when the telephone surprised me. I might as well admit I get the quivers anyway when Norton calls. I'm like a fifteen-year-old schoolgirl in her first love affair, it's delightful. Can you have a love affair with a publishing house? Everything is so new, so exciting! There is always a note of amusement in their voices, as if they also were having a good time. They really like my manuscript, it's extraordinary.

It was a year ago—I was making a Christmas eggnog then too—that the academic publisher had sent back "Peacocks" to me "ready for the press." A covering letter had bade me light a fire, pour a sherry against New England weather, sit in a comfortable chair, and read their edited version as if it was a book I had never seen before. I surely hadn't! It was unrecognizable, torn to bits, castrated. At the end of twenty pages I was shaking with a rage that burned until Norton poured honey on its still smoldering ashes. No wonder I love that Voice. I lift my eggnog ladle to it and its three sets of readers. Full.

My annual struggle with Christmas is upon me. I try to ignore the crystals from past years that slide between my fingers. In my childhood, in our children's childhood, cookies and a glass of liquid refreshment for Santa Claus would be set by the fireplace where stockings hung limp, to be found Christmas morning sagging with lumps and treasures. The cookie plate and glass would be empty. Who had been last to bed, woke up first? Kittens tangled themselves in ribbons and tissue, standing on unsteady legs to bat, and break glass ornaments. At midnight service the bells on our daughter's full red pettiskirts jingled as we walked the quiet aisles of Trinity Church. One year a son was so engrossed in a book that he would unwrap nothing else, and behaved impossibly about going to the annual festive dinner at his grandparents'. Do you spank a child on *Christmas*? There was the Christmas morning that his older brother sharpened his appetite by shoveling our Buffalo driveway—a hard job—so we could maneuver the car out. Just as he finished, we were bundled into coats, our arms full of packages, the snow, heavy on our slate roof, came roaring down, obliterating his efforts. In my own childhood one year the Tree was erected in a bedroom where my mother lay ill. My father lifted me in his arms to touch the angel that blessed us from its tip. The Tooth Fairy, my brother irreverently called her as, grumbling, he carried pails of water for fear candles wavering on the tips of evergreen should set a fire. No colorful strings of electric lights in those days.

I won't send cards this Christmas I promise myself, even as

I wander through stores picking up a box of them here, another there—ribbons of love to connect me to Oregon, Arizona, Texas, Louisiana, Florida, Maine: to England, Mexico, Africa. I won't decorate my rooms, I say firmly, it takes too much time, makes a mess; then I go out to cut greens to arrange traditionally on my mantelpiece. I won't have a tree. At the last moment I rush to town, buy left over ornaments, hang them on a small evergreen by my door, wade through thorn bushes to hang more on a sapling at the bottom of my drive. Their globes of silver, scarlet, gold, emerald will catch falling snow, tinkle in the wind. At the end of a dock someone has nailed a tree, scraggly and inconspicuous (unless a gull perches on its tip) in the daytime, a melody of dancing lights reflected in the waters of our pond at night, wishing all his neighbors Good Cheer. You *can't* ignore Christmas.

When I was small the parishioners of the Unitarian church across from our home would gather next door in a group of lantern-lit forms I watched from my mother's open window. Wrapped in mufflers and warm caps, the women with muffs, they went about the snowy neighborhood singing carols to widows and shut-ins. When I grew old enough to join them my voice piped among theirs. Yellow light streamed from windows, doors would open, I could glimpse a Christmas tree inside. I was proud to be included, begged to carry our lantern.

As young marrieds, no babes yet to keep us at home, Brad and I spent Christmas with friends in a rural New England village where carol singing also was a custom. Round-eyed, rosy-cheeked Beth stoked us amply in their farm kitchen. The herbs she raised and dried hung on one wall, rugs she braided for sale were always in process in the corner beyond the fireplace. Steve was an orchardist and musician, like his father before him. Our last year there he had been left along the roadside by a hit-and-run driver. Now he was living with his strong body on crutches, an empty trouser leg strapped under his belt. He couldn't accompany the carolers about the village green and snowy streets, he said at supper, but Beth would drive him to old Mr. Perkins' pharmacy, where her husband annually warmed the singers with mugs of hot chocolate, and from there up the hill to the hospital.

He refused our sympathy. "I've sung there since I was six years old," he said flatly, "with my father. And I'll sing this year even if from a wheelchair. Dad's ghost will push me if you won't."

"Don't feel sorry for me," he admonished, seeing the tears in my eyes. "If I let this get me down I'll never do anything. I have Beth, that's more than many men have. I have my music. I'm writing a book about my father and his music, under contract." He grinned at Brad. "Maybe you will come up this spring and prune my apple trees?"

We all laughed, the tension broken. Brad was not the brawny type. In our partnership I carried the wood, hauled the water, he did the thinking—a very satisfactory arrangement. Only without him I have had to learn to think, which hasn't come easily.

We had set out that night, lanterns in hand, a light snow falling. Bundled as in my childhood I was warmed also by memories of the years when I had skipped excitedly between my parents, my nose buried in a small ermine muff a grandmother had provided; by memories of our daughter later, equally proud, her nose buried in the same muff, skipping between Brad and me.

Villagers joined us along the Green. The Historical Society had set candles at every window of the Captain's House, but these days no coachman in uniform greeted the revelers, no aproned maids in frilly caps offered platters of cookies and chocolates. A Boston man wanted to buy this property and turn it into an old-fashioned inn. Over our hot chocolate at Perkins Pharmacy there was discussion about this. The Historical Society couldn't afford to maintain it, but the villagers wanted to meet the man first, be sure of his honesty before they voted.

There was much talk of Steve, too. Obviously he was liked, everyone was proud of his courage and stubbornness. They were trying to persuade him to run for mayor because—for a while at least—he commanded such respect that they might get a few bylaws changed, and purchase a new location for the town dump.

"Wasn't it Emerson who wrote, 'On the debris of despair you build your character?' " the man next to me had asked as we straggled up the hill to the hospital. "Steve's family goes far back in this town—every one of them a stalwart."

We unbundled our snowy coats in the waiting room. Learning that Steve would be singing, the doctors had come in a group to honor him, and of course the staff was present, and a considerable number of summer people come up for the holiday, on their way to midnight service at the church. They lined the corridors as we moved between the wards, singing along with us, it was festive. And in each ward as Steve, on crutches, greeted those who were bedridden, not able to get about as he could, not having a Beth beside them, his head lifted, his rich voice poured out, silencing every sound. It was like cream, like velvet, lit with love and prayer. He ended our ragged carols with "O Sanctissima," singing this again in the lecture hall, where the mobile patients were gathered. If there is a God, I had thought, then He must hear this, He will put his hand on Christmas Eve on this plain, sturdy man and heal him. Steve was a plain man, almost nondescript, with mousy hair and a snub nose. Only the quick, mischievous look in his eyes, his sensitive mouth, told of the intelligence and wit inside. His voice hung in the silent hall.

Next day the word went around town like wildfire. Whether at the hospital or at midnight church service, where again Steve sang, again maintaining his thirty-year record, someone hearing him had asked about the empty trouser leg, the recent accident; had arranged with the hospital for him to be fitted, when he had sufficiently healed, with an artificial leg that would function almost as well as the lost one, that would make him whole again. A Christmas gift. How wonderful people are, what money can do! The gift was anonymous, no one had learned the donor.

Steve had been dazed when he was told. He had held tightly to Beth, tears in his eyes. Then he had brushed them aside, looked at Brad.

"I won't need you for pruning after all, my boy," he said. "I'll be able to do it myself. But you can come up anyway," he had finished with a huge grin.

January 1983

When Lisa, who is illustrating my manuscript, came for supper tonight, I asked her to sketch a snowman, forgetting that snow isn't as abundant in the sea air of Cape Cod as when we lived in Buffalo, so she might lack experience. She drew one, then three while I cooked, set our table, lit candles. They all were grumpy. Did you ever see a *grumpy* snowman? She apologized, saying she was feeling grumpy herself after a long day teaching art to teen-agers. Feeling better after our meal she produced a cheerful one. She hadn't known, though, that a proper snowman must have arms for hugging, or for holding brooms. As she lives in a fishing village, he wears a fisherman's hat with an owl's feather tucked in it!

Our daughter once worked for Scribner's. Following the progress of "Peacock's" manuscript she advises me *Don't let your publisher print anything* without you seeing it first, so I am writing my editor's assistant—I don't know the protocol of his office, to whom I should write—asking if I may see what they plan to use in their catalogue? I am nervous about what I sent them. I get carried away, say things I never should, my ego goes up and down like a squirrel. At the moment it is in a January slump and I am certain I made a fool of myself. I'll sleep better if I learn what my lines were edited to, if they are accurate. I tell her that I'll have more of Lisa's sketches to send by the end of the week. I can get good copies made now, a friendly realtor by the post office bought a new copying machine for himself at Christmas and is willing to barter for cookies. He can eat only so many at lunch, though.

My postage bill is horrific.

I'm in a bad humor. I'm having trouble getting permissions for quotes I've used in "Peacocks" and we can't go to press without them. They aren't easy to obtain, I find. The person at the other end forgets, uses my request as a bookmark or to light a fire, I guess. They are authors, they must know how necessary a permission is. Sometimes it is a publisher I must write, they may refer me to the owner of the copyright. It takes *time*. I am charged $25 a quote, and two copies of the book when it is published. My bad humor is alleviated as I wonder (smirking) about the reaction of the press I broke my contract with when they receive *their* copies, restored to my original form, with Norton's imprint on them. They gave me the permission I wanted promptly, I concede them that.

The one being the most difficult is, of course, the one most important to me. If its owner doesn't respond to my last urgent telephone call I'll have to ask my editor, with all of Norton's prestige behind him, to work on her. He has a persuasive voice. The other I lack is for a verse from the anthology of a private school. I'll use it anyway and if they sue remind them that

Brad put two students through their expensive curriculum. It took years. We used to visit, the headmaster loved us. Brad, anyway. I just ate his wife's good lunches and minded my manners.

I am writing Norton please advise. There's a lot more to being an author than you'd think.

I have further problems. My editor is of a different generation so his use of words, his meanings are different from mine. Today he is critical of my saying, at the end of a chapter "Sweet dreams." What is wrong? I ask him indignantly. Isn't that what your mother said when she tucked you into bed at night? Didn't you have a mother?

His copy editor is still younger, a feminist. She corrects my "ladies" to "females"—not even the common ground of "women"! I write her a cross note on how to me "female" is a biological term not politely applicable to my friends. An animal. Also—I laugh so hard over this that promptly I forgive her—she claims the paragraphs from Ecclesiastes that I copied word for word from my St. James version of the Bible are incorrect. And adds, to my complete mystification, that I must get permission to quote these! A visiting granddaughter solves the mystery. She must know the words of the Psalmist only from a rock song in the sixties, granddaughter explains; she had no churchly upbringing. Becoming an author is shaking me out of my ruts. It's rather fun shaking Norton out of a few of theirs, too.

I am snowed in. Glistening beauty piles high on my window sills, knee-high drifts block my front door. The garage door is frozen shut. By opening the sliders of my living room and tossing shovels of snow outward I have managed a path of sorts to my bird feeders, to the gratitude of a variety of parishioners. A flicker prospects for corn, a myrtle warbler clings to the suet feeder. At the bottom of the hill Canada geese and duck tip up along the marsh edge where a stream keeps a small opening in the ice. A Great Blue heron has joined them, his stance impassive on his thin legs.

I am supposed to be a Bird Lady but I'm not any longer, I live on my past. Over years I have handled some 50,000 birds—I don't know how many—which qualified me. Before that I birded in the urban parks of many countries under the identification of "wife accompanying official husband," but in those early days there were few foreign bird guides. It wasn't until 1959 that, with a naturalist, an adventurer really, willing to take a few trustworthy characters like me with him, I began exploring Central America and the Caribbean, going to areas then primitive now become fashionable, known to all bird tourists. (Probably because we talked so much about them.) Tours in those days were in their infancy, we were setting the pace. Then I was as enthusiastic as birders are now to leap out of bed before light, drive many miles to see what species might—and as often might not—be perched high in a forest tree, be foraging on the verge of a stream, be flying inside a volcano. With the years I have become lazy, rarely going now to see what a hurricane, an unexpected storm may have brought to shelter on Cape Cod, to pause before setting out on its return journey. I let birds come to me—a goshawk hunting from a neighbor's tree, a sharpshin chasing a dove into my big window; a descent of juncos, as this morning, scratching in the snow with cardinals as they did on my Arizona mountain. There they competed with a flock of feral peacocks for the food

I scattered. Blue snowbirds was my mother's name for juncos. In the shadow of snowdrifts today their backs do perhaps look blue. (But not very. My mother wouldn't have had binoculars.) In Paris a merle (that's a blackbird with a clear, fluting song) used to ornament the lawn of a fine old residence to which I walked my man to work. In an unpeopled park in Spain ducks would cluster about my feet, tug at my shoelaces, begging crumbs from my lunch. A similar group of panhandlers followed me through an open door on a Massachusetts refuge once, to share a privy with me. On an Adirondack lake one summer a Canada goose had lost part of her upper bill, perhaps defending her nest from a raccoon, and was starving. I mounded corn in the sand at the water's edge, where she could slide her lower mandible under, and so feed. At first her mate, distrusting me, swam at a discreet distance back and forth, calling in distress lest I hurt her. After a week when I came out of my cabin in the early mornings, no one else around, both would skim across the water to my feet, follow me tamely about on the grass like dogs.

One fall on that lake I often paddled my small canoe to a hidden cove to watch an osprey work on the construction of what, next season, became its nest. If I stayed half hidden in the reeds in summer, remained immobile, the birds accepted me. The male would fly with a fish to his whistling mate, supervise as she tore it into bite-sized pieces for their two young. There was a rocky slope on the far side of their cove where I skinny-dipped, lay sunning until I was dry, or energetic enough to resume my clothing. Unexpectedly rounding the point in a boat one day, two men caught me.

"Just looking around," they called as they passed. "Got more than we expected."

On the Florida Keys, to the delight of tourists at marinas,

under special license I banded Brown pelicans. Tourists would gather to watch me lure—and with luck catch—an ungainly bird by its bill, inspect it for injuries, cut away fishline that might be entangling it, fasten a numbered band on its leg, and let it go. Their joy was even greater the day a Great White heron stole behind me as I was giving my educational talk and sneaked from between my sneakers the mullet I used for bait. Mullet, when I first started banding pelican, were considered trash fish, I was given them free. Two years later I had to pay $2.00 for one, I was not pleased to have it stolen.

All this, reasonably, qualified me as a Bird Lady, but the expeditions of long ago are blurred in memory, along with names of the foreign species I so excitedly listed, still have in notebooks packed away, to be thrown out by my heirs with the stacked boxes of photographs I took. It is easier now to sit, as today, watching a lone, unseasonable robin hunting berries on snow-laden bushes, hunting crumbs jays may have missed.

Mending, watching the activity outside, the geese tipping up, my mind drifts through those years when I counted Least tern colonies in borrow pits and on commercial roofs in Florida; when I waited in a Trinidad rain forest for a trogon to return to its hole in a termite nest; watched a lek of manakins snap their wings on a courting ground while an unseen bellbird clanged its metallic note from the same nearby tree, year after year. In Quebec woods ruby-throated hummingbirds might fly to the red bandana hanging from my pocket or, more satisfactorily to us both, discover the vial of sugar syrup I held in my hand. Brad built and set out for me in a marsh behind our camp, tree swallow boxes at a safe distance from where moose gathered, hooves flattening a large yard on the muddy verge. Where are those boxes now? The fox kits that played games on our small beach, the bears that shared raspberry patches with me, the moose—are they still there?

My past is pleasant to wander in on a snowy day, often picturesque, but it is gone, I tell myself firmly, gathering up my sewing. What matters now is today, and what I am going to do tomorrow.

I crumble crackers and a slice of bread, break a piece of crust from yesterday's pie to toss out in the hope that the lone robin may find them.

February 1983

The sun is frost-bitten today, the sky and pond both pewter. A circle of gulls flutter in the wind like scraps of paper, but winter holds no fears for me. This weekend I'm setting out with a group of zealous researchers from Manomet Bird Observatory (plus my long-time mentor and friend Chan Robbins of the U.S. Fish & Wildlife Service) for Belize. We will study birds that nest in our northeast woods and winter in tropical rain forests. Belize is a Connecicut-sized country lying between Mexico and Guatemala. When first I went there its name was British Honduras.

I say this weekend, but it's hard to schedule a trip when you deal with a small, suspicious foreign government; arrangements don't necessarily go smoothly. We have local connections so there shouldn't be the problems of the year when I flew with the two men of National Audubon's Research Department on their first survey of wading birds around the Gulf of Mexico. The military in Belize wouldn't, couldn't believe we were flying their coast just to look at *birds!* Our small plane was searched each day, the gun we carried for emergency landing cost us a fortune in bribes. Officials were convinced we were running arms or drugs across the Guatemalan border, and certainly we must be spying. On our last afternoon we flew too far south, lured by the cays and bird colonies of the magnificent, blue, islanded Bay of Honduras and were late returning for the curfew we had been given. We could hear the orders and alarms they were broadcasting for us and about us, but our radio malfunctioned, we couldn't reply. As at last we taxied back onto the field, two military planes armed to the teeth (or wings) were taking off to shoot us down. It was mighty scary.

This time we will be living more safely on Dora Weyer's plantation, Parrots' Wood, with no problems but rain, flat tires, overcrowded vehicles, more rain. There will be parrots and martins, white egrets riding the air above her pond, not the herring gulls that float over mine.

March 1983

I am back from Belize. Out my window the marsh is still edged with ice floes and mallard ducks. A skim of ice swirled by the tide is slick on the pond. Gulls ornament this, huddled in a circle. The chipmunk that lives under my terrace wall appeared this morning to welcome me home, assessed the season, then went back to sleep for a few weeks more. Maybe I will do the same. Aaaaaaaaaah, it's wonderful to be where the temperature doesn't rocket up to 105°, my sneakers can dry.

As I am replacing the shorts, quinine pills, books on tropical birds with the heavy sweaters, books on Western birds, banding equipment, and needs for unknown Arizona territory where I am to make a survey for the Arizona Nature Conservancy, UPS delivers a package to my door.

Galley proofs "to be gone over carefully for mistakes, typos, misspellings and *returned as soon as possible.*"

Nobody warned me of this! Indignantly I dial Norton's 800 number, which, as usual, is busy. When I do reach my editor he is friendly but unsympathetic. Printing must be scheduled well ahead of time, these proofs can't wait until I may have an empty evening in Arizona, doubtless far distant from telephone or post office. It will be an easy task, he soothes me, it won't take long.

Not take long! Four midnights later and I still haven't finished! His copy editor—I could wring her neck—has changed all the commas which let my sentences run on pell-mell the way I like them, to colons. Irritably I change every darned one of them back. Tedious. Words, phrases, spellings of my generation trouble her. She has replaced them with the equivalents of *her* generation. I change them back. I've never used printers' graphics so I have to hope someone in those offices can translate the squiggles I make in the margins.

Editor calls to make sure I will finish before I leave—a mistake on his part. My complaints singe his wire. I admit, grudgingly, that his girl has caught some egregious errors, for which I thank her, but I can work on these galley sheets only at night, when I am tired. Probably I am making as many more mistakes as I am correcting. Mellowing, I tell him he has permitted me three sentences he had asked to have deleted. I appreciate this, I say, and hope I have been equally generous. We argue about putting my photograph on the book jacket. No, I say. *No. NO!*

I'm not usually difficult, particularly with men, but I have only a week to shift, both scientifically and sartorially, from tropical rain forest to the Arizona desert where I am headed. I haven't time to be polite or diplomatic if I am to reinstate all those commas. I tell him I've been to my doctor to get two botflies excised from inacessible regions of my back, if that will differentiate me from his other lady authors. I'd hoped to encounter a jaguar, botflies were a comedown.

I am making another bird survey for the Arizona Nature Conservancy on the eighty-one-square-mile Muleshoe Ranch east of Tucson. Like the two former ranches, it will be far from friends and supplies, I will be on my own. Perhaps it is the being alone that creates the sense of adventure I seem to thrive on. In a way it's like figure skating, like controlling a spirited horse. The success, the grace depends only upon you. The sun is brighter, the stars more brilliant, the fragrance of grasses and rain, of animal droppings are sharper. No one tells you what you see—or miss seeing. You paint a new world around yourself, cope with its problems.

I am late leaving Tucson. I gave a program at the university, as usual talked too long. The students had really good questions, on land uses and water tables. Now drizzle mists the windshield of the Wagoneer I have been loaned. Don't try to drive north from Willcox if it rains, the Conservancy men warn as they wave me off. In Willcox, once a famous cattle center, now just a dusty town except when spring rains flood off the mountains, I stop to buy food, soap, toilet paper. I'll stock up properly after I've seen my quarters. I bought gas, the men had insisted on that.

It is starting to rain lightly. A purple cloud hangs over the mountains north where I am headed but heck, the ranch is only 30 miles and the road doesn't climb, I was told, just twists through the foothills. Off I jounce in my borrowed vehicle. It takes *two and a half hours* to drive those 30 miles! How was I to know it had sluiced rain up there all morning?

The paved road quickly becomes gravel, then mud, then deeper mud. Nervously I cross the washes, The jeep rides high but skids alarming toward ditches on either side. A rancher, going the other way, passes me.

"Be sure you are in four-wheel drive," he calls from his window. "There is real trouble ahead of you."

Another—the only other—vehicle flags me down with a second warning, then sees I am minus my gas cap—my borrowed gas cap. The driver gets out and stuffs the hole with a rag; judges my inexperience and looks anxious. As he should: I am coming under that purple cloud; the desert darkens, the foothills hem me in. At the other Conservancy ranches, also without traffic, far from paved roads, I had been on solid rock and knew where I was going, which here I don't. Turnoffs worry me. No signs identify them.

I made it finally, in the dark. At a shallow, wide river the road ends, my lights show a gate on the far side. I navigate the water, drive a steep hill to the ranch house. My pride is enormous. I sit in my vehicle loosening my muscles, beam at scenery I can't see, realize I forgot to buy peanut butter. Carrying my gear through an ancient iron gate—these buildings had been a hospital in the Civil War—an unadvertised Shepherd pup knocks me off balance. I spill everything in the dark.

I find my quarters—a big cold room with the electric light that had been advertised. This is a single bulb, hanging midroom, wan, not meant for reading. The full bathroom would be a luxury if it functioned better, if there were hot water. I scrub the counter and the shelves of an adjacent closet, unpack my clothes.

This morning they are soaked. It rained hard in the night, the roof leaks. There is no hot plate (also advertised). I must use the kitchen in another building. The hungry pup welcomes me, is pleased to help. Wide windows frame a magnificent valley. The river curves away among sycamores, horses are feeding under them. Steep cliffs, slopes tier up to distant ranges. Sixty square miles, no one living on them but me. All sparkling with snow.

Today two men from Arizona Fish and Game Service drive in. They are checking on mountain lions, not on me, I am a surprise to them. No, I say regretfully, I haven't seen any lions, just barn cats that rove up from the stables. Damn, damn, must I always make bird surveys where there are cats? I haven't seen the mail box I'd been told about either. They laugh—it is 14 miles down the road. I think I've been through this before.

The telephone in my quarters rings out but not in, I learn when I call the Conservancy office. The nice ladies there are worrying that I am alone with rattlesnakes and bulls, burros and cattle; a recent storm had washed out fences, am I all right? Yes, I reassure them, except for a huge bull with one of my nets hanging from his horns that stands in my best bird area glowering alarmingly at my red jacket. The Shepherd pup guards me, barking and barking. It barked at me for a while, too, but I am getting it under control, letting it into my room at night out of the rain and cold. Love works wonders. Or is it just food, and a warm place to sleep—typical female wiles? The manager who was also to guard me (if not share my room, attempt to put his muddy feet on my bed) is four hours over the mountain helping his wife have their first baby.

Birdwatchers have been trying to call me, the women continue, to find out about the Gray hawks I am keeping my eye on. Gray hawks in the United States are mostly in Texas. If the birders come up will the hawks be here, can they see them? How do I know? Birders don't want to travel my road unless they have to. I don't blame them.

I will have visitors, I am comforted. Soon. People will come to bathe in the hot springs that seep everywhere through the grass, keeping my sneakers always wet. The water seeps into catch basins, sending clouds of steam up into the clear morning air. Very pretty. But bathers won't come when snow is on the ground, ice tinkleds on the bushes, that bull roams.

I use my one-way telephone to call Norton's 800 number, make sure I have no unfulfilled obligations; ask my editor if his treasurer scutinizes his telephone bills, will inquire about charges from Arizona. He laughs. London, Paris, Japan—to a big-time publisher the Arizona desert is just a suburb.

April 1983

Making my morning rounds early this spring day I take a couple of hummingbirds out of my nets—not easy when my fingers are clumsy with cold at 6 A.M. Hummers are delicate, their tiny claws clutch the mesh. Females are brown and look alike. The breasts of the males sparkle scarlet, gold, azure, emerald, their colors identifying their species. I hold the tiny creatures in my hands to warm them, or tuck them inside my sweaters. (This may be the Sun Belt but I live in sweaters.) I place a drop of syrup on their bills and send them off with a blessing, in Spanish, they have flown north from Mexico.

After breakfast I go up the creek, jumping over shallow rivulets, watching for animal tracks. I go out of my way to a pond where an endangered fish lives and is guarded by a fence to see if the Great Blue heron that eats small fish, whether or not endangered and fenced, may have been stalking about. I go further, to see if the thrasher chicks have fledged from their messy grass nest in a cholla. They stand on prickly cactus branches I don't dare put a hand near, curious about me, hoping I have brought them breakfast. I am repaid for wet feet by seeing a Zone-tailed hawk that looks and flies so much like a Turkey vulture I have surely to see the bars on its tail. It soars over the jagged red cliffs, hunting. What can raptors find to eat on those bare rocks? For a further bonus from the cottonwood comes a thin, high scream. When I turn a Gray hawk flies off a nest. One of my tasks is to document these hawks. I am now seeing them every day, but they are not yet incubating. So far the most exciting, unexpected bird I have recorded on my sheets has been a Common grackle, an overabundant species in my Cape Cod yard. That's the glamorous ornithological life I lead!

Still Arizona

Wanting to hear Easter music I go outside for the holiday. In the flesh pots of Tucson I have dinner with two real, professional authors. I had met them on previous trips but now my book is in press they admit me to a different level, to the brotherhood. They grant that Norton's reputation is impeccable but after a second martini they warn me very seriously to be on my guard, to be sure how the fine print on my contract reads—all publishers are devious. When I tell them how protective my editor is, guiding me as if I were a six year old, holding my hand, they become even more concerned and hastily pour another drink. For me too, that's more than I'm used to.

My contract. I don't dare tell them that while that man at Norton keeps assuring me me it is on his desk, ready to mail, it hasn't yet emerged from his over-papered precincts. Is he bamboozling me? Are publishers any worse than stockbrokers or plumbers? How am I to know if he is real, can be trusted? All Norton is so far is disembodied voices, scrawls on yellow flags. How come I have such faith?

On my return route, at a desert party the guest of honor expounds on his enthusiasm for scorpions. Delighted by my immediate interest.

"Come" he says, picking up an infrared flashlight, a long-handled pair of tweezers, "I'll show you. The road will be alive with them in the dark." Within a few yards he tweezes enough of these creatures that I have painfully learned to avoid, shaking out my sneakers each morning, to fill a jar. We stand, talking under the stars. No one raises an eyebrow when we return with our catch but our hostess, a bit miffed that I, an unknown, had removed the lion of her party. And perhaps the friends I am visiting, who give me a quizzical hopeful smile. They would like to see me settled in marriage.

I am home! I hope never to go away again! If I had a husband I would beg him to leash me to a chair. (He'd prefer the stove.) If I had a husband I wouldn't have gone to Arizona. I'd beg him to take my sneakers, my sleeping bag and sweaters, jeans and tee-shirts to the Salvation Army, my travel agent's address out of the file, to censor my mail. Why do I get myself into these ventures? Twenty years from now who will read my reports, who indeed will ever have heard of me?

I survey my comfortable, shabby, orderly living room. A fire is waiting to be lit, seven lamps are each bright enough to read by. My son doesn't know I'm back but maybe he and his wife will share their dinner. I ignore the carton of mail they have left on a counter. Though—should I look? Might there be a communication from Norton? No. Norton doesn't use stamps, they telephone. I ignore the red light on my answering machine. Tomorrow will be soon enough to learn any obligations. Day after tomorrow. . . . I light the fire, pour a glass of sherry.

The tide moves in and out. On my early morning walks it creeps through the marsh grass along our lane. Crabs move in the shallows, schools of small fish flicker beneath the surface. Sometimes a clammer works with his rake, uncommunicative, his back turned toward me. My presence is immaterial to all this, I am not a participant.

150 years ago my hillside was farmland. A mill dammed a small river, now just a stream meandering with no force through a cranberry bog into a reed-grown pond becoming another bog with the slow processes of nature. This carries fresh water into our salt pond, keeping open in winter's ice a small space where

Canada geese and ducks gather, occasionally a green heron. Native Americans camped by this small river, there is a midden hidden under the pines on my hill. Sheep grazed where bare hills are now grown to oak and pine, lady slipper, wildflowers. Back through its human history, long before that, when the glaciers had pushed and halted, leaving their graveled moraines, the tides had gone in and out. I watch boats swing with the current, in summer when I swim I can feel its slow tug.

At a bend in the lane, this morning, I can see my son moving about his kitchen. We are both early risers, he to drive 25 miles to teach his college classes, me because I walk before breakfast. My relationship with my children is not necessarily day-to-day sociability, chitchat. It is a submerged bond, flowing deeper, that can be counted on in times of stress; of joy or despair.

I find my children and grandchildren are peripatetic in my life. We are farflung, our interests different. Although we share basic attitudes, values shift over the generations, as words over our years have shifted meanings. Is it better to live closely, to be secure, to know that if you reach out a hand you can count on one another, or should you keep on expanding your perceptions, hoping these will take you beyond ossifying viewpoints; to trust the depth of your bonds?

I lift a hand in greeting to this man by his window, grown older than his father when he died. Over the years he has taught many of the people who have entered my life here—a carpenter, lads who clear my drive when I am locked in by snow and ice, a women helping me select a sweater, another taking blood pressures in our pharmacy. He must be a fine teacher, sensitive; warm smiles light their faces when they learn I am his mother.

If I am out before he has come to fetch his daily *Boston Globe* I pull it sometimes from its green box holder, scan its headlines, sometimes amuse myself by reading my horoscope. Today this bids me attend carefully to my finances, heed an emotional hunch, be kind to a stranger who may influence my future.

My granddaughter Sarah is a professional photographer. When she wrote she was going to New York for the Christmas holidays, please, I had petitioned her, would you go to W. W. Norton and photograph my editor and his office for me? My curiosity is enormous. Take him for me from every angle—the shape of his nose, his haircut, his hands, his smile. Take his assistant too, we talk often, she is friendly. Look to see if she has pretty legs and tell me if he is the kind who notices legs, if he notices yours. I want to know *anything* about him, all I have is a voice. Come here at New Year's. We will read in front of the fire, make hot chocolate, you can shovel the snow that Santa's reindeer knock out of the clouds as they leave my roof.

Today, three months later, her photographs arrive. I could cry. I had expected Norton to be like the old-fashioned Boston publishing houses I have been in—a waiting room with panelled walls, old prints, flowers and books on low tables, the receptionist discreetly off in a corner. Norton looked no more glamorous than my insurance company—small cubicles, corridors crowded with equipment, the inmates hurrying by, telephones ringing, she says. My image of an editor with a Fifth Avenue address had been of a mature man, formally attired, behind an orderly desk, secretaries jumping to attention. The photographs of this man, whom I really know only from a handful of scrawls on yellow post-its, bears no relation to the one I've fantasized from a warm voice over the telephone. I don't want him to have arms and legs, a necktie, receding hair! He is just an ordinary fellow who eats, must balance a checkbook or a love affair, who probably loses socks and wallets, can be cranky. He looks like my gynecologist, says my friend Betsy, coming in, finding me studying the photographs spread on my table. I am embarrassed to think of the letters I have written to that dour Scottish visage. How could I have? Unsmiling. Well, it had been brassy of me to send Sarah in, why should he smile for us?

When Betsy leaves I reach for the telephone, dial his number, by unusual luck find him at his desk.

"I need to hear your voice," I demand. "Your photographs have arrived, wrapped in birchbark for reasons known only to Sarah. A few months late but I expect you haven't changed. Do you suppose if I line them up on my desk each time we talk I will get used to you?"

He laughs. We are always laughing when we talk. He had had copies in his mail too. "Which one do you like best?" he asks.

"The one that's out of focus" I reply promptly. "And the one of your assistant. What an unholy mess your office is— books on the chairs, on the floor, papers piled everywhere, slurping all over your desk! No wonder you never find the notes your telephone operator puts there saying 'Please call Mrs. Fisk.' I am indignant to have my preconceptions so wrong."

From his voice I had thought I knew this man, discerning intelligence, generosity, humor, but each person is like a shuttered house. We may peer in windows, rap at the door, but only rarely are we admitted, and then only so far. Only a few times in life do we stay, welcome and loved: drink coffee or wine, eat dinner, sleep with the owner, scramble eggs for breakfast. There are too many closed doors, too many halls where only children may run. Mostly we stand outside, noting how the shifts of light, of sun and shadow, alter our perspective. Curious, frustrated.

Could our friendship have grown, I wonder, if instead of concentrating on the timbre of his voice, his pauses, I had been in his office distracted by his haircut, his ears, the style of his necktie, his telephone constantly interrupting us? No matter how well we think we know our friends we see only the small slice they permit us.

May 1983

Today I am to be at the Audubon Sanctuary again, where I work two and three times a week, sometimes four as school classes, natural history groups come to my table. What do I do there? I'm not sure. Their calendar lists me as a bird banding demonstrator. I put a small bird into a small child's hand, carefully, so she can feel its delicate bones, study it, release it to fly to Mexico, to Venezuela. The adults watch the child's face, the look of wonder, of delight, the dream that flies off on those fragile wings. I hold a bird to a man's ear to let him hear the rapidity of its heart beat—400 or more times a minute to his 72. That's why, I tell him, birds must keep stoking their energy, why they are feeding and singing before dawn, which makes him grumble and cover his head with a pillow; why, if he goes away in winter he must have someone keep his bird feeders filled. We can last a few days without our calories, a bird can't. I show an older woman a bird's broodpatch, the blood vessels distended as her own had been when she was pregnant. I watch all their faces, a reward to me for the time I spend at this. It's hard to know what you do when it is yourself. I try to change attitudes, to interest people in wildlife. It belongs equally in this world with us.

It's a warm morning and I am eating breakfast on my terrace peacefully, not a care in the world. A few days ago I turned housewifely, cleaning, scrubbing the open shelves that separate my living room from the kitchen, washing and realigning the glasses on them. We lived a formal life in Washington, a lot of glasses survived for cocktails, highballs, wine, sherry, champagne, liqueurs, rarely used now. Some of these were my father's, an aunt's. They provide a screen, catching sun or lamp or candle light, stirring memories.

A breeze stirs the pines. Idly I watch clouds, diaphanous, golden in the sun, drifting from branches. Lovely. The breeze dies, whispers again, more clouds drift, settle. I come alert. I lift my arm from my chair, see where it has been lying in golden dust. The gold is on my arm too, on the table beside me, on the railroad ties edging the terrace. It shimmers on my coffee, on the surface of my bird pool. Pine pollen!

I had forgotten, absorbed in housewifely energy, this annual fertilization rite that each June, if I leave my windows open, gilds furniture, books, mirrors; drifts in golden piles about the feet of the piano, in every corner. If I dust my cloth turns golden. I will have to wash each surface, my screens next week. I have just *finished* washing those screens, setting them in place for summer! I run fingers through my hair, they come out sticky.

By night my bare feet—it is hot—have left trails about the pine floors. The cover to this typewriter has gold in its folds. Unless it rains we are in for a golden week as pine blossoms continue to ripen. Look on the bright side, I bid myself, at least I'm not expecting guests.

June 1983

By the far side of my river terns nest where each winter storms scour out a crescent of sand and pebbles, leaving a sparse growth of Ammophila breviata regulata (that's beach grass). It is a small colony, flown up from South America to make shallow scrapes just above the tide line, raising a handful of incredibly camouflaged chicks despite the hazards of fox and skunks, high tide and blazing sun. John Hay, who studies their colonies on the Cape, has written, "they live on a tightrope of survival." They rise to attack any intruder in a cloud of white wings beating the air, of ebony heads and coral bills, their cries "a ragged shred of ocean music tossed aloft," as Thoreau heard them. Henry Beston living alone on a lonely ocean beach may have been describing them when he wrote, "the lovely sight of the group instantly turned into a constellation of birds . . . spiralling flight, the momentary tilts of the white bellies, the alternate shows of the clustered, grayish backs. . . . In a world older and more complete than ours they move gifted with extensions of the senses we have lost, or never attained, living by voices we shall never hear."

I am always quoting Beston's small book *Outermost House*, written 60 years ago, when the great beaches of the Atlantic coast were empty. There are still a few empty pockets left here and there, like my crescent. The birds don't mind my drifting up in a canoe. They dive about me, catching small bait fish to carry to their mates, or to feed to small chicks that run, tumbling over pebbles, to beg from them. When I land to count nests or eggs and young, to band the chicks, they come above me in a screaming swarm, dive-bombing, scraping the protective hat I must wear with long pointed bills. The moment I retire they settle back on their nests, preen, resume fishing, leaving only one or two to escort me, still scolding vigorously, still swooping at me. To observe their behavior I must lie flat at a distance in the grass. A guard keeps an eye on me, flying over in threat, crying, but as long as I am prostrate I am in no real danger. I spend many hours marveling at the elegance of their flights against summer skies, their arrow-like dives, their incredible selection of only their own begging chicks to feed. I do this instead of attending meetings, going to parties. It vexes my friends but feeds my soul.

August 16, 1983

Day of arrival of *The Peacocks of Baboquivari*. Erma J. Fisk, author; W. W. Norton, publisher. $14.95. ISBN 0 393-017583, whatever that is. I should write this paragraph in capital letters.

I tore open the wrapping at the post office counter, our postmistress as excited and curious as I, so many times she has handled that sturdy manuscript box, a relic from the publisher I broke my contract with. It had a sticker on it insuring it for $400. Imagine! Would I be worth that much to W. W. Norton, Jean? I asked her. We leafed through the pristine pages, discovering which illustrations of Lisa's had been selected—I had been incommunicado in Arizona during that process. We lifted the jacket to admire the binding color—

Arizona blue, as I had asked—and found my initials in gold there, which left me speechless. Sitting in my car outside I hunted up additions I had written to see if I had slid them in so skilfully Norton would never know. Yes, they were there.

I couldn't wait to take this gaudy jewel to Lisa, to hear her whoop and holler (in her reserved New England manner). We crooned over our firstborn—I had never written a book before, she had never illustrated one. When I look at a book I see print, typos, words, what the book *says*. I found two typos right away, didn't dare hunt for more. Lisa showed me other dimensions—how the designer had used space, given variety to our pages.

Some authors might celebrate with champagne and a party. I pulled out the vacuum cleaner and furniture polish, long overdue. A Norton author mustn't live in a dusty home. I must remember that I am, in the words of the Kirkus review, "a remarkable woman" and live up to this. Should I buy a new pair of jeans that won't—yet—have a hole in the knees? I'd rather be dear than remarkable but I guess I'm the wrong shape. I won't fight the reviews.

It's a good thing Norton printed so many promotional cards for me to distribute. Nantucket has called and wants 50 more. How big is Nantucket? Boston is asking for more. I brought out the photographs of my editor a granddaughter took for me last winter and set them about my desk to share my joy. I should study these photographs before I write him my impulsive letters, he looks pretty crusty. I suppose editors have to build a protective layer of crust. I tacked the out-of-focus one by my desk and have blown kisses to it all day.

The excitement of becoming an author is mounting. Today I took a packet of the promotional cards to a bookshop where my local granddaughter works, to ask if the proprietor would place them on her counter. A young lad listened to us chatting, eyes wide.

"Are you *an author?*" he asked. "Would you autograph one of those cards for me?" I was as excited as he was. Imagine being asked for my autograph!

In my mail is a letter from a travel agent, a friend I've not heard from in years. She wants to put *Peacocks* on her mail order list, she has seen the review in *Publishers Weekly.* "Is it an adventure story or a personal journal?" she asks.

I have requests to speak in October in Buffalo, to a Rotary Club in California—a bit far! If I write 10 letters a day, sending out these cards—who can write 10 letters a day?—it will take only 25 days to cover my list. Except that daily it grows longer.

Peacocks isn't to be released officially until mid-September, but a bookshop in the busy Hyannis Mall had asked me to participate in an Authors' Festival, could I arrange to have books there? I am putting my toes into a wholly new world! I had called my kindly editor, laughing, laughing, I was so excited.

Today, mid-morning the day of the festival, a truck drives up to my garage door and unloads a carton for the festival, another for me. I swallow a sandwich, a glass of milk and reach the mall as I had been requested, promptly at noon. Outside the bookshop, in the side central corridor, a rectangle of tables is set up for some 30 Cape Cod authors. We are flanked by benches and plants, a steady flow of shoppers. We each have a chair, a big name plate, and books stacked, ready to be auto-graphed (and bought). I am placed next to a Cat Man. *Poor Planning* for a Bird Lady! He wears one long, dangling earring and never stops talking but soon Lisa arrives to keep me com-pany, charm everyone, I can ignore him. Some of our friends arrive to support us, be amused by all this fanfare.

What happens at Book Fairs, I find, is that authors wander about chatting with each other and buying each other's books. It is hot, by afternoon our hoped for customers have gone to the beach. Those who do come drip ice cream cones on us. Lisa and I have a neat time, and buy ice cream cones ourselves. A friend of a friend who is selling his book on sailboats comes along to talk with us. Across the table smiles an author who claims I had once written him a fan letter. (I should be more careful whom I write. To whom? Who? Where is my school-girl grammar?) He invites me to his home—for tea, cocktails, or to look at his sketches. (He turns out to have a plump little wife, right on guard.) Ensconced behind the biggest pile of books sits a man with a fine face etched by years. In a second-hand store in Tucson my mountain spring, far from the Cape Cod beach he had written about, I had found one of his books, loved it; been homesick, fallen in love with his jacket photo-graph. I would have been happy to join him at *his* beach cot-tage, for tea, cocktails, etchings, or whatever. Alas, that had been an early photograph. Now he is elderly, with wispy white hair trailing on his collar. He gives me a fatherly lecture on reading the fine print on my contract. (Obviously my inexpe-rience shows.) He has a wife too, darn it, she hadn't been mentioned in his book.

Afterward the shop gives us a party in a nearby restaurant. Exhilarated, I introduce my new friends to rum sours, we have a hilarious time. Driving home I keep falling asleep, it is hellishly hot, but I safely make it. I sit right down and write Norton, asking what other party-minded bookshops they know, and sign my letter Alice in Wonderland.

September 1983

A woman from a Boston TV station calls today, wanting me to appear on a panel of Older Women in New Careers. I am flummoxed, and refuse. I'll be on Nantucket. How could I get back and forth to Boston? It would mean polite clothes, taxis, overnighting in a hotel. My birds are more important. Maybe next month, I tell her.

A couple of booksellers I tell about this at dinner scold me roundly.

"Idiot!" one explodes. "Think how many books that could sell for you. Don't you know how hard it is to get publicity like that? Forget your birds! She won't ask you again."

I am going to have to consider priorities. Which is more important to me, my birds or this book that is so astonishingly changing my life?

October 1983

I am returned from Nantucket. It kept raining, the migration was poor. Somehow this year banding warblers and red nuthatches doesn't seem as important as the excitement of having a book published has introduced into my life—the reviews, the calls from friends around the country, the requests to lecture.

This new life is nonsensical. Why do people who chatted with me perfectly normally last year (if they bothered to chat at all) now fall all over themselves when we meet? It's just me, exactly who I was then. Has my freedom to call Norton's 800 number, being splashed, complete with photographs, across the pages of local newspapers, built some sudden magnetic field about me, a nimbus? This morning a young man came to my door to buy my book, and pay for two more I'd sold him yesterday at a meeting. Last fall he barely noticed me, I was just a white-haired woman instructing him in feather edges. Today—well, between my arithmetic and his nervousness it took both of us to figure out the tax, get his change right. I get nervous and sign 1893 under my autograph instead of 1983. At parties I am given those social kisses and smiles that aren't worth a damn. It's ridiculous. Fun, though.

A man at our small post office stopped me on the step today.

"Aren't you Erma Fisk, the author?" he asked (in capital letters). He wanted me to sign two books his wife had bought at a party the museum gave for me (because parties bring in new people, help build membership, I am a Trustee). There was almost a timidity in his voice.

Why? I stood in the doorway of a bookshop the other day and attempted to estimate the number of books on their racks. Here today, gone tomorrow. Piled conspicuously if the subject is timely, the author famous. Lined up in the window if the jacket colors won't fade. Then shoved back for next week's crop, placed on shelves where they must be hunted for; then returned, or discounted or shredded.

I signed this man's books on the hood of his car. Another man joined us, chatted, examined a copy of *Peacocks* from the supply I now carry on my back seat; bought it. We had an autograph party right there on the step, laughing, which made other people stop. I sold two more copies, forgot my shyness and left with new friends only I will never remember their names. All through this I am so embarrassed. I feel like Alice in Wonderland, as I wrote Norton. The world has shifted around me, its proportions are gone out of whack.

When people compliment me I don't know what to answer. I shuffle my feet, look about for a means of escape. I'm having to develop a veneer, a patter I hear myself giving out, which embarrasses me more. I feel dishonest. Sometimes these people are merely being polite, sometimes they mean it. Requests for an autograph baffle me. Why? What meaning can Good Wishes and my name on the flyleaf carry to someone I don't know? I joke with them. They can't give the book to someone else if I've written their name on it, I tell them. I say my name is splattered all over the pages, if they explore under the jacket my initials are there in gold, too.

Their attention is like the coffee and brownies served after a program that give me the quick calories I need, moisten my dry throat, loosen—if it is wine they offer—my tongue. If I can write a personal line I try to for I am learning how many lonely people are Out There, how painful and destructive loneliness can be. We all reach for a hand to help us on our way, unaware that if we will just put one foot in front of the other, eventually we proceed to a different outlook on the world. The scenery, the figures, the challenges change, some of the obstacles diminish. I didn't consciously put this in *Peacocks,* but it seems to matter more to readers than the bird journal I thought I had written. People thank me for giving them courage (which I could use more of myself). I don't know how to deal with this.

A man came up the other night after a program. "Thank you," he said quietly, and was gone. Another day a man I didn't know waited until my well-wishers thinned, then leaned down, kissed me, was gone. A girl leaving town, her car packed and running beside us, approached me.

"I was to be married," she said. "My fiancé was killed. I couldn't have gone through this summer without seeing you here, knowing the grief you too carry inside; learning from your book that it can be surmounted." Tears filled her eyes. Tears filled mine as she hurried into her car and away. I can't describe what this does to me.

"You have answered the questions for all of us," wrote a woman from across the continent, "and supplied many of the answers with your life. Thank you for your book. I hope **you** are writing another one."

What can I answer to the pain, the exposure, the cries for help that come through fan letters? To the fellowship that comes from them? I go back to my pages sometimes, trying to find in them what others see, but I don't.

When dusk settles outside my windows, in the empty hours when I falter—don't we all?—I remember these people. They have cut deep. I guess we don't any of us know what we do, the impact that unknowingly we make.

November 1983

I had my first formal Bookshop Signing today. The shop was small, but we managed to prop Lisa's illustrations about. A small table had been set out for me with wine and cheese, a pen, a stack of books. The friendly wife—how can you tell wives these days of separate names?—had made a platter of cookies which attracted customers. The owner appeared taciturn until I watched his eyes—he talked with his eyes, and his mobile eyebrows. The wife was chatty: I guess it takes one of each to make a good couple. Obviously their customers liked them.

Things were slow until Lisa arrived, poured me a second glass of wine. I began to feel more comfortable. Lisa is wonderful with people, soon we had a group about our table. She gets strangers laughing and chatting, which sells books. I can see I have a lot to learn. The Bishop came, which was dear of him. He tried the cheese, helped himself to cookies, and laughed at me.

"You don't sell books looking at your feet and mumbling," he instructed me. "You have to pretend you are an Important Person." He raised his voice. "After all, how many of my parishioners rate a book review in the *New York Times?*" Heads turned, and he winked at me.

I'm not much of a churchgoer, but the Bishop doesn't hold this against me. We have served on boards together, he and Lisa are old friends. He moved about, praising her sketches, greeting people, helping himself to cookies. The Bishop likes cookies, it shows. I like cookies, it shows on me too, only today I was nervous, I stuck to wine. We didn't sell too many books, but the proprietors seemed satisfied and said the Christmas trade would absorb the rest, so Lisa and I signed the leftovers, finished the cheese, and left. The afternoon wasn't as bad as I'd feared, but I wouldn't want to do this every week. How do other authors sell their books?

Fan letters are arriving in response to the promotional cards I sent out. Old friends emerge from the woodwork, introducing me to their spouses over the telephone—second or third spouses sometimes, I have to be cautious. Today a long lost friend inquires if I would be willing to farm-sit his sheep for six months, he wants to return to a western university to earn a further degree. I am tempted, surely I could get another book out of that experience! Another writes—"Your book is just like your letters, only better typed." Obviously she missed the many typos. I am going through my pages looking for ones to be corrected in the second printing. I was a gamble for Norton, the first printing was small.

Yesterday I talked at a Book Luncheon upstate. Delightful owners, excellent lunch. My colleagues were a dowdy woman in gray wool pushing a cookbook; a shrill feminist who upset our digestions and talked too long; then a quiet man who said more about the need for teaching children to read than about his book, stacked by the lectern. I liked him a lot. We were an interesting mix. The cookbook sold best, to our mortification.

Driving home I stayed with a friend overnight, then detoured to a bookshop she recommended. A young man at the front desk listened somewhat skeptically to my story. It takes courage to go into a bookshop, claim you are an author, offer to sign your book—if they carry it. He studied *Peacocks'* jacket, the Norton logo, regarded me more carefully. Putting two fingers in his mouth he gave a shrill whistle.

"Hey, Jack," he called over the stacks to his manager. "Come look. We have a Real Live Author here."

No wonder my ego balloons! In *A Time To Dance, No Time To Weep* Rumer Godden wrote, "A writer's life is necessarily such a lonely one, so uncertain that we flourish on praise." My friends fuss at me for going away so often, "working so hard," but I can't call it work. Today I've a call from a college asking for a program to be followed by a signing only the bookshop has sold out, can I arrange to get more copies for them in time? Gad, what a swelled head I am getting. When will the second printing be available, I ask Norton.

It is accepted that the elderly become queer. They are forgiven because of their age, but doesn't our freedom to say and do what we want come because now we are free of conventions that formerly restricted us, we don't care what the neighbors think?

A man stopped by this morning to return a book his wife had borrowed. I was just stepping out the door to set on my platform birdfeeder the remnants of our Thanksgiving turkey, bones that had fragrantly simmered all night for soup. He gave the platter in my hands, then me, a disturbed look. What will be a feast for crows obviously to him is garbage. If I take these hunks of turkey to the town dump the gulls will profit from them. I'm not studying gulls, I quit that ten years ago, I'm studying crows. I want to learn more about the flock in my neighborhood, see if they can be tamed, if they will come to recognize me as a friend, a sort of Demeter. I'm interested in their relationships, pecking order. Some days I count two, one on guard, one feeding; some days six, but there may be more. They arrive in my yard at first light. When they glimpse me they fly swiftly off, maneuvering between branches with a great flapping of glossy violet-black wings. On bitter days last winter they came even to my doormat where I might have spilled corn thrown out for small birds. Crows are famed for their wit and intelligence. They are said to recognize faces, certainly clothing; the walks, the intent of hunters; even to pass information from one generation to another. Omnivorous, they eject what they cannot digest in pellets, like owls. You might trap, and mark one once, but you will never catch that individual again.

A grandson who understands my interest tried to explain this deviation from conventional suburban behavior to our visitor, met with a polite but baffled "oh." Of course, but unfortunately, the crows do not appear while we stand there. Later grandson and I, sitting inside immobile as furniture, observe our ebony panhandlers slipping through trees to argue over our Thanksgiving bounty. We laugh, wondering what our visitor will report to his wife, whether she will stop by again to borrow another book.

"She's a bird lady," she will tell him. "All of them are queer. Even the young ones."

I can't see that watching a flock of disputatious birds is any queerer than watching a huddle of football players run and tangle while you hunker comfortably in an armchair, or on a hard bleacher bench. You can learn a darned sight more, watching birds. Cardinals peck warily in the bushes about my feeder. About them oak leaves are deep gold and copper. They harmonize with the carpet of pine needles below where a towhee scratches. The small black berries on an ilex at my window will be emergency food to spring grosbeaks and orioles traveling north. The branches scrape against the window in the wind.

December 1983

I am returned from a Christmas interview at a Cape TV station. I wore the blue blouse they had advised, which pleased them. They used some of Lisa's illustrations to decorate our chatter, which pleased me. I had missed their turn off in heavy rain so I was late, which didn't help my nervousness. I'm not comfortable performing for television, perhaps because I am not in charge? Fortunately today I was soothed by the painting that hung over the couch were I was seated—a seascape by Carolyn Blish of a winter beach. Surely the footprints in the snow were those of my friend Matt whom I used to visit at his coastal home on my migrations. He had told me that Blish also stayed with him, painting from his deck in the dunes; that he had persuaded her to add the gulls that now fly in all her seashore paintings. This same print hung in his hall and I've seen it in banks. If it weren't so large I'd surely have it on my own wall, I love it. In the glare and confusion of lights being set up about me it was a blessing, helped me to give an adequate performance as the camera moved about, impaling me. What coincidences pop up in life!

Afterward the camera man offered to run the tape for me, but after a minute I couldn't bear to look at myself pontificating. In those days when I had stopped with Matt I may not have been lissome, but I wasn't yet plump and grandmotherly. Maybe now that my records are up to date, my home in relative order, my book is selling well, I should quit. I've lived long enough.

I can't quit, there are programs I've promised to give, work I've offered to do. I better go drink some eggnog. I made too much for a party, a pitcher full is left over. That will make me plumper.

Eating lunch I watch a fox walk along the edge of the marsh, hunting duck for his supper. So far I've not seen him catch one. He turns his head as if he knows I watch, and admire his thick winter coat. I write a grandchild that perhaps I will buy a duck—a dead one—at the market and put it out for him on Christmas Eve.

January 1984

Trying to learn more about the publishing business I drive to the parish house of a local church for a program on "What Happens When You Have a Book Published." Our speaker is a poised and confident lady author in a fashionable green outfit, She is full of statistics and practical advice. Expect to Be Patient, she warns us. Treat Your Editor as a Friend, Not an Enemy. Use the Back of Junk Mail for Carbons. She lectures us knowledgeably on advances, on knowing every word in our contracts. Contract? I had stuffed mine, when it came, in my safe deposit box, not understanding it very well, trusting W. W. Norton.

I leave the parish house with a serious sense of inadequacy and a couple of cookies slipped into my pocket in case I should skid off the road into a snow bank and become hungry. A nice-looking fellow listener watched me pilfer these, and chuckled. He was an exnewspaperman, he said, who hadn't learned anything from the program but maybe his wife had, she is trying to be a poet. He asked if I were an author? I said I didn't think so, but when he found out Norton has me in charge he said I must be, and filched another cookie for my pocket. He knows the president, he said, and would like to nourish his property. I didn't get his name, I always forget the important things. Good cookies, though.

I haven't told anyone I am going into the hospital, I don't want even my near and dear to know. My disposition will be too fearsome, I'll be groggy, I'll burst into tears at a kindly word. I have written notes to my son, who will have to fetch me home, and to my daughter, lest she worry. I'll mail these as I pass through the electric hospital doors in case I conk out on the operating table. This would mortify Dr. Smith. Imagine having a surgeon named Smith, how dull! I won't conk out, this is a routine operation, delayed payment for the joy my babes brought me. I needn't be afraid, but of course I am. Or is it the prescience of boredom, of not being the mistress of my body, my hours?

Every other winter I have taken trips; at random as I've been asked to assist researchers in Mexico, El Salvador, Grand Cayman, Peru or have visited my families in California, enjoying their young. I've had no goal in mind, just taken whatever came along. I look at today as just one more such expedition into foreign country. The food will be more familiar (if less interesting and tasty). I will have to accept a different culture and different mores, see how life and death are handled in another texture. Associating as usual with strangers I can learn as much from young feminist nurses, and doubtless a bitchy older one, as I might observing Mayan Indians, fellow scientists, or the culture and habits and language of relatives one and two generations younger than I. It needn't be all wasted time. As on my other trips I must adapt, stifle criticism, broaden my viewpoints, enjoy.

I know I'm scared because I keep dropping things—my breakfast egg, a coffee cup I never have liked anyway. Last night I made a list of adjectives reviewers have showered on me these last few months—doughty, gutsy, cheerful, clear-thinking, high-spirited, brave—to keep under my pillow for when I hurt, or can't sleep, or strangle on pills. Only I've lost it.

My entrance through the sanitized hospital doors is so slapstick I forget to mail my possible farewell letters to my children. I am clutching a hairbrush and a satchel of books I won't get to read—a Sarton journal I was given for Christmas, Annie Dillard, a slim volume of Vincent Millay whose sonnets have accompanied every hospital stay I've made. In the bad hours her images paper my walls, her music blots out corridor sounds. A heavy whodunit came unexpectedly from Norton in my morning mail, I've brought that too.

I'm not on the computer a receptionist tells me coldly, I can't be admitted. I haven't taken an important test, either. I'm not at my best when going in for surgery. I don't care about her damned computer, I answer. I am there, suitcase in hand, by my doctor's arrangement. I had reported for tests, as required, been sent dressed and undressed up and down corridors, is it *my* fault if one is lacking? Is there any reason I can't be tested now, it is only 3 P.M.? Yes. Too late. (Saved me $50.) I stand my ground until they stash me on the maternity floor, perform the humiliating jobs nurses invent to keep patients occupied, I'll bet even if you come in for ingrown toenails. They grudgingly fed me an unattractive supper at five o'clock, then went away, leaving me with bleak hours to fill until any normal bedtime. Normal by my standards.

Do you know how many minutes there can be in an hour, how many seconds in each minute when you are uncertain of your future, a cipher in an impersonal room full of frightening equipment, your insides frozen with worry, your roommate moaning behind her curtain? I open the whodunit from Norton in the hope it will transport me elsewhere. Immediately it does. The offices of art magazines are new territory for me, I explore them with a soigné murderess. Suddenly, moving about his office talking to police officers, are my editor and his assistant with her curtain of shining blond hair, all the accoutrements of that office I had seen so briefly at Thanksgiving—plants and coffee machine on the windowsill, files and piles of paper on his desk, books piled on the floor, paintings on the door. It is unbelievable, a gift. And he hadn't known I'd be in hospital, need a friendly hand holding mine when he mailed it to me! I read that page a second time, gluttonously. A few pages further on there they are, again in the room with me with those policemen, laughing, sending out for beer and coffee when most I need company. I'm not feeling courageous or doughty or resilient. What a godsend! I read happily on until a nurse comes in, turns out my light.

Another hospital day. How do I know what day it is? I don't even know what *time* it is, my watch was taken away, there is no calendar on the wall.

Somehow my editor has tracked me down. He called this afternoon, sounding smug. As he should, no one else has managed this, not even my Big Sister, who keeps an efficient finger on me. When he asks how I am, I reply "Dead." That's because a few minutes ago a student nurse found my blood pressure so low in alarm she asked permission to telephone my doctor. (He had laughed, she told me later, said Mrs. Fisk wasn't used to lying in bed for days at a time, not to worry. If I died it would be from boredom or frustration. He is right on that, nothing to do, but sleep is killing me.)

While editor and I are talking the nurse returns, tests me again. That's all student nurses do, take your blood pressure and if you do succeed in an hour's quiet sleep bring ice water to wake you up. Thanks to his making me laugh, my surprise at hearing his voice, her needle jumps so high she brings in another nurse to check her machine. I've been telling people all fall that Norton has given me new life in my dotage, here is the scientific proof.

The nurses call me Erma, which infuriates me. At my age I deserve the dignity of Mrs. Fisk. There isn't much dignity of any sort in hospitals, but the nurses are always weary, there is enough ugliness in these corridors without adding my ill nature to it. I yearn to hear the babies crying in the nursery, but it is sound-proofed. I have permission to walk up to see them tomorrow, though, and to make tea in the kitchen.

I brought a copy of *Peacocks* with me to hunt for more typos, but my roommate promptly bought it and won't loan it back. She is so miserable I can't argue with her (or reach her table when she is sleeping). It makes me laugh that I can sell that book even from a hospital bed!

February 1984

I am home, comfortable in the pillows of the living room couch. Sun pours through geraniums on my southern windowsill, picks out the flowers and bright jackets of books my friends have brought. The room is Christmas all over again. Outside a mallard and his lady are digging at corn in the snow. The weather has been bitter, they are too hungry to be afraid. The pond is frozen clear across.

My family won't have to read my longhand writing they complain about because Nancy, a gangly redhead who teaches knitting in the village, has appointed herself my secretary. She brings my mail, types my answers, puts out birdseed, piles up firewood, heats my soup, cheerfully keeps me company. I did her a small favor last summer, she claims this is a payback. She made a Christmas sweater for my granddaughter Alice with horses prancing across it, she wants to see her in it. She is starting a musical one for Douglas but wants to meet him first. To see his style, she says. She is studying the effects of color on personalities and actions, and takes this very seriously. (My daughter, Amanda, sounds to her apple green in her letters.) She is also studying astrology and will tell you about the tall, dark men you are going to meet, with their pockets full of money and tickets to Paris. Greece is where she wants to go, she just hasn't found the right man to take her. She says when my supply of gift casseroles runs out she will cook Mexican dishes for me. The world needs more Nancys. I don't understand why some man hasn't snapped her up. One did, she says ruefully, but it didn't work out. She is wary of being hurt again.

Our lives change. What was valued, necessary to us last year, imperceptibly loses its urgency, becomes discarded. People you had thought you loved, occupations that engaged your eager attention, where are they now? Correspondence on a cause once vital is laid aside to be read another day. Across the room at an exhibit you see a face dear to you as your face was dear to him a year ago. You each give a nod of casual friendliness. If you are near enough you greet each other with a pricking, a stir in memory of happiness, of quarrels. You may smile at each other ruefully, make a date for lunch, but the hot, animating flame has died. We move on to new work, new loves. And if there are vacuums, if at times the heart cries out, we busy ourselves investing our energies elsewhere.

It isn't until years later that you learn each project, each relationship, long or short, has left its mark, changed obliquely your understanding of yourself or others. Like books on your shelves, dust has covered them, silverfish have chewed the pages. Cleaning out your library you may read a page or two—or refuse to. But the books get set back on their shelves, you don't give them away.

My spring calendar dazzles and frightens me. Becoming an author has turned my life around. I am scheduled for talks to breakfasts, churches, garden and reading clubs, colleges, a Rotary. I remind myself that program chairmen have monthly slots to fill. They are looking for someone new (and preferably noncontroversial), someone who does something offbeat. I am an age, they tell me persuasively, where older people relate to me, and young people who think 50 is moribund are astonished that I have survived so much further quite cheerfully.

I hope I teach these latter to look at their seniors with more interest. It's made me look at people differently. My own values are changing, I see my own tolerance extending.

March 1984

At tea yesterday I was talking too much as usual, saying I wished I were small and cuddly, wore ruffles, and got kissed at parties. Everyone laughed.

"What's wrong with wanting that?" I demanded. "I'm built wrong? I must appear competent, everyone thinks I am, but I can't change a tire or handle a rude salesperson. If I lock my car I leave the window open: staplers defeat me, taxi drivers don't hear when I ask them to turn off their radio, I can never figure what to tip. Because I live alone I suppose my ineptitudes don't show. What I need is a companionable man to do all the things I don't like to. In return I'll gladly handle the mail and the garden, take trash to the dump, cook his dinners, feed his friends. I know—women don't have to do this any more. The young of both sexes try to persuade me of this. Never mind, *I* do. I don't need a career to prove myself, give myself an identity. It's too late. Besides, I like to cook.

"Actually I have right here on my desk a photograph of me with ruffles up to my ears, taken during an interview with that 'competent, gutsy, straight-shooting author.' The *Washington Post* took it, they even printed it. I should have it on my bathroom wall in place of the mirror."

They laugh again. It's hard to get people to believe me. It's aggravating.

My audiences—well, this isn't entirely true, it's a generalization—are preponderantly older women, of an age that was confined by the traditional roles. They are eager to hear how I managed to break out from a life once patterned much like their own; wistful to think what they might have done, what they see their daughters doing. They don't listen when I tell them, with exasperation, that they aren't too old to build new lives.

"You were so brave, alone on the mountain," they insist. "You have led such an interesting life."

Their daughters wouldn't think so. Those who can work it in with childrearing and husbands, or who forgo these for wider living than their mothers ever dreamed, are out running the world, or learning to. Pushing for family planning, child care, equality in the marketplace. Moving up in scientific and economic fields. I envy *them*.

I've returned from New York to find an alarmed request on my answering machine for confirmation of a local talk. *Where was I?* (Very happy in the big city, being cosseted, eating an excellent stew with a gourmet cook, going to exhibits.) I have soothed the lady, washed and ironed my blue professional blouse, and am on my way with Lisa's illustrations, my Arizona slides, pen and sandwich.

My audiences are always different, which is why I can keep on talking. The second this week was a big, merry group that meets monthly, serves a trestle table full of fattening, home-made nibbles (at 10 A.M.!). They specialize in local speakers—scientists and politicians, a fire chief, a salvage expert exploring coastal wrecks. They are traveled and sophisticated, were laughing before I began, had me laughing immediately, we had a fine time. Maybe I changed—a little—their attitudes toward wildlife. I educated them on the Nature Conservancy and its aims. Quite a lot bought books. The seller's discount goes to a local conservation organization so I educated them on that, too. When I went shopping later we recognized each other in the stores and laughed some more.

Friday is to be a men's garden club. Probably they are expecting a talk on roses and insects, they will be disappointed. Sunday is a Book Brunch where I'll be on the platform with a strident feminist, an Australian poet and a mystery writer known for his egotism. That ought to be a challenge! But I'm to be last, I won't have to talk but a few minutes, just remember to comb my hair and wear lipstick. In Boston next week I will be sandwiched between a dog breeder and a sailor. People write books about anything! Library groups are the most attentive, ask the best questions, although they don't buy my book, they plan to borrow it. Reasonable. The one that scares me most is a business college for Women in Corporate Management. The professor claims to have read my book so she knows what she is getting into. Then comes a writing workshop in Boston that ought to be fun—or a disaster. Graduate students of various ages and backgrounds. I'm to persuade them to rewrite, revise, pare to essentials, take off the protective armor we all hide behind, be honest. It's a wine and cheese meeting in a private home. I'm going to need wine to get away with any of *that!*

I write my editor—"You see why I am having such fun? Our book is like a skiff floating me downstream, eddying into backwaters, exploring small inlets. It is giving me a wonderful life."

Nights with a fire burning, the ends of fat Christmas candles shining on the piano, I am working on my current onionskin sheets—clarifying, deleting, adding. What a good time I am having!

I am writing a second book. I missed those friendly voices at W. W. Norton, my privilege of stopping in to see them when I passed through New York. I no longer had an ethical right to dial their 800 number (free!) to chat, to take up their time. Once *Peacocks* was printed, out in the stores, they were busy handling other authors.

One day I called them. "I miss you," I said. "I think I'll write another book." They laughed tolerantly, not believing me. Surely at my age I was a one-book author.

I started it in Belize. Why should I stand about in the rain of a rain forest where I wasn't really needed? There were plenty of others eager to do the work. Younger. When I am dead they will be educating the next generation with what they are learning here. So often I remained on the plantation, helping two Doberman pinschers guard it. From jaguars? Interlopers? I baked our bread, edited a mystery our hostess-cook was writing, wrote myself.

My sheets have a so-so title, which gets explained: an introduction that pleases me, a finale that is all right; bits and pieces I like that perhaps my publisher might like. I haven't yet found a way to pull these together. I'm not pregnant with this book the way I was with *Peacocks,* I doubt I can pull it off. My reviewers have made me self-conscious, too aware of what they liked when what matters should be what *I* like. Also a book has a mind of its own. It needs to grow and my climate isn't right. I haven't time to structure it, handle the transitions. There are too many interruptions, too many trips to give programs, sell books.

People on buses and planes, once a Cuban who had no English working on my stalled, recalcitrant station wagon on an empty Florida road, proudly show me photographs of their children, grandchildren, spouses; beaming proudly. I travel with a carton of my books, set them out in their bright jackets on tables at programs, beaming as proudly. This is commercial, but I explain that a percentage of every sale goes to a local community group; a second percentage, the royalties, to a conservation organization; and the third is kept by my publisher, helping, I hope, to pay my editor's salary so he can buy sneakers for his daughters—a human touch that seems to please my listeners.

You can't believe how exciting it is to spread out my books, or to see its jacket bright on bookshop tables, to chat with the proprietors. I need to get *Peacocks* well launched before I worry about another book.

April 1984

Tonight I am in Woodstock, Vermont, listening at midnight to the calls of injured Great Horned owls Sally Laughlin is rehabilitating in flight cages in her woods. Woodstock had a poster advertising my program at each end of their village green. I swelled up like one of the blowfish I used to catch as a child, fishing with an aunt in the whaling town of Sag Harbor, Long Island. I hadn't brought a camera with me, and it was raining so I couldn't commemorate this publicity for my family. They seem astonished by their formerly domestic mother's activities. When will I have time to bake cornbread for them, bring over a pie for dinner? I cover my typewriter when anyone comes, I don't tell anyone, even Norton, after their laughter, what I am doing.

Back on the cape my hours are quiet. I am typing reports for the Feds and Massachusetts—a sort of ornithologist's IRS, equally onerous. My sheets are only a pale echo of the numbers I used to have in Florida. There aren't many birds migrating or resident along the edges of my marsh, and I've had more important duties to perform this year than banding a few robins, catbirds, and jays. If the royalties on *Peacocks* amount to enough to buy a Jonnie-acre of green space saved on an Arizona mountain, I wonder who will feed on it, where will it be? I'll have to live long enough to find out, to visit it. Always something to live for . . .

When first I came here I didn't have robins and catbirds—just a song sparrow or two in the tangles, a woodpecker hammering in the woods. The hillside had been sheep pasture, now long since grown to pitch pine and a variety of oaks, some of these flaming scarlet in autumn. Over the years I have built up the soil a little, scattered wildflowers, bulbs, native plants; leaving dead trees for nest holes. My gardens would never rate a glance from the Grubbers Club, but hummingbirds come to coral bells and bee balm, swallowtail butterflies decorate the dill and parsley I grow for their caterpillars to munch. I produce insects as well as flowers, bird food as well as tomatoes, an abundance of slugs. Who eats these, I wonder? Horrid slimy creatures, they must be of some use. A small boy who helps his smaller sister at a lemonade stand sells me earthworms to plant in my compost heap, but they must be the wrong kind, they don't reproduce. Or the robins and skunks find them. There are different kinds of worms, I learn, some of which like compost, some who don't. Live in the country, your neighbors teach you oddments.

I built a shallow bird pool, mixing my own concrete, finding its shape easier to envision than to achieve. Now I see prints of nocturnal visitors about it, enjoy the splashing and dunking of birds that drink from its leaf-dappled surface. Slowly this has brought robins and catbirds, this and berries on wild shrubs I planted about it. And doubtless my thorny raspberry patch! Orioles dip into the syrup of my hummingbird feeders, flirt and sing their spring songs in the still leafless oaks. A pair or two remain to weave their hanging baskets out on slender locust branches where even red squirrels daren't venture. Bird books claim that orioles don their flashing black and orange wedding splendor south of the United States, before they migrate, but over the years that I have weighed, measured, banded, and photographed them in spring I have handled only ones still making do with last year's broken and ragged tails for a rudder. That's what banding does—provides little bits and pieces of information to confound those who bird only with binoculars. I set out orange halves for them. Catbirds come to these too, and tanagers, for calories. I must fasten the oranges under chicken wire lest they be carried off by marauding crows that raucously harass a pair of Great Horned owls nesting each winter high in a pine down river—if you can call owls' shapeless bundles of sticks a nest. The crows also search out robin and blue jay nests, taking eggs and chicks to feed their own young—as doubtless so do the owls. Only owls work at night, so while I hear their low-pitched calls, I don't see them at their evil work.

Red squirrels ballet up and down my trees, hunting woodpecker and flycatcher holes that might contain eggs. **My** neighbor shoots squirrels, but they belong in our world as much as he does, I tell him indignantly. If I—and he—put out seed to attract birds for our enjoyment, they and their progeny attract natural predators. Or neighborhood cats, which are morally the worst of all, they have plenty of food set out for them in their kitchens. Plump quail provide food for hawks, the raccoon prowls at night, snapping turtles pull under small ducklings swimming in line behind their parents along the pond's edge. Everything has to eat. My seed helps many a small bird through winter's cold. Someday I plan to search under the nest of those big owls and their rapacious young, break open the pellets they eject to find among tiny mouse and shrew bones shiny government bands I have put on chickadees, finches, and the large-eyed titmice that come to my feeders. Is this proportion of natural death from hungry predators any worse than the death humans deal out with guns and bombs and chemical poisons, without the excuse of hunger?

Live and let live. If my neighbor wants only decorative cardinals and friendly chickadees in his yard, where does he draw the line? I ask him. What about rabbits? Fox, skunk, raccoons? The neighbors' dogs, children? He gives me hard looks, I can't seem to get through to him, but he has his gun out of sight, I notice, when he asks me over to identify a bird, to advise on what flowers might be distasteful to rabbits. If I were to shoot anything—I don't tell him this, he would—it would be the far too many glossily beautiful purple and green and ebony grackles that strut about snatching corn I scatter for smaller birds. The grackles roost by the hundred with red-wings in a swamp down the lane. At dusk they set up a terrific racket, their version of the song of spring peepers. Arguing about who will sleep where, I guess. One year a mallard brought her half-grown brood to my pool. Its concrete bottom disappointed them, but they found corn the grackles had missed, and seemed satisfied.

Last week our daughter gave a bash for me in her home in Washington, within sound of the chimes of the National Cathedral. Her invitation was a panic—My Mom Wrote a Book! It panicked me as I hunted through my wardrobe, the racks of shops within reasonable distance, for an outfit for this occasion. I found nothing that pleased me until—yes, there was what I wanted in the furthest corner of the furthest garment bag in my closet. If you wait long enough fashion repeats. The skirt was a correct length, the peacock colors flattering, the fabric far better than what modern shops offer. I used to wear it to diplomatic receptions. The glamour of those days would give me sheen, confidence.

What a joyous party it was, her home full of flowers, of music, of merry people! I felt like a bride. Friends from her lives, from mine, from the government years Brad and I had lived in Georgetown. She is known for her parties, but she outdid herself this time. I'm told the food was delicious. Someone brought a plate to me out on her terrace, but I didn't get to eat anything. I couldn't greet people with my mouth full and was afraid of dropping mushrooms on the books I was signing. Occasionally something was popped into my mouth, I swallowed hastily. I was so overwhelmed I never even finished the glass of wine brought me at the beginning so I wouldn't be shy. I needed to write something different on each flyleaf and often I couldn't even remember the name of my well-wisher! How many attractive, generous friends she has, I thought; and what a lot of friends her father had had, too, who came to shore up his widow, and because they loved her.

"Better than a wake," Jeffrey Bond had said with a twinkle. "We kept hoping you would come back to the District, marry one of us." He had stopped, really looked at me, still holding my hand. "But you couldn't, could you? None of us measure up to Brad."

His eyes had created a moment of silence about us. If I could have married anyone it would have been Jeffrey, he was our closest friend, the children's courtesy uncle. He had a new wife with him. Lovely and young, she came along the line and took him away.

Amanda had thought of everyone—Brad's office manager, the secretary I had thought long dead but there she was, white-haired, fashionable as ever. Finally the crowd on the terrace thinned, then parted for a tall man with keen blue eyes, a firm nose and chin. Authoritative. I've met him, I thought, he is so good-looking I couldn't forget him.

"Don't I know you from somewhere?" I asked. There was a hush in the circle around us—the white-haired guest of honor, this white-haired handsome man. He told me his name, I shook my head. In blissful ignorance I asked, "What do you do?"

The group delightedly closed around me, informed me— when he had left—that he was an eminent news commentator. Everyone in the District knows him, listens to him probably twice a day! And TV commentators have strong egos, they told me, laughing. It goes with the job.

Oh, well—country mother I don't have TVs in my living room, kitchen, often bathrooms as they do. I don't brush my hair, fasten my bra listening even to a handsome man of his status. When I caught his face today on the morning news I was still mortified. But what I most remember from that afternoon are the friends and the flowers, my pride in my child, her pride in me—My Mom Wrote a Book.

The next day my program in Virginia went off well. In New York I called Norton from the airport. They have had to order a third printing. I flew home on wings.

May 1984

I have been alone, peaceful and relaxed all day. The telephone has not disturbed me, no one has strolled across the brick walk I personally laid and am so proud of. The doorbell has not rung. Make it loud, I had instructed the man who installed it, so I will hear it if I am upstairs. Now I don't hear it even if I am in the living room if my hearing aids are turned off! That's what age, with its sneaky indignities, does to you.

When I was making bird surveys on remote Arizona ranches I didn't mind solitude. I had the challenges of my work, of new birds to study. A golden eagle might drift lazily over a canyon, a hawk soar in the morning thermals. I would watch foxes stalking rabbits, chasing them in a sudden burst of speed

(speed on both parts) into a tangle of brush; waiting a bit, then slipping away disappointed. Deer might stand on the hillsides, ears pricked, assaying me. I might find sign of mountain lion, coyote. Cattle pressed against a fence, eyeing me soberly, an occasional ranch horse skittered down the slopes, as unused to humans as I became. Life flowed at a different tempo. When humans did arrive, their noisy vehicles spitting smoke and gravel—friends, a rancher, my sponsors, climbers with bulging backpacks, I welcomed them but they were from another world. When they came in a group, spreading about, usurping my land with their cameras and picnics, chatter and incessant questions, astonishingly I found I resented them. Military planes flying over with an intolerable, echoing racket were unwelcome reminders of wars and murder, bombs and drug runners, shopping malls and the polluting plumes that some days rose through my translucent air from smelters down desert.

On days when I am undisturbed here at home, writing, I am not alone. Standing by my desk, moving about my rooms munching an apple, cooking a cheese omelet so real I can smell it, are the fictional characters I am creating. Like real people they refuse to be pigeon-holed, go off in directions I've not planned, laugh at my attempts at control. They may be built from people I have known—or thought I had known—but there is no time sequence. An echo appears from 30 years ago, or here is someone I met at dinner last night.

Writing, I am aware of but not seeing the sunlight on my table, the marsh beyond my trees. It's like being enclosed in the fairyland of one of those delicate (and expensive) glass Christmas ornaments that catalogues lure us with. Which is reality?

The telephone rings. A pert-voiced young dental assistant reminds me of my appointment. Reality with a capital R.

I drive many miles giving programs. I don't mind. New England is beautiful, I crisscross its back roads, I have friends en route. Instead of stopping for coffee and doughnuts or ice cream cones in towns, I stop in bookshops, although it embarrasses me to go in, holding my book half hidden, offering to sign any copies they might have. Often the managers know me from the signing that Lisa and I did last fall at the New England Booksellers meeting. This signing is nonsense, but the shops seem to like it. Some put stickers on the jacket which obscures its illustration or the promotional comments on the backs. Some more intelligently insert a marker saying "Author Signed." Both claim this increases sales. Since I am trying to raise royalties for the Nature Conservancy I pluck up my courage. That W. W. Norton published me gives me status, often I get a friendly red carpet rolled out, the offer of a cup of coffee.

Today a friend led me into the Dartmouth Bookstore in Hanover. Ignoring the clerk at the cash register, to whom in my ignorance I would have applied, he led me to a back desk. The young woman there looked at us inquiringly, saw the book I was bashfully clutching, and ran out from behind her desk crying, "Are you Mrs. *Fisk?*" Spontaneously she hugged me! Penny, her name was—a shining lucky penny in my day.

Further south, chatting with the women who ran a big shop, I explained that I was in town to talk at St. Paul's School. One asked if I would be willing to come back, address an anniversary meeting of her wildflower club? I get many engagements this way, by word of mouth (sometimes, as here, mine). I was enjoying New Hampshire in the spring, I said, I would enjoy it equally in the fall. What a good excuse to drive north through its flaming foliage! Of course I would come.

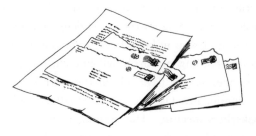

June 1984

I have heard nothing from Norton about my just completed manuscript, "Parrots' Wood." The key to my post office box wears thin. Our postmistress sympathizes with my discouragement as daily I inquire for a package.

Writing a book is like a love affair. While it lasts you are deeply, emotionally involved, the rest of the world exists through a haze. You perform required social and business motions, but your real self is turned inward. Surges of happiness, insecurity, despair pulse through you. You wake in the night with the need to express yourself, fall asleep later in a glow of satisfaction.

Finally your pages go to your publisher. You hold them to you, bid them godspeed. Then you wait. And wait. The yoyo of tension you have been on gradually loses its elasticity, you reenter your former world. When at last the manuscript is accepted and returned for revision the passion that absorbed your days and nights is spent. It is just something—some-one—you once loved that it is now pleasant to see, recalling past pleasures. The relationship has become casual. Working on proofs you remember the emotion that once drove you, and marvel that it did.

The physical birth of a book is also like that of a baby, the date of emergence as uncertain. Decisions on illustrations, typeface, color, publicity announcements are not unlike the practical necessities of outfitting an infant's room. And at the end, when these decisions are out of your anxious hands, again you wait.

At last it is over—the professional consultations, the exictement, the queries of your friends; the more aloof interest of bookshop managers, the chore of proofreading again and again. Occasionally, like a postcard or telephone call from a former lover, you may get a friendly call from your editor, as indication that he too has been a participant in this love affair, this birth. Or you may not. Months later your book appears in the stores. Receiving congratulations you try to remember what sparked you, how it was conceived.

July 1984

I have a decision to make about who I have become and I can't come to grips with it. I know it's troubling me because I am dropping things again—my breakfast egg as I was taking it from the fridge, the pot of honey I wanted for my toast. An egg on the floor is bad enough to clean up, but half a pot of honey is impossible. After peeling apples to cook in a lemon syrup I have let these burn, and the cookies I was baking for a museum party tonight. I recognize these signs of behavior. They will continue until I make up my mind.

One of the problems of living alone is that you have no one to tell you what you are doing wrong, which a spouse or a family is happy to do. Your children, once they are grown, won't, although they daily did before. Your good friends don't—that's why you stay good friends, they accept you as you are. Your not so good friends might like to but you aren't going to pay attention to *them.* Men my age—if they spoke out it would only be because somehow it affected their comfort or convenience. Besides, there aren't many men my age. The younger men I work with are fun to be with, not critical. They don't pat my knee, wax philosophical or judgmental. I lay awake last night, tabulating, trying to make up my mind. I pulled the sheet over my head, made myself go to sleep, woke up with my mind still circling. It isn't that big a decision. It won't matter ten years from now, even ten weeks from now. Why do I plague myself with it? How do other people sort out their lives? Keep from being hurt? Maybe if I chop up the small pine that blew down in last night's wind across my path the physical effort will help. What is wrong with me these days?

No, I can't chop. I have to don polite clothes and drive up Cape for a luncheon.

On my way I stop at the post office. Now, this very moment I hold in my hand the manuscript of "Parrots' Wood," returned with a formal letter of acceptance from W. W. Norton & Co.

If I were the lachrymose type, tears would be spilling down my cheeks. Norton has gone overboard, that man has never written me like this before, I can't believe it. Praise on those yellow flags? I will lay them away as jays do acorns for gray days when the world offers no sustenance. Who knows what green shoots might someday push through the ground they have wintered in? I should be rushing out to buy champagne, summon my friends to celebrate. Instead I'm crying. I never cry. I must be hungry, or have been up too late last night.

I ripped open the package with its letter open sitting outside our small post office, selfishly preempting a slot other people needed to use, getting more and more hysterical. Now I am clutching the manuscript, holding it on my lap, on my way to this luncheon. With pleasant people so I don't mind going, though it's 30 miles and I keep getting lost. I don't know this part of the Cape, and I have to keep stopping to read those yellow flags.

Only stupid people get lost, and my polite shoes are uncomfortable. This puts me in a critical mood. I look at myself, at the Author I have turned into (which is the reason I've been asked to this luncheon). I don't like who I see a bit. She is brassy, sophisticated. It's as if there were two women inside my skin, no relation to each other, who won't get along. Like sisters sleeping in the same bed, each jockeying for the most comfortable side, quarreling, neither one winning. I used to have to sleep with my sister, I know about this. One woman is the real me, content to keep a home, make visitors welcome, do bits and pieces of ornithological research off by myself. That's the woman I'm used to, comfortable with. But all of a sudden she has split and now here is this impostor in party clothes and lipstick, driving down wrong roads, I've just had to backtrack, I don't know where I am: going out to be a public figure, however minor. I know I wrote *Peacocks* but I don't feel any connection from it to me. This second book, I'm beginning to know its pages by heart too, writing and rewriting them, but it has no relation to me either. I can't adjust to this Author Woman that people write letters to, ask to address their organizations. I need a nice, comforting, fatherly editor (in a pin-striped suit) to tell me it's all right for me to be aggressive, that's how books are sold. I need a nice, comfortable friend to laugh at me, tell me maybe I'm not all that agressive, and besides, my new friends don't know any better, they think I was born brassy. I want someone to see I don't take the Bloody Mary I'll be offered, keep me from assuming my public personality as if it were a fashionable suit.

Then I really look at myself. (I'm back on the highway again, I know where I am, five minutes more to go, I'll be only a little late.) I see that with every program given, every book autographed, I have become bolder and more willing to stand up for myself. I laugh at people who used to frighten me. I talk at parties and don't care if I hear myself saying something stupid. This New Woman is rather fun to be. But she upsets me. She talks too much. She acts Important. People listen to what she says, which certainly they shouldn't.

It's like being in a love affair. You see yourself with different eyes. Traits, a personality you didn't know you had, are uncovered. You feel desirable, rush out and buy new clothes. Like a love affair it won't last, but it will change you, you will never be able to go back to who you were. You are going to have to adjust, learn to live with a different self. How all this can be happening to me is baffling. I don't *want* to adjust!

Now that I have this philosophy off my chest—I had a very pleasant luncheon, kept relatively quiet, sold some books out of the back of my car, I am writing Norton that, yes, they may send me the contract they offer. Their letter is pretty legal. If I die tomorrow will they read Proof? My children surely won't. No, I don't plan to put my head in a plastic bag, or choke on champagne, I'm having far too much fun. Norton doesn't like my title, I don't like the one they suggest. We will have to wrangle. How nice. I'll need to clean the manuscript up and rewrite some, but after that letter I can lick tigers.

August 1984

I am struggling with my manuscript of "Parrot's Wood," wishing there were more of those companionable editorial yellow flags to help me. At the moment I am writing—and rewriting—a clarifying insert Norton demands. It has become two pages instead of the short paragraph they probably expect. Don't be in such a hurry, I admonish them. A book, a poem, even just an insert has to grow. From a seed planted by wind, by chance, by a yellow flag it must push its way through soil and leaf litter, thrust into rain and sunlight seeking nourishment. Whether it blooms or withers is a gamble. All our efforts are gambles, be they omelets or children. Or inserts.

An editor, I continue, complaining, is there to make sure the stakes that give this seedling support are set solidly; to search its stems for slugs and beetles, or for pearls of insect eggs, chrysalides of butterflies that may attach to it. I may build the root system but I need a discerning eye to pull weeds, clip a shading branch. I am grateful for your yellow flags, I say, I just want more attention.

September 1984

There is a nip in the air, a summer blanket is inadequate. I fetch a quilt with delicate flower tracing on its creamy surface that I bought on impulse one day, and spread it on my big bed. In the Depression days of the 1930s Brad bought that bed, also on impulse, for $9. Solid maple, broad, originally with tall posts, it was our son's ten years later when he contracted polio. Little was known about polio in those days. Sister Kenny had recently been in Buffalo instructing in the care of this poorly understood disease, and our pediatrician felt I could provide better care than our teen-ager might get in a busy hospital. As polio was then thought to be infectious, the family was banished to Grandmother's while I stayed alone with our child, sterilizing dishes and sheets, packing him every two hours in woolen blankets kept steaming in an electric boiler provided by a new air force family down the street. Testing for weaknesses Dr. Arnold said I need not bother to pack the little finger of the left hand, the rest of his body would tax him enough. From the depths where our son lived in fright and suffering, a voice protested—That's my best milking finger, *I need it!* His illness was traced back to summer weeks when he had helped a farmer with chores, at a Canadian camp. No one else contracted it, it was a freak occurrence.

The bed, that's what I'm talking about. When our children were grown, out in the world on their own, when Brad and I moved to Washington it became ours, by a window looking out on a magnolia tree. Widowed, I had its posts cut off, put it in storage. Now on Cape Cod I lie in its comfort, though I admit I feel selfish when a couple hoping to sleep in the same bed together must accept the conventional twin beds of the guest room. Mostly young people visit me, eager and lusty.

A granddaughter in her twenties often curls up on it reading and napping all day when she visits, ignoring the lure of summer outside. I will leave it to her in my will.

"What did you find hardest when you were widowed?" a man asked the other evening. Several of us were sitting about a comfortable living room after dinner, looking out over Pleasant Bay. The distant barrier beach lay like a shadow under brilliant stars. Empty dessert dishes were scattered on tables, a fire crackled, lighting our faces.

Conversation ceased, everyone looked at me. There were other widows in the group. A widower had asked the question.

I considered. All right, I thought. He asked seriously. You know the answer. Let them have it.

"It isn't what an older woman is supposed to say." I hesitated then, looking at them. Not everyone likes frankness. "We're supposed to joke about needing a husband to gas the car, take care of bills and taxes—all that. So we do. But it isn't that. You can buy a lawyer, a carpenter, doctors, but you can't buy love. What I found hardest, what I still miss after all these years, is having a man who comes home because he wants to come home, because he wants to spend the evening in my company, slap me into bed at night. For years you have been desirable, you took this for granted. Suddenly you are not and you only need look in a mirror to see why. It's a tremendous adjustment. Perhaps at sixty if you are handsome still, gregarious, wealthy—perhaps if I had returned to our friends in Buffalo, or stayed in Washington participating in the social life urged on me—going to square dances, concerts, exhibits . . . But I couldn't. I couldn't pretend to gaiety, handle the necessary chitchat. I moved to a different part of the country, immersed myself in a field of work where no one knew me, where gradually I worked my way through loss, created a new identity. But if you want to know what I missed most—and still do—it is that. However I and Jane and Susan cover it over when we leave here tonight, we go home to an empty house, a cold bed."

The room was quiet. "Have I embarrassed you? Is it indecent of me to talk of this? At my age?"

Jane is our most recent widow. I reached out my hand to

her. I looked our widower in the eye, smiled at him too.

"Probably you will marry again. Not one of us—someone younger. I hope you do. I wish you happiness. What you need to wish *us* is strength. I doubt you men realize how much your friendship means to us. A substitute, but an essential one."

A boat was homing out on the bay, its lanterns bobbing through the dark—some fisherman coming late to the light and warmth of his cottage. I fixed my eye on his lantern, followed his passage; wishing him safe return, a woman waiting for him.

October 1984

This wooden house is full of creaks at night. Propped on pillows reading, or writing in bed, twisting sentences over and over until they satisfy me, I hear footsteps stealthily mounting the stairs. My door knob clicks—or is it just the click of my electric blanket? My breath becomes loud, ominous in my ears. That rustle—or is it just the movement of my cheek on a pillow, my leg tensing under the sheet?

Often outside I sense an animal, catch the whiff of a skunk or raccoon digging for insects in my path. A Great Horned owl may hoot, acorns clatter on the roof. I enjoy these natural sounds. It is the creaking, the clicks that trouble me. I hold my breath, I try not to panic. I tell myself this is a holdover from childhood when a sibling tortured me with tales of a bear that awaited me on the dark stair landing, of a hand that would reach for me in my bedroom before I had reached the comfort of a lamp. Once, in an old home in California where doors were never locked at night, I awoke with fingers pressing on my throat. I could utter only the useless gurgle of nightmares, colored by a mystery I had been reading before I slept. It took horrifying moments to realize this was only the family's pregnant cat seeking entrance to the warmth inside my blankets.

Hearing sounds in the night, no neighbors within reach, I have trained myself to realize they are the house talking to itself, to me. I pursuade myself to sleep. That's what happened the night I was burgled in South Florida, only there it used to be Cuban tree frogs that alarmed me, jumping at windows for insects.

Have you ever tried to decipher, in the morning, a page you had scrawled at night, at 3 A.M.? I've trained myself to do that, too.

December 1984

I am paying for my bird-banding activities by working on reports. Early up, late up, totting figures; three whole days of this between Christmas parties (which muddle my figures). Souring my disposition. To restore my ego I go to bookstores, sign *Peacocks* for the Christmas trade. They complain about not being able to get their orders. How can I make money for the Nature Conservancy if the stores can't get books? I report this to Norton. They reply, austerely, that they fill orders if they come directly to them, that is, if the shop is recognized by their credit department, which the Peter Rabbit Wildlife Center, the Robin's Nest, and such usually aren't. Most shops obtain their supplies from distributors; a big order is more apt to be filled promptly than a small one. The publishing business is a lot more complicated than I've realized. I should stay away from it. Only I'm having too much fun.

January 1985

Some of my friends won't answer their telephones before noon, they even disconnect them. I understand this. If you write, paint, do research, are immersed in a lonely process, an interruption can throw you off balance. But I live alone, the telephone is my link to the outside. It lets me know, often, that I really exist, even if the voice at the other end only needs to chat about their own affairs, is seeking information, a favor.

"How *are* you?" invariably they ask—a stupid question. No one really wants to know about your aches and pains, misfortunes in the money market, family affairs, your car's dead battery. My answer depends on my mood and how well I know my inquisitor.

"Rolling with the punches," I say sometimes, the cheerfulness of my voice again depending on my mood. Or, "Plodding along, putting one foot in front of another."

The most courteous answer, I've decided, for people I don't know well is—"Sitting here, trying to grow old gracefully," which seems to amuse them. Of course, some days I am bursting with stories of my own to tell, keep *them* on the phone when they are restlessly wishing to be off. It's a risk we both run.

If I counter with, "What are you doing these days?" my real friends may say, "Scrubbing the toilet . . . babysitting a grandchild . . . studying travel folders to see where we can't afford to go." A man may say, "Into a new love affair . . . thinking of buying a racing car . . . taking my dog to the vet." These are sensible answers, I can relate to them. They make me feel better about my own humdrum activities.

My other complaint at the moment—it's January, a bleak and fretful month. In January I am always complaining.

The telephone rings. I limp across the room. "Erma?" asks an unknown voice brightly. My hackles rise. Erma is what my siblings, my lawyer, my medical men call me. I accommodate to these, although I grumble. But a stranger, speaking to me at a party, after a lecture, or on the telephone, trying to sell insurance—where have *manners* gone? When you don't know someone, if the relationship is business, the hope of a donation, perhaps even a desire to express admiration, wouldn't you be further ahead to use the formal, polite address of Mrs. Fisk? Indeed yes! The familiarity baffles me. For more years than I care to acknowledge I have been Jonnie; or a number on my checks, Mastercard, various licenses. Then I wrote a book. My editor called. After our months of working together he knew me, of course, as Jonnie. Which of my names would I like on the jacket?

"Well," I had said, slowly, thinking, "Erma is my legal name, I suppose we should use that. It will look well in print if you use the J. And then maybe no one will know I wrote it? It isn't all that good a book, you know."

Erma is a woman I have come to dislike. She gives lectures, wears high heels, permits photographers to pose her; has practiced a gracious Thank You for those who congratulate her. If the telephone rings, I limp across the room, and someone asks, Erma? it takes character to answer politely, having learned the next remark may be—

"Oh, I suppose I shouldn't call you that, but I feel I know you *so well* after reading your book."

Oh dear. I have laid myself out on paper, I have no more privacy than a bather on the beach. Someday if I am cooking, my hands are buttery, if I've not yet had my lunch, my self-control is going to snap, I will hear myself saying frostily—

"Yes, this is Mrs. Fisk speaking." That will be bad for sales.

Convalescing from flu I have been gorging on journals, wanting to see how other women live, what they think about, what stirs them. This one fills her pages with flowers, the weather, her cats, the difficulties of fitting writing into the necessary chores of her days. An intellectual, she discusses philosophy and political news over lunch with her friends, detailing the menus. (They sound delicious.) But these friends come through—to me at least—only as background for her constant temperamental swings. There is always a barrier; she doesn't let us inside. I can look at her but she is aloof.

This one is warm, loving. I come to know her husband and children, I'd welcome her as a friend, I could count on her. A teacher, she relates to people. She will weather the midlife crisis she writes about.

This next one is so turned into the midlife crisis that absorbs her, an affair with the husband of a trusting friend, that we hear of nothing else. Her family are only a painted backdrop against the excitement, the difficulty of finding time to sleep with her lover.

Another spends her time rolling on couches and the floor with *her* lover. Her anguish becomes so boring I can't finish her pages. I sympathize with the mess she is making of her life, but I don't really need to know every sexual detail of the lovemaking that ultimately loses her a husband and a beloved child (and, no doubt, sells the book). When the flush and happiness of the affair fades she will be left with long, empty years to deal with. (That's my elderly voice speaking. She may marry again within a few months, how do I know? It happens.)

This woman is my age, neighborly, with a host of friends. She also writes of flowers, cats, food, but adds the birds and animals she watches outside her windows. It is a domestic scene, wise and observant. Friends compensate for the losses that over the years we must all endure, accept. I'd like to take tea with her, I'd learn.

This one, an outdoor woman, rebuilt her life after the collapse of hopes, after pain and divorce. Now she is a beekeeper traveling the country selling and delivering her honey. She would be a fine companion, I think, letting you comfortably into her truck, her life. Or do I like her because I am also an outdoor woman who has had to rebuild *my* life? I wonder what people will find in these pages? I had better go stir my porridge instead of thinking, I smell it burning. What readers find in the book I wrote as bird journals never ceases to astonish me. If we could stand aside, see ourselves as others see us? No, I think not.

In today's mail is a letter from the Florida Game and Fresh Water Fish Commission requesting the locations and estimates of size of Least tern colonies I found in that state from 1970–1975. I moan. I suppose I have these somewhere in the jumbled cartons of files in my mouse closet. Their request will demand patience, time, trips to town for xeroxing. But what did I do all that work for if not to have it useful, even if 15 years later? Condominiums and golf courses now nest by the beaches where terns used to hover, carrying miniature fish to their miniature young.

Unhappily I dump out the cartons onto my table and set to work, watching a Great Blue heron fly over the pond, trailing its long legs. In a February thaw fog has shrouded trees on the far side. It creeps along the shoreline.

Over my desk hangs a large painting of Common terns that Chris Pineo did in 1971, back in the days when the tern study on Great Gull Island was relatively new; when supplies, and water in hogsheads, came over Long Island Sound in a fishing boat, to be carried ashore over an alarmingly rickety dock. When our only bathing facility was the jellyfish-laden, cold, salty Atlantic. Chris was young, and shy. He kept his door closed—quite a trick in the warp and rubble of the old army barrack where he and I lived, brushing our teeth leaning out of our respective windows, sleeping among the broken glass and fallen plaster on the floors. As we became friends he let me see paintings he was working on for the American Museum of Natural History of the resident birds on this small, sea-sprayed island they owned. Afternoons he might row me out to his lobster pot in the hope there might be some of these crustaceans big enough to eke out our crew's supper. He measured them conscientiously, putting back those that were too small, as usually they were. Later his fine paintings were exhibited in the windows of Abercrombie & Fitch, the famous New York sporting goods store of those years. When I left he offered me my choice of one, as a gift.

What I most wanted was his delicate rendition of Spotted sandpipers emerging from a clump of grass, but the Director of this important tern study, Helen Hayes (not the actress) was studying Spotties there, living in blustery weather as early as March, sleeping rolled up by an ancient stove that was the only heat; living on peanut butter, jam, and enthusiasm. Helen was the young instigator, mastermind, cook, and beloved leader of what became a long-term research project, still ongoing on this small, eroded, former Spanish-American war army post (expensively fortified, no shots fired). She had learned, through color banding, that once a female Spottie lays her eggs she leaves the household chores of incubation and feeding to the male; picks up with another mate, nests again. This was a behavior published when the feminist revolution was noisily fighting for the recognition that men were involved in parent-hood too. I'm surprised the organizations shouting for wom-en's rights didn't put a Spottie on their banners. Helen had asked for this painting so I settled happily for a pair of Common tern perched on a driftwood stump—a pleasure every time I look at it.

Over my stairs, shadowed in dim light, flies a Least tern, given me by Cal (for Caulion, no wonder he shortened it) Sin-gletary in my Homestead days. His fine photographs then graced

Audubon and other fine wildlife magazines: It is from his black and white early days. The year I left Florida to winter in a small rock cabin in the Arizona mountains, Cal gave me a huge color photograph of a Least tern brooding its chicks, to keep me from being homesick. Did you ever try hanging a large picture on an irregular rock wall so that it is secure, and straight? I can advise you.

In my kitchen, stained by smoke and water when young vandals had set fires in my three-roomed Florida cottage, is an Eckelberry drawing of Sooty terns flying against the background of Soldado Rock, a 200-foot crag off the coast of Trinidad where once I spent a marvelously uncomfortable night with Richard and Margaret ffrench. Overhead, shifting in air currents moved clouds of seabirds like shadows against the bright stars. Under our cots silently terns moved their eggs from their scrapes in the rock to a safer distance, so that when we woke in the morning our area was empty.

There is a story to every painting in this home. How did I get into this? I am sorting files from Florida for the Fish and Game men. If I don't reply to a letter the day it comes in it becomes obscured in the pile. I don't envy friends jaunting off this winter to warmer climes; to Ghana, Morocco, to the excitement of glamorous (in the travel folders) cruises. I have more than enough to do right here, paying my dues for past pleasures.

February 1985

The past swirls in without warning. Yesterday a man called.
He was new on the job, his editor had ordered him—to get
rid of him, I decided—to write a column on Why People Go
Birdwatching.

"How did you happen to call *me?*" I asked. He had been
given my name by an ornithologist I haven't birded with since
I left Florida, whom occasionally I meet at conferences. Instantly
I was returned to hot, arduous hours I had struggled through
mangrove roots and mosquitos on the heels of this kindly scientist, being patiently instructed in plants new to me. In gratitude for these sudden memories—the wide Florida skies, the
limestone rock that had sliced my sneakers, the raucous cries
of waterbirds we startled—I consented to talk with this young
reporter. It was obvious he knew nothing about birders and
what we do and, I soon concluded, had little interest. In my
most teacherly tones, trying to open his eyes just a little to the
vital resources of the natural world, I gave him a short education. He sounded surprised when I asked that he send me two

copies of what he would write. Why should he? I educated him a bit on that, too—courtesy toward those whose time you usurp, the report on his accuracy that I would supply to his editor, who is a neighbor.

Last night as I dressed for dinner—that is, I was shifting from jeans to a long skirt and ruffled blouse; from sneakers to slippers suitable for the home I was bound for, the telephone rang.

"Damn," I muttered. "I'm late already. Can't I ever get anywhere on time?" But since I never know who may be on the end of the wire, what change it may bring to my life, I answered cheerily.

"Jonnie!" The voice was as resonant, as welcome as it had been 15 years ago when its owner and I used to sprawl in the languorous dusk on the steps of the National Audubon research station on the Florida Keys.

"Do you remember," the voice asked when the usual exclamations and trading of vital statistics had been accomplished, "that when you were working on Least tern colonies I did a survey for you on the Keys? You were hollering, writing, speechmaking to get protection for them. An architect from the Midwest wrote you, asking for particulars on roofs where you had discovered them nesting. He wanted to know the designs of such buildings, how large they were, how near to water. Would you know how I could get hold of him?"

"Richard!" I exploded. "That was 15 years ago, how could I possibly remember?"

Richard waited. I thought. Least tern had been a focus of my life for many years. Working for the U.S. Fish and Wildlife Service I had pinpointed their breeding colonies along the Atlantic coast. They are more important to me than promptness to a dinner party.

In Florida I had located colonies on the flat roofs of shopping centers, industrial buildings, condominiums, banks. This research project was at first all my own because ornithologists couldn't believe that the robin-sized opportunistic birds were finding these nesting habitats safer than their traditional beaches become rutted by vehicles, usurped by people, paved for parking lots and airports. Those beaches, those rooftops I had climbed to, the people who had helped in an eventually increasing protection not only for Least tern but for other sand-nesting species—plover, skimmer, willet, oystercatcher—are burned deep in my memory.

"Wait," I said. Richard waited. "Horseberger. I can't believe I remember, and that isn't quite it. Notre Dame, I think. I was sure he was a kook, except for killdeer no birds would be nesting on Chicago roofs! But I answered his questions as best I could, sent him copies of articles I'd written, newspaper photographs. When he thanked me, asked for more, his letterhead showed him Chairman of a Foundation studying something so esoteric I couldn't even spell the titles of its Board members, much less pronounce them. He was a renowned architect. I wrote him about Lou Greene in Fort Lauderdale. She had first alerted me to the roof nesting, on a Port Authority building there. She and Ed used to climb 60 feet up on an outside ladder to photograph and monitor a colony of 200 nests. They talked me up that ladder once, on a windy day, it was hairy. Skimmers also tried to nest there, but their eggs stuck in the hot tar under and gravel and broke. Lou got the Port Authority so interested that ever since they have built their warehouses to our Audubon specifications. A public service, they consider it.

"Horseberger. Rich, I haven't kept papers and letters from those years. Migrating north and south every six months I had to jettison anything that wasn't current. My only tern files would be on the work I have done here, on Cape Cod. If I have those."

Richard waited. "I'll look," I promised him, "but there were only three letters, I wouldn't have kept them."

Rich told me more about his family, his job. I told him about my new career as author and lecturer. We sighed over the days we had worked together on the Keys. Lazy mornings out on calm shallows of the bay studying the Reddish egret that were his interest; the cold beer and good lunches at bay-side restaurants that refueled us. As we wound down I suggested he try to find out who had run the Department of Architecture at Notre Dame in the mid-seventies, see if there was a name like Horseberger, which made him laugh. He wants to put notes in architectural magazines suggesting that buildings be designed like those in Fort Lauderdale, to incorporate space and safety for birds since man is so rapidly obliterating their habitat. A very fine idea, I told him, I'm in favor of it.

I wasn't too late to the dinner party. My excuse was at least unusual, it was accepted. Today, without optimism I haul out some 20 pounds of files I have kept on terns—newspaper clippings, articles, photographs, journals. I am amazed as I sift these to find how much work unwittingly I had done, the impact my small crusade to help one small bird had made as I dealt with federal employes, refuge managers, bank janitors, IBM vice presidents, state game men; the hours and weeks, in rain or shine, I had happily tramped beaches. While the birds are still not thoroughly protected, effort has been made, recognition of the decline of their species grows annually. Not fast enough, probably, to save them.

As I return the last box to the closet I see a solitary manila envelope. Photographs, I remember, sent me by a German in thanks for material I mailed him one year. I pick the envelope by the wrong corner, its contents spill out. Photographs, yes. A sheaf of material I once sent to the *Miami Herald* for an articles they wanted to write. (It had taken a call from my lawyer to get this back) And then—astonishingly—

Eureka! In bold black ink, the entire margin needed to list the officers, trustees, advisors of the Environic Foundation International, is the name and address of Patrick Hoorsbrugh. Well, pretty close to Horseberger, as I puzzle over his signature. The letters told me why he was interested in my information, but most of the words weren't in my out-of-date dictionary.

A mouse died in the wall of this closet sixteen years ago. Its memory is still fragrant. I keep wine and liquor, manuscripts past and possibly future, cartons of the books I take to sell at my lectures, a manual typewriter for emergencies, and a large assortment of file boxes and cartons from my past in this closet. Regularly I promise myself to take these last to the town dump so my heirs needn't. Thank God I haven't. From now on they are reprieved, blessed, they will live in this house as long as I do. Dr. Patrick Hoorsbrugh! I wonder if he is still alive, if Richard can locate him? Of course he won't report to me— biologists are too busy to write social letters.

JONNIE FISK
28

March 1985

My dentist is a dour fellow, not surprising when you figure he spends his time poking into mouths. While he picks about mine he asks about little brown birds he has seen, and the shorebird lookalikes he notices on weekend vacations. He pulls a small notebook describing these from a pocket, reads to me while I am speechless with my mouth propped open. Overtime—a lot of time, a lot of fillings—I have educated him to some extent into the realization of wing bars, bill differences, tail shapes; have promoted him to the easier identifications of herons and grosbeack. We are friends.

After 50 years of conventional domestic life; gardening, housework, child raising, my wedding ring had to be cut off a finger enlarged and grown arthritic. One of the indignities of age (every day seems to bring a new one). My beloved had arrived in Boston our wedding weekend with no ring to bind the ceremony. We made a hasty trip to the secondhand shops of Beacon Hill—in 1926 marketing was less competitive, the better stores were closed on Saturdays. Our anxious search had only enhanced the value of my circlet to us. We were in too much of a hurry, too dazed with happiness to ask its history.

The elderly small town jeweler in Florida who snipped off my golden ring had eyed it with disparagement. It was too thin, he pronounced, to be enlarged. The flowers that had ornamented it were long gone, it was now just a delicate, useless piece of metal shining from my past. Seeing my distress, he could, he suggested, make a small cross from it. Perhaps. He wrapped it on cotton in a small box—a casket.

I have felt extraordinarily naked without it. While after 26 years of widowhood practically no one uses anything but my nickname, or my legal, professional name, no Mrs., I like people to realize that my children and grandchildren are legitimate, the honorable issue of Bradley Fisk, with excited assists from me. I had brought the ring north with me. On a recent dental appointment I offered it to Dr. Charles. To use for a filling, I suggested. I'd bet it was better gold than the modern stuff he charged me for. He was shocked. Use a wedding ring to fill a tooth? He summoned his laboratory expert from his wizard's den below stairs. They conferred over my head as we waited for novacaine to work its magic. They inspected my knuckle, measured my finger, conferred again.

Today a slim golden circlet proclaims me the relict of a warm, loving man, my families definitely legitimate. Tonight I will place it under the Bachrach photograph of Brad, seeking his second blessing on it while I sleep, hoping to dream of him. That photograph has its own history: painful. Some other day. One memory triggers another.

Unfortunately I believe that when someone dies they are gone. They are not in heaven, not looking down as, in spite of common sense, I often childishly hope, not sitting at a table in the clouds drinking ambrosial wine with friends, noting our mortal troubles and triumphs. Their spirits do not roam the sky, are not reincarnated—they are gone. Only as they are remembered do they live. I rub my slender, shining golden circlet. We create our won happinesses.

Nursing a bad throat I am being lazy, sitting at the big window looking at wind ripples chasing across the pond, at the glisten and gloves of raindrops on my bushes. Two fat gray squirrels chase around a tree trunk. An equally fat vole has pushed his way up through pine needles to glean corn the quail missed. It must be a male, females have better sense than to come out in this weather. Besides, by now they should be caring for a litter deep below my terrace. You study authors and their habits, I tell my editor on the phone as I watch; feed them. I study voles and their habits, feed them. They resemble plump mice. They make tunnels under the most expensive lawns, chew the bulbs and roots of garden flowers, are incredibly prolific. Valuable creatures, one of the bases of the food chain.

The quail don't leave them much. A covey ran through the yard a while ago, pecking at yesterday's leftovers. It is easier to add quail than the bank statements spread before me. The quail file erratically in broken formation through last fall's chrysanthemum plants, pecking; scattering under the feeders. The dominant male stands guard on a log. Sometimes I count 11, sometimes 9—or do I miss a couple, their streaked brown plumage the color of fallen leaves? On sunny days they rest in a hollow in a circle facing out so they can see danger approach, as the pioneers ringed their covered wagons on the Western plains, watching for Indians. Spiny lobsters migrating off the coast of Bimini do this, too. Quail are as big as the sharp-shinned hawk that comes looking for a meal. I doubt he takes one, their camouflage is so good I often use binoculars to make sure they are really in their hollow. Doves are easier pickings for the hawk, slower moving, although he misses them often. A winter bird has a hard time of it. No casseroles in his freezer.

Yesterday before the rain I stood at this window and looked over the pond glimmering through marsh grass, narrowing into a small river. A Great Blue heron stood on its edge, a hundred gulls found water deep enough to float in. The curving shores were edged with shafts of ice in pewter, bronze, silver, crystal. A flounder fisherman in an old boat with a mast but no sail was breaking a wide circle of open water that spread out, closed in again, sent ducks up from the edge of the marsh. My view is never twice the same.

Emily stops in at noon, bringing grapefruit, croissants, and frozen lemonade with honey and a small bottle of rum to soothe my throat. Coming down from the bathroom she pauses on the stairs, looking for any new photographs in my Rogue's Gallery. On one side are Brad and our children at different stages; citations, historical items. On the other are men I have worked with, who have cared for me since I've been alone, who have eased my path.

"How come you and your editor are good friends?" she asks, studying his face. "Nice eyes. How old is he?"

"Younger than my children," I tell her, amused. "It's a telephone friendship. He has an 800 number so we talk a lot." Editors—the ones I've known, need to build a special relationship with their authors. They're like doctors, only it's what's inside your head and heart they're concerned with, not your bones and lungs and allergies. I've dealt with only one woman, English. She accepted an article on Striped owls by air mail before air mail was common and didn't change a word so I thought she was great. I'm not sure I'd take criticism well from a woman but maybe that's because I'm a widow, happy to be associated with a man, even just his voice. I judge people by what flows without their knowing it over the wire. You deal with essence, you learn as much from pauses as from their words. The man beside him is my broker, he lives in California. He has a cheery, protective voice but not an 800 number so I don't call him as often. The next is my CPA, he lives in Miami. I thought I should put them all in one frame—protective icons.

There are two other photographs in that frame but fortunately Emily doesn't ask about them. They are of men with whom I worked in foreign countries. Often I pause on the stairs, regarding those faces, thinking how empty my years would have been without them. They don't fill the vacuum but like flowers, like candles and firelight, their voices make my home less lonely.

Emily has brought my accumulated mail. After she leaves I plump my couch pillows and lie, sorting it. Mail full of unexpected lumps and interest. I set aside the newspapers and magazines, drop on the floor highly colored, high decibel brochures on trips I can win to Hawaii or the Caribbean; on kitchen equipment, cameras. There are bills, orders for my bird-banding booklet; letters from people I know, from strangers. These letters are gambles. One is from a woman asking if I might be willing to give an opinion on a manuscript. Her letter is shy, hesitant. People have helped me all along my way, surely I can take time to help her. Another is from a woman who wants me to critize a book she has written. I don't like her letter. If I approve her pages, she says, would I pass them on to my editor? (The book is already in the mail.) I don't mind being used, really, often there are interesting results, but I do appreciate courtesy and there is none here. A naive young couple who have written and illustrated a bird book ask advice on marketing it. Always there are pleas for funds, from the local firemen's association to the many conservation organizations and nature centers I have been involved with, talked to. They are all expanding, increasing staff. I would like to help each one but how can I? Their newsletters pile up on my desk, full of information I could use if I had the time to read it, if I could remember it. Oh dear.

Here is a program request for next fall. How do I know where I will be on that date, if I will even be alive?

I get letters from lonely women needing letters in *their* mailboxes; wanting to know how I have managed my widow-hood. I haven't time or strength for them, I can't be leaned on. One showed up at my door the other day. I couldn't be rude so I made tea and spent half an hour listening to her blather about my being a role model.

"Find some work to do," I told her finally. "Never mind what it is. It will get you up in the morning, involve you with people, demand responsibility. Most people aren't as lucky as you are, look at your life that way."

This wasn't the advice she wanted, but what more could I say?

Also in the mail Emily has brought are postcards from farflung grandchildren, two wandering in India, two making their way on a shoestring on bicycles through France; and a request for information on the Asa Write Nature Centre in Trinidad. I get these often. The Centre was Spring Hill Estate in 1959 when first I went there, one of many visits over 14 years. Well past its day as a producing plantation, its mountain rain forest had not yet become a mecca for tropical naturalists. Dr. William Beebe of the New York Zoological Society, famous for his undersea bathysphere explorations as well as for his tropical research, still lived, elderly and ill at Simla, a few hairpin miles down the fern-edged walls of the mountain road. Also elderly and ill, equally famous naturalists of a past period came from England and Europe to live inexpensive winter weeks in one of Asa's three guest rooms, enjoying each other's tales of past adventures, past glories; her native food, the beauty of her then unspoiled valley, the flowering trees and shrubs shading, overrunning, her verandah. Richard Meinertzhagen was one to whom I brought cold drinks and tea cakes, his eminence as an ornithologist and colonial soldier unknown to my ignorance.

Or do I remember his name only because I read it so often in the piles of rain-stained scientific papers that cluttered the tables of her verandah? Asa rarely bothered to bring these inside during showers.

"Jawnie" she would protest in her deep voice when I spread them out to dry, knowing they must be valuable. "Don't trouble yourself." She was not a naturalist but a marvelous raconteur and hostess. Her rich voice sounded through the rooms all day berating her one crippled servant—whom an hour later she might affectionately drive to church or family 15 hazardous miles down valley.

Slowly her home became a stop for naturalist tours, bringing her in a little money, although the price she charged for lavish lunches, or the $6 a day for five meals and laundry if you stayed, was minimal; as was the two cents apiece she might get for the grapefruit we delivered in her battered jeep to hotels in Port of Spain. She was better known at the hotel back doors than at the front, as she explained to an English Commissioner's wife who had left a formal invitation to a Garden Party at the Queen's Hotel. I was disappointed we had missed this gala occasion, but as Asa pointed out, my luggage didn't include white gloves and a wide-brimmed garden hat. By then I had learned many back doors, the huts and homes, pig farms and cockfight yards, of various Trinidadians; the hospital, the economic edge on which she carelessly lived, ignoring it.

Bit by bit over years she turned her dilapidated home into an inn equally dilapidated but made glamorous by her lusty stories of our predecessors, of her life in Iceland, of the royalty it had been her task—hardly a pleasure, she sniffed—to entertain. Her uncle?—her father?—had been high in the government. A judge? A prime minister? My attention was more focused on tropical tanagers and hummingbirds in the tangle of flowering shrubs about us than on the history with which she regaled her guests. One birder more sedentary than I one day counted 33 species in an hour in a pink-flowering tababui tree off the verandah. Alas, birds were more important to me than tales of bygone royalty.

A formal, faded photograph of Asa at her presentation to the Court of St. James hung in her formal drawing room with its furniture of an era equally faded. For a time mine hung beside it, my shorts and sleeveless blouse in sharp generational contrast to the dignified elegance of her gown. I suspect both are long gone now. For a while my face also hung in the hearts, as did theirs in mine, of the managers who succeeded each other once the Centre had been set up, but they too are long gone, none of them could last under Asa's autocratic interference. I sympathized with them the winter I had to take over, run the Centre. Even without Asa to countermand my orders, make me reach for soothing libations, when after six weeks I finally escaped I vowed never to set foot south of the Carolinas again. What a book I could have written of those weeks! If I'd had time, if I'd known I was going to end up an author in search of a subject!

"How come you are so special?" Don Eckelberry asked one evening. A group of us were spread about his and Ginny's room discussing how to keep the Centre alive until Asa died, before she destroyed it entirely. Only that night at dinner she had accused a dignified lady from Boston of being a Lesbian. The woman had stood, turned to me, folding her napkin.

"I don't have to stand for this," she had said. "Can you recommend another inn for the three of us?" Asa had glared at me as I wrote the name of an excellent place in Tobago, thinking how badly we needed this lady's money.

"You are the only one of us she hasn't publicly accused of

sexual misconduct, deviancy, or drunkenness," Don had continued. "How come you are spared?"

Asa and I had a special relationship. She had cared for me lovingly like a mother after Brad had died in Guatemala, when I had been unable to return north to face our children and friends. I had cared for her lovingly like a daughter one fall when she had had a heart attack—and no wonder! All those chocolate cakes with rich sauces poured over them that she reveled in at tea time (carefully slicing off rat nibbles)! Her gusto for living had turned into culinary appetite. She would be guiltily angry with me for refusing the two and three helpings she urged; even angrier if I managed not to appear for tea at all. At the end she turned even on me. She couldn't prevent my pushing her wheelchair, my visits to her room, but stubbornly she refused to talk to, even to look at me. All forgotten the winters I had been there catching birds for Don to paint, the dawns I had set nets down on the flats, or up in the ridges collecting data for Richard ffrench's invaluable *Guide to the Birds of Trinidad and Tobago*—a book that Asa herself had instigated, that brought her the many bird tours, the conservation organizations now supporting her.

"That's why," I tell my children angrily, "I'm going to quit life before I hurt all of you like that. I won't put you through that hell."

Although it is a question, I ruefully admit, of knowing, of recognizing when the time has come. My father died of a heart attack after a good dinner and an afternoon at the horse races, my mother after an afternoon's swim on Cape Cod, Our son slipped into sleep watching a movie he had helped to produce. My heart isn't all that good either, so I am up for grabs, I just haven't decided on my druthers.

Where was I before I became entangled in this? Sipping a

rum and honey lemonade Emily made for me before she left, immersed in memories of Trinidad, reading my mail.

April 1985

A trash truck in town has a bunch of artificial jonquils tied above its gaping maw. Daffodils are bright on my hill, sturdily raising their heads after three days of rain. Forsythia brightens corners, green furzes lilac twigs but the oaks are not yet even budded. Weighing the cold wind that bends the tall pitch pines I opt for my typewriter instead of the brisk walk I like before breakfast to limber my joints. Early passersby on the road below are more disciplined than I. A neighbor who bundles groceries at the supermarket—to get away from the women in his house, he tells me cheerfully—walks his old dog. A teen-ager or two reluctantly scuffle toward the school bus stop. A jogger in a red jacket is new. A middle-aged couple in ski clothes and caps march by, determinedly making their daily circle about the pond before their breakfasts. Squirrels chase under my squirrel-proof feeder, hunting what titmice and chickadees spill. The feeder swings like a big soap bubble in the spring wind, its clear plastic reflects blue from the sky, green from the pines. The raccoon returned in the warm weather last week, after a winter's absence, but must have gone back to sleep, my suet feeder hangs undisturbed. Last week he pulled it into branches I can't reach, although the bough he must have used is so slender it's hard to believe he can navigate this. Or do big, glossy crows send it swinging loose in the wind as they flap off it? A skunk made small holes in the pine needles of my terrace last night, digging for insects. I'd think it too cold for insects. Last summer's chipmunk is back, running along the wall, pauses to look at me. I keep planning to tame him with peanuts but I don't take time.

My spirit soars with Spring.

I drive to Cornell—a long way but even leafless that New York landscape, once I cross the Hudson, is beautiful—rolling hills, farms, rivers, the history of the Erie Canal flowing beside me. When we lived in Buffalo I drove this road often, on my way to our Boston or Vermont relatives. The names of the small towns I go through are a litany.

My lecture at the Laboratory of Ornithology is to men and women who know far more of my subject than I do but they are nice about it. I worked at the Lab one summer, then was on the Board of Directors, so many of them are friends willing to accept my amateur status, interested in my new writing career. It is exciting to be there. I am a dilettante in that academic world, but just breathing its atmosphere stimulates me.

I drive further west to Buffalo, where Brad and I brought up our children. I give programs at the Museum and at the Club, see old and dear friends, am Author in Residence—there's a resounding title for you!—at our children's school. Life hasn't changed much there. It's a world I moved out of when Brad died. If I had stayed our friends would have sheltered me, I might even have married again, but I couldn't stay, I had to grow new roots. It is a very different culture from our coastal one, I have a lot to mull over on my way home.

At Williams College I stop and am again brought into the academic environment, into efforts to save our planet's resources. I am queried as to what I am doing in research now that I am living—retired is how it is put, rather critically—on Cape Cod. This intensifies my mulling as I head home.

I repack my bag and drive across the state to talk at a regional conference. I shouldn't have. Almost everyone there is a colleague from some stage of my ornithological life. They remind me of who I really am under this Joseph's coat of authorship, of where I had taught myself to fit into their community. This took me 20 years of striving, I can't just discard it. They are interested and amused that I have written a book (some even buy copies), but they pressure me on what am I doing now in the field? They set me back into the niche I had carved for myself, not noticing how dusty it has become, how rusty I have become. Their genuine feeling shakes me. It makes me anxious to quit this publicity nonsense I have slid into, playing all this time, being flattered, laughing, laughing. (How many years since I had laughed like that?) It's been wonderful. But now I need to work at projects quiescent in my mind, to answer letters spilling overlong on my desk; to fulfill social obligations even if this means learning to cook again; to dig a respectable garden, take care of this house I had built, stand on the lectures I've given.

"*Ave atque vale,*" I wrote my editor. "When I've made an honest woman of myself I'll come back." This worries me. Can you go back? How much have I changed?

June 1985

Father's Day

Well, it was Father's Day when I put this sheet in my type-writer, now it is three days later. I am celebrating the day a little late by baking health bread for my student colleagues. They eat too many potato chips for their good. None of them are fathers.

All week I have been out on a barrier beach with them, "consulting." They live in a shack in the midst of wild roses and poison ivy, study, at the moment, plover, deer, crows, tree swallows. They have set out at least 50 boxes for these last in the marsh; to my critical mind too many and too close together, but the birds don't seem to mind. That for old lady consultants! They are giving me, they say, I haven't seen it yet—a tee-shirt that says "Consultant" on it.

When I was young I used to go out with young gentlemen

at eight-thirty at night, now it is at six in the morning. It's an imperfect world.

The bread smells delicious. I will eat a crust for my supper, claiming it should be tasted, tested, before giving. That's fair, isn't it?

July 1985

When I decided to go back to being a Bird Lady I had forgotten that in nesting season I work 12 hours a day out on one beach or another, and that I am woefully out of shape. Why doesn't it rain? My family and friends complain they can't reach me, don't they have telephones that function at night? Just because I am retired doesn't mean that I am home all day washing and waxing and making strawberry jam!

What I have been doing mostly this past month has been driving at 6 A.M. to the sand dunes of a barrier beach 30 miles away. In a parking lot at that hour empty I transfer into the front seat of the truck of a graduate student who is making a long-term study of Piping plovers. These are small, plump shore birds five and a half inches long that live most of the year from the Carolinas south to the Gulf Coast of Mexico, briefly flying north to reproduce. In the last century they were annually shot by the thousands by hunters, egged out by hungry fishermen. With legal protection from the Migratory Bird Treaty of 1918, they have made a comeback, but no one is sure how viable their population is. In some states they are an endangered species, as each year they lose more of their sandy, solitary habitat to summer homes, vehicles, kids, dogs. There is worldwide anxiety about their survival.

In the hope that with my years of experience I may have learned a couple of things he hasn't yet, young Eric takes me out with him. (And because I have a banding license, which he doesn't yet.) He needs someone to talk with, he likes the cookies I bring, I can observe from one side of his truck while he watches out the other. Birds accept a vehicle, it is a perfect blind for observation and photography. I find it also comfortable for catnaps when the sun is hot and no wind—or plover—stirs.

When you study a bird the first need is to catch it, mark it in some way so it is individually recognizable, so you don't need to catch it and handle it again. Then you can tell which bird belongs to which nest, with which mate; with binoculars recognize it next week, next year, for as long as its colored plastic leg bands or wing flags don't fade. Eric needs both male and female from each nest. We catch them by placing, carefully, a large cage of light-weight wire over a nest whose four eggs (once Eric has located them) lie well camouflaged in a scrap in the sand. One side of the cage is propped on a stick, a string runs from the stick to our truck window. A quick pull will drop the cage over bird and eggs without damage to either. Very simple, if you don't watch the clock. Once the bird is trapped one of us then extracts it—carefully again—places a numbered government band on a leg, accompanies this with colored bands in a predetermined and recorded order; carefully measures and examines our catch, then releases it to resume incubation. The trick is to note which way today's footprints patter to the nest, which way the wind blows, so as to be sure which of the four cage sides will be the front door, so to speak. And then to be patient. That is the trick.

When we invade its territory the bird, naturally, leaves its nest. It protests loudly, flutters, drags a wing as if injured, to lure us away from its precious eggs. When we retire to our truck shortly it returns, bobbing characteristically, crouching as if on a false nest to fool any watching enemies. It walks warily about the wire addition to its home. It is unhappy, but in this species the urge to incubate is stronger than its anxiety, so after considerable fussing, inspecting, circling, maybe flying away, then coming back to repeat the sequence, our bird walks in, walks out, in again, finally settles on the eggs. We give it a few minutes to warm, or cool its treasure, then pull the string. All this demands patience. If the bird has been trapped before, this year or last year, perhaps even the year before, it is reluctant to enter. If it stays away too long we must dismantle our trap, return another day, so as not to chill or overheat the eggs. A bird's safety comes first, science second. I am more patient than Eric, that is why he needs me.

Only there are two plovers attached to each nest, trying to protect it from two-legged or four-legged enemies. In the way of our modern human generation some avian species split after a love affair, leaving a single parent with the domestic burden. Plovers share family duties. As with humans the female invests more time than the male, sits most often on their eggs. We tell the sexes apart by the amount of black on their orange bills, and on the black collars encircling their necks. Eric is keener at this than I am, that's why I need him.

Are you still with me? This is a $50 lecture you are getting, be appreciative.

We may already have banded one of our pair—yesterday or last week, or last year, so there is a 50 percent chance that once we settle back in the truck it is the banded bird that returns to incubate. We know about that bird, we don't want it. We must sit, and sit, until at some undetermined time the unbanded mate arrives to take over the duty. You see why there is plenty of time for sleeping? Only one of us must stay awake, be alert to make sure the birds don't unobtrusively trade off while we nod. On a gray day when the beach is empty a deer may pick its way from behind the dunes, wade out to sand bars, swim from one to another, gambol. I'll gladly sit all afternoon to watch that. If it starts to rain a bird mustn't be kept from its nest. If a clam digger comes along with his bucket, or a vehicle noisy with children and dogs, the bird just about to enter our cage flies off, our vigil begins again. Hazards are many. Research is a slow and patient occupation, not for everyone. On a hot day it is a somnolent one, almost a necessity to perform in congenial company. I've been lucky with my companions.

If we get our bird we drive down the beach to the next nest, repeat the process: keeping, as we drive, a sharp lookout for chicks that have hatched. They can run as soon as they are dry, they crouch from approaching danger in previous wheel tracks, are easily run over. Their camouflage is magnificent, meant to foil foxes and kindred predators but it evolved long before the days of beach buggies and Day-glo jackets.

We settle at our new location. Eric pulls out his notebooks, pores over his neat columns of data, discusses them with me. I pull out today's cookies and a thermos, check his recitations, sleep.

So that tonight at 1 P.M. I am still well awake, the day's mail sorted, letters written to go out tomorrow. The night is still, and hot, the tide gleams high in the pond. I'll swim before I go to bed. At this hour I can safely drop my clothes on the dock and skinny dip.

August 1985

My Beach Boys have returned with a Chinese man from an excursion to the Canadian West. They want me to go out in their truck with them tomorrow, hoping I can cope. He has no English.

My experience doesn't run to Chinese. Turks, Latins, Europeans of several tongues, Asians, yes. When we lived in Washington, because we had been abroad (however briefly, never enough to learn the language) I was asked to volunteer for a government agency that brought scientists to the States. My task was to meet their planes in the confusion of National Airport (there was no Dulles then); to pluck some hapless man whose name I would have on a slip of paper, that had been given to me over the telephone but not phonetically, from the line of debarking passengers. I would welcome him to our country, trace down his luggage, put him in a taxi with instructions to the driver, instructions to him as to what to pay the driver, and wave him off to whatever office or hotel was his assigned destination. I couldn't talk their languages, often they couldn't speak ours, but I had arrived at too many international airports myself not to recognize and sympathize with the bewilderment that identified them. They were always men (this was in the 1950s) but unexpectedly they might arrive with a wife and child, even a baby. This meant hasty telephone calls, hasty rearrangements of destination, unhappy comments from the other end.

With planes not necessarily arriving on schedule I might have to meet X at one end of the airport—fortunately in those days it was smaller—and Y at the other. Within minutes.

"Stay here," I would gesture to the first confused arrivé. "Don't move, I'll be back."

Off I would dash to find my second hapless charge (and family), then consolidate them and their luggage. I can't believe now that I actually did this, and successfully. I have clear memories of swift, frantic dashes through the crowds, my panic if X had disappeared, my incompetence. Somehow I managed. When arrivals were leisurely while we waited for luggage we would try to talk. I would ask where they were from, what their field of study was.

"I work with the underground," one middle-aged man told me proudly, pleased with his command of our language. Since I had friends in the CIA, knew they were trained not to talk, I explored this surprising statement further. He was en route to the Colorado School of Mines. . . .

Always they would ask me please, please to go with them in their taxi. Setting out alone with only a piece of paper and foreign currency was traumatic. My compassion level was high, it had to be. You put all you have into a job like that. I might meet one of them later on the street, at a reception. His face would light with recognition, with gratitude.

For a period after arrival my charges were immersed in classes at American University to acquire our language, our culture. When I could I would snatch an hour to attend these. I had another volunteer job trying to help foreign doctors, also recently arrived, with their English. I had no training for this, I needed help. Their teacher was a slim, quite gorgeous colored woman. Nowadays that adjective would be "black" but she wasn't, she was a golden café au lait who taught as much with body English as with her sentences, walking back and forth with a grace most people can't begin to match. How I wish I could go back to those days! So many opportunities I missed, so much more I could have done with training.

I couldn't teach my doctors in a formal frame as she did. They came and went with the exigencies of the hospital—an ambulance clamoring outside our window, a messenger at the door summoning one—or four—of my class away. While their English was scientifically correct—more or less—none of them had the street language of the poor and largely black patients they tended. Instead of grammar I concentrated on pronunciation using medical words—A as in scalpel, B as in bandage (different *a*s)—I've forgotten that alphabet I worked out, so useful to them. I knew from bitter complaints that they understood only a small percentage of words the staff used, of hastily given instructions. These were men—and one Korean woman—of intelligence, forced to go through American training under doctors whose lectures were delivered rapidly, in monotones, from heads bent over notes, with no regard for their students' lack of ability to understand them. I was enraged that the hospital wouldn't let me don a uniform and accompany doctors on their rounds so I might learn and teach the words they most commonly used in the wards. One finally did sit down with me for an hour to go through his lowest denominator vocabulary. I told him how my men had had an argument only that day asking me to determine whether "take down" means to reduce a temperature or simply to write it on a chart? They didn't know. God help their patients! He sympathized with my requests, but not the hospital hierarchy so I used the only tools I had—patience and friendship.

One year a Turk, well educated, high born, entered the class late, recuperating from pneumonia. Wan and bewildered, needing proper food to build his strength, when I asked how best I could help him he led me to the cafeteria to show what he could select that would be within his religious diet. To him hamburger of course would have ham in it—a no-no. A few weeks later he detained me to ask if gin and tonic would be acceptable, within his father's rules? Lonely, he had picked up a street woman. She had taken him to a bar, rolled him. A week later he asked if, having slept with her he must marry her? He was frightened of his fellow students, no one was helping him. I appealed to a Colombian, also high-born. Enrique had set himself up as my protector in this medical maze. One day I was asked if I would write on the blackboard a list of the words and phrases used by lower-class hospital patients for their private parts. Me, raised in a Victorian family where tooth brushing was the most physical fact of life ever discussed? Enrique had sprung to my aid.

"This is not a suitable subject for Dear Our teacher," he had pronounced firmly. "I, Enrique, will speak with you after class when she has left."

Dear Our teacher—how that phrase they used rings in my memory. How I wish I could better have helped those men! At a Christmas party a colleague and I set up we suggested they each describe how Christmas was celebrated in their country. Grown men, singing a carol, they broke down, in their own language they sobbed in homesickness.

Magazines, TV, rock songs blasting from my grandchildren's radios have increased my vulgar vocabulary. I find this limited. With all the richness in the English language, all the expletives, the similes that could be used, why must writers, young people, middle-aged people express themselves in just a dozen overworked, unattractive words that have lost their punch? The slang that baffled my doctors in those hospital wards would surely enrich many of the modern novels I read. Occasionally, to amuse myself, I mimic them. I am regarded with astonishment, with disapproval. I am supposed to act my age.

I've managed to break my new rehabilitated typewriter. I surely need a man to take care of me. Not a second husband, nor a Chinese, though.

I'm distressed when I'm asked how I write. It is a common and friendly question but how can I write when my days are shredded by social activities, domestic chores, unanswered letters? I am not a professional with an orderly schedule, a housekeeper, someone to make a dash to the supermarket because a guest is unexpectedly coming for dinner. I write preferably in the early hours before my stomach grumbles for breakfast, before the telephone rings. During the day if I am in the grip of a book, even of letters that need care in their composition, one part of my mind is sensibly aware of where I am, functions automatically, the other is floating in another world. Words, scenes, sentences flood in on me. If I don't immediately capture them on paper they are gone, I can't reconstitute them. I've said this before. It explains my glazed expression at meetings, or in the midst of chatter. If I'm driving I pull off the road, pull out a notebook.

I also pull off the road because, mesmerized by the efficient straight Interstates I must take (because they are quicker and I have been late starting) I become aware that I am weaving, falling asleep. If I am not near a rest area or a parking lot I drive off onto the roadside grass. This upsets state patrol officers. They pull up beside me, beep their horn. They come to my door to make sure this white-haired woman is not slumped in her seat with a heart attack. We discuss weariness, hearing aids, the possible danger to a lone female. If I have stopped to write, they may find me again some miles further down the highway, be displeased.

Today was intolerably hot. Lulled by the monotonous Massachusetts Turnpike I pulled off to nap. Of course my windows were open! But you'd hear, sense, wouldn't you, someone approaching your car? When I came to on the seat beside me were scattered a handful of colorful children's candies—life savers, gum drops, a lollipop. I had been aware of no one. I drive on more soberly. When I stop at a crowded Howard Johnson's I carefully lock my windows.

My light blue VW Rabbit looks like any other except the window behind the driver's seat is plastered with stickers of conservation organizations I belong to, have worked with. These bring me many questions, new acquaintances at shopping malls. Once at Brigantine National Refuge in New Jersey a car pulled up alongside mine. The driver looked me over, said, as he placed his telescope—

"You must be Mrs. Fisk."

My California son, traveling with me, was mightily astonished. As was I. The percipient birdwatcher had noted my Dade County, Florida, license plate. He had been once to my banding station in Homestead. Many people came there over the years, I didn't remember him. Joe Cadbury. We became

friends later at the Maine Audubon Camp, a really nice man. I don't need to see out the side window of my car that identifies me, I don't have a head that twists like an owl's.

Returning to my car at Howard Johnson's, licking an ice cream cone before it melts entirely, three small children run up with their mother. Had I liked their candy? they ask, laughing, delighted to encounter me a second time. What a coincidence, what a grace note in both our days!

I've been really frightened only once in the many thousands of miles I've driven each year—from the North to Florida, to Arizona, to California, to Canada, to Cape Cod. Migrating, alone as always, within twenty miles of my Florida cottage on its lonely lane I was following a big tractor-trailer down an empty two-lane highway that led south from the Tamiami Trail to Homestead, grateful for its lights that illuminated my way. I was unaware that the high beam I had needed earlier on a dark, narrow road flanked by canals was still on. At a turnoff—there were few in that agricultural country, there were no houses—the trailer slowed, deliberately jackknifed across my way. With hostility, evil in his every step, a bear of a man came snarling toward me. All I caught of his words was a menacing "I'll teach you to turn your high beam off" only he didn't say it as simply as that, his words and intent were brutal. If I angled out into a field, if there was no ditch, he had left me just enough room to get by him. He reached for my door handle but I was gone, fleeing down the highway before he could straighten out his rig, come pounding after me. A mile further south I could leave the highway, zigzag through a series of empty, dark roads that would lead me to the safety of my lane, my dark cottage behind hedges. Which I did.

Once I was safe I didn't realize how deeply this encounter had shaken me but now when I drive on a warm summer night often I am returned to the soft air of south Florida, the smells of dust, of vegetable fields stretching into the night, of his exhaust. I see again that hulking shape rolling toward me, hear that ugly voice. He marked me. I am careful about my high beam at night.

The thermometer at my window reads 94° and I am grumpy. Definitely grumpy, I realize, as I load my car with bird-banding equipment—notebooks, tools, nets, poles, a metal rod to make holes for the poles, a heavy mallet to pound these into ground that hasn't felt rain in a month. I should be watering my tomatoes, neglected because I have been away so often. Instead I am on my way to our Museum of Natural History to give a banding demonstration. At 2 P.M., an hour when birds aren't flying, particularly in this heat. I knew better last month than to schedule this program but the new naturalist has a passle of young day campers to keep occupied, weakly I had consented to help him. Now I must pay for this lack of judgment. I cast a longing look at a book that came in the morning mail, at the hammock I so rarely get to lie in, fill a thermos with the lemonade I'd like to drink in the hammock and drive off. Grumpily.

No one is about at the Museum. I cart my gear to a shady spot, open my folding table, gather up my poles and nets. Where I had placed these in the spring is grown to waist-high bushes and poison ivy. I clip a narrow path, tramp down its edges. I pound holes for the poles, string a net, tangled because I take them down in too much of a hurry. The feeder along the big museum window is empty but I anticipated this and scatter a jar of seed in the hope of enticing a blue jay, a red-wing, chickadees, perhaps a nuthatch. Immediately I snare a chipmunk I didn't anticipate. I'd forgotten to bring heavy gloves, fortunately he shakes out with only a little assistance.

A song sparrow flies by, is caught. I extricate it, hang it on a branch in one of the thin cotton bags I stitch for this purpose and work on Net Number 2. An elderly man raps on the Museum window, then comes to a door, agitated.

"A bird is hanging in a bag on that bush. It can't get out," he informs me. *Do something."*

Holding half-strung Net Number 2 above poison ivy I explain why the bird is hanging there, say I need ten more in similar bags. I am too hot and hasty to be as gracious and explanatory as I should be, he is bewildered. I have given research and the Museum a bad name.

Ordinarily someone would show up to help me, at the very least bring me a chair and a glass of cold water but today the area is somnolent. I fetch my own chair and water, sit by my table, watch chickadees fly up to my net, back off. Birds' eyes are far sharper than humans', they recognize danger. I still chide myself that I am here but gradually the quiet and shade relaxe me. Children the age of these campers will be either a rapt audience or resentful that they aren't engaging in a sport. It is a gamble.

The naturalist arrives with his charges, all eager, all wanting immediately to explore the nets, expecting them to be dripping with colorful birds. Fortunately a redwing, then a jay is caught. The children watch me extract these, pleased to see them bite my fingers, to see the original song sparrow escape as I reach my hand into its bag. I move into my instruction, teaching with the aid of the live birds and with the fine photographs I cut from magazines that pile up on my living room tables about bills, feet, plumages, food, habitat. We acquire several interested adults with good questions. I am doing something I have been doing for twenty years, that I thoroughly enjoy when it goes as well as it does now, making me feel useful. I net enough birds to let each child handle one, even the usual fat, overeager boy pushing ahead of the others, who predictably is upset when a waterthrush I am about to put in his hand pecks him. Waterthrush are our earliest migrant, I am pleased to have this one, I can talk about migration. I dismiss the fat boy, put the warm, five-inch bit of feathered life instead in the hand of the smallest of the group, who has been waiting his turn patiently, hopefully, eyes alight. He examines it with keen interest, smiles when he is pecked. The look on his face repays me as he releases it to fly on its long journey.

I am again hot when I have finished packing up, carried my gear to my car, sipped lemonade from my thermos. But what else do you have to do? I ask the woman still grumping inside me, complaining. Instead of lying in a hammock reading a book about how someone else contributes to our planet I have shared my mite with a score of people who may now look at other lives with more respect. The woman who had asked me how to teach a cat not to eat birds had been unhappy when I replied astringently that cats are animals that we human animals keep for our own pleasure. They should be kept indoors, or on a swivelled leash away from bird feeders, near a tree where they are free to sharpen their claws, climb. If each of the fifty to eighty million cats estimated to be in the United States catches only one bird a year, I said, that still removes from the avian population . . . She had stopped bristling though when I placed a bird gently in her hand, letting her feel the small warm body equipped with senses she lacks, as Henry Beston wrote; with abilities she can never aspire to.

A breeze has sprung up, the fiery sun is sinking. It hasn't been such a bad afternoon after all.

November 1985

Today I am cleaning bookshelves, finding manila envelopes of letters and articles that once mattered to me, vignettes the

New Yorker had printed in its early days with a check for $2.00 and a friendly scrawl from E. B. White: scraps of my past put away to reread, to savor. The task had begun with vigor on a rainy day but now goes more slowly.

I sit at my table reflecting on the small deaths of the spirit that scar us. These come unexpectedly, paring you to the essential bone; milestones on your passage. A letter from a woman you loved, once radiant, adventurous now become raddled, suspicious, lying; from a man once an integral part of our Saturday nights who left his wife for a younger woman, shutting the door on their children, on us; from friends who have betrayed my faith, diminishing me. I wonder what miseries haunt their midnights? If they do? Can I be sure I wouldn't have done the same? When faith is betrayed is it their fault or mine? Do I expect too much, build images to meet my needs? Ah, there's the rub that haunts *my* midnights. Put not your faith in princes, nor in their strength, wrote a Psalmist—a tag doubtless misremembered from my childhood instruction. I lose faith in myself—a small death nibbling at the person I thought I was.

Once at a jazz concert, in a tent, once at a poetry reading on the grass in the shadow of Washington's unfinished Cathedral I chanced to see lookalikes of men whose lives had been woven with ours—friends over many years, many good, some bad. Both now are dead. Removed from my physical surroundings I became anchored in an ambience of memory, a disturbance far stronger than the music, the voices I was there to hear. Our pasts, I think, become our strengths.

As also they reveal our weaknesses. On the Florida Keys, where highlights of an Audubon Christmas Count were being reported, a woman sat across the room from me. We were

clumped on hard chairs, weary from a long day in the field in
and out of cars with telescopes and binoculars, pushing through
vegetation scrub, through mangrove swamps. I judged this
woman was in her early sixties, as was I: with a solid figure,
hair like mine pulled tautly back from her face, her sneakered
feet firmly planted on the floor. She was the image of the widowed self I had not yet been able to accept, remembering how
I had been at forty, at fifty. That's how you must look to other
people now, I told myself bleakly. Sensing the lonely years she
must survive she is wishing, however subconsciously, that she
had a companion beside her, a man to love, to care for. But
what man would give her a second look? She would be acceptable to work with, have useful skills, a sense of humor, but to
take to bed?

I know *you* don't subconsciously hope for this, I told myself,
losing track of what birds were being reported, in what habitats. You are contented in what you do, in your new friends.
But deep below these everyday occupations if this is what you
are hoping for, forget it! I returned to the bird listing, joined
in the arguments. But inside me that evening something died.
Over the years, wanting not to, I have remembered that
woman—her sensible clothing, her gray eyes that passed over
me, the constriction she had given my heart. I see her still in
my mirror.

I've gone on. I have built a new woman, a new life. Satisfactory, cheerful, almost contented if I don't look back, if I
don't sort through old letters, photographs, scrapbooks. I'll
let my executors do that, take them to the town dump; clean
my home, make it fresh and welcoming for whoever comes in
next. They won't know about the small deaths of my spirit.
They'll have their own.

I've washed the bookshelves, this won't need doing for another year (or more!). I discard the manila envelopes, restore, carefully alphabetized, the books. I wonder with what my successor will replace these, what she will keep in her manila envelopes?

March 1986

A fox must have set up the ducks from the marsh. They rise in a flock of shadows against the lowering sky, are skeining across the river. A Great Blue heron flaps ponderously behind them. Our winter has been cold. Some snow, but no big storms since Christmas. I'm too old to be living this way but I pay no attention. Wellesley, Chicago, New York, Connecticut, enjoying old friends, meeting new ones. Talking, talking: at Plymouth, my local grandkids' school. Today I'm packing for a research trip in the Bahamas—sneakers and shorts instead of heels, a hat, and my formal manners; teen-agers instead of their parents. How exciting it is each time to come home and see the red light blinking on my telephone answering machine! Wonder Where Next?

After the Bahamas is to be Boston again, Albany, New Jersey, Pennsylvania: to honor a woman who singlehandedly saved Least tern colonies on the Delaware coast. From this last I can stop in New York City on my way home, see those nice people at Norton. The last time I was in New Jersey my lecture hat was searched at the Atlantic City airport. To see if I was carrying drugs in the hatband? We were fogged in, I was two hours late for dinner at the other end.

Why am I doing this to myself at my age? Because it's such *fun*. Because I want to cram in everything I can before I die. Besides, what else do I have to do? Get my hair cut, my teeth cleaned, eat lunch with friends, stuff envelopes for organizations mailing fund appeals? Join a reading club, nap in the afternoons? These trips, these invitations to speak are a gift. Undeserved, but I'm not about to turn them down.

April 1986

I have a friend, Susan, valuable to me. Since we both travel, she is involved in Boards and Committees, we see each other only off and on but the bond is close. She is modern, resourceful, energetic; always knows a good travel agent, a reliable carpenter, a pleasant, old-fashioned hotel in a town I will be driving to. It greatly surprised her that I wrote two books that in their small way have become successful. It distresses her that I exposed in them what, to her conservative way of thinking, should be kept private.

She tries to improve me; urges on me mechanical kitchen

tools, extolls the benefits of a new car to replace my battered one. I listen dutifully, hug her, would go out of my way for her any time, which she knows. But not enough to buy a new car!

She is uncertain as to when I manage to do my writing since she never catches me at it unless I am correcting proof, grumbling mightily at a copy editor whose demands for precision are foreign to my style; grumbling equally at myself for the typos my hasty typing produces, no matter how careful I try to be. Today Susan has asked me for lunch, just the two of us, serving an excellent cold soup whirled up in her Cuisinart, a crisp salad with lettuce washed and dried in another gadget.

"What I have you here for"—she eyes me authoritatively over iced tea fragrant with lemon mint and something else I don't analyze—"is because I want you to use my word processor." She raises a warning hand. "I know, we've been through this before, you say one wouldn't help you but you haven't really tried, have you?"

She knows the answer. I am entirely comfortable with a pencil and a yellow pad in bed, or sitting at my typewriter looking out the window at birds and squirrels, a neighbor's dog, a rabbit, a fox. I *could* use a Cuisinart to make my soups and mayonnaise but an ancient blender does the job quite adequately. I like to beat eggs with a fork, it's peaceful. I'm not interested in a microwave because it cooks faster. I suppose I am bright enough to learn to handle the processors and computers that are second nature to even my youngest grandchildren (although their handwriting is execrable), I just don't feel the necessity. When my neighbor proudly demonstrates his electric snow shovel—

"What's wrong with muscle power?" I tease him as we attack our respective driveways. "How am I going to keep in shape if

I don't shovel snow? I'm too old and brittle for skiing."

I let Susan lead me to her study, set me at her desk with its assortment of equipment. Actually she now has two desks, pushed together—one for letters, a telephone, address files, the normal essentials; one for mechanical aids to her business affairs.

"Write something," she commands me.

After a minute my fingers tap but my eyes wander to the garden outside. There everything is orderly—grass, edges, shrubbery neatly clipped, flowers blooming in disciplined colors and sizes. No robins run across her emerald lawn hunting insects; no song sparrow carols from a bush; no dead branch hosts chickadees. Susan and her gardener do not tolerate litter, nor insects that can be chemically discouraged.

Looking over my shoulder she pounces. "You've misspelled 'encircling.' Now look"—she pokes a button here, a button there—"you see how easy it is to correct?"

The square of the screen she is reorganizing cuts down my view of her yard, is as offensive to me as my misspelling is to her.

"If I were really writing," I say slowly, aware that she is trying to help me, to make herself a part of this activity that excludes her, "I might rewrite those sentences three times before their sound pleased me. Maybe tomorrow, maybe next week, maybe next month. I might not worry about the spelling even then—that's a copy editor's job.

"I could learn to use modern aids, I suppose." I smile at her. "But I'm not going to live long enough. I'm trying to write another book before I die. I can't wait while I learn to fiddle with buttons."

She sighs. To please her, obediently I swivel my chair from the antiques and paintings and subtle color arrangements of her room that are as important to her as my sentences are to me. But the flow of my words, the idea that had been germinating has been interrupted by her need for mechanical perfection. I can't remember even the thrust of what I had started to write.

May 1986

Outside in morning sun I paint windowsills, trying not to get green spots on my turtleneck. When I'm done I fetch the shovel and cart and clean up the leaves carpeting my drive. I spread them for mulch on the sandy bank along the road. Someday long after I am gone the pink roses so characteristic of Cape Cod will bloom for passersby. I have stopped erosion on that bank this way, some of the roots I have planted are sending up shoots already, I want to look down from heaven and see a mass of them, with a song sparrow singing from the topmost branch of each. It's a pleasure, a part of Spring to accomplish small tasks without hurry.

The sign at the foot of my drive needs painting. I can't pry the top off last year's can. You lose the strength in your hands with age, an indignity that annoys me. I was raised to consider men Superior Creatures. If something is difficult, whether it be tax accounts, hanging a picture or pulling the cork from a wine bottle I look about for a man, so today my immediate thought is to carry this paint can down the lane to the boatyard and ask young Chris there to deal with my problem. But those winter months I lived alone on Baboquivari have left their mark. As I wrestle ineffectively first with a screwdriver, then a can opener, I find myself thinking—

How would a man solve this? His hands would be stronger but also he would know a trick or two. *Think like a man, Fisk.*

In my mind's eye I give my can to young Chris, who might also fail to pry off the lid. I watch him run his eye along the shelves, halting at a tin of turpentine. He would pour a few drops of turpentine around the can's edge, I think. And so can I, I have turpentine. And so I do. Five minutes later I proudly carry the opened can down the drive to the sign I wish to paint, patting myself on the back with smelly fingers. Only— only I wish I could think more often like a man! A lifetime of being a helpless female is hard to discard.

My calender instructs that at noon I am to talk to a prestigious group at Wellesley College. Food at the Wellesley Club is first rate. I dress carefully in a rose suit that shows up well even from back rows, lovingly polish and pin on the silver Pegasus that flies me through all my performances (and distracts attention from my tired face). I'll need to leave early, Wellesley is a good two hours away and I have a stop to make.

Carrying breakfast to the table by my front window I look

out and freeze in dismay. Last night I forgot to close a Have a Heart trap I have been setting out in the hope of catching a feral cat that is terrorizing the neighborhood bird feeders and domestic cats. (A Bird Woman is expected to have a range of skills.) This is a large trap, meant for raccoons. In it now stands a large skunk, very handsome in its white-striped, shiny black coat. Caged animals upset me; I can't bear to go to zoos, see living creatures locked. Without stopping to *think* I set down my toast and am out the door. Talking in as soothing a voice as I can muster I walk slowly toward the trap. Since I am neither nervous nor afraid (I said I hadn't stopped to *think*) the animal remains quiet, does not threaten me with a raised tail. Or is it too confined to raise this?

Carefully I release the door, prop it open. Skunk and I contemplate each other, skunk silent, me still murmuring persuasively. I don't have time to fool around, I become impatient first. Clumsily I lift the heavy trap as high as I can, balance it against my hip, shake its tenant out. Skunk stands there, continuing to contemplate me. Then with no *Thank you* no raised tail (or is that no raised tail its *Thank You?*) it turns and ambles away unhurriedly. Then and only then, brushing dirt from my suit, now disordered, do I remember why I am wearing it. We once had a small cocker spaniel that encountered a skunk, we were giving a party in the country. It was a week before the cocker and I, who had had to bathe it in tomato juice while our guests choked on their dinner, were socially acceptable. My dress never was. Today I would have had to bury my prized rose lecture suit.

Five-thirty is too early. I don't need to leave until eight so I lie in bed, worrying about what to pack. Southern Connecticut will be warm (and beautiful—apple blossoms, white violets carpeting the woods below white dogwood—where four of us are to gather). But it will be really cold in the northern clime of Cornell University, where we are driving to a conference. I'm told there are only screens in the windows of the summer cottage where we'll sleep. No heat, the communal washroom a fair walk down the road at night. Should I take ski underwear? Surely a flannel nightgown, a flashlight.

I'm not eager to go on this trip, I have something I want to write pushing at the edge of my consciousness, the embryo of an article not yet formed. I woke with sentences, arranging themselves in my mind. Perhaps before I leave I can put some of these on paper. It will be a week before I am back at my desk again.

Bahnofangst (try to pronounce that!) is the vague anxiety that besets travelers, the feeling that a trip is a mistake from the beginning. I keep this word written in a notebook to remind myself that while I always hate to start off on trips I always enjoy what is at the other end of them. I meet old friends, make new ones, splash merrily in the sea of what has been my trade. If I fall asleep during papers the fringe benefits are delightful. Sometimes unexpected. Last year this annual conference was held near the District of Columbia with heat and comforts. Bunk beds. (In my college days we had a whole room to ourselves.) In bunk beds if I shift from one side to the other the body above me is disturbed, and vice versa. Thrashing around I disturbed some insect, it bit my eye in retaliation. This swelled and discolored. Holding ice on it proved impractical, there was no nearby pharmacist to sell me an eye patch. I was a mess to see, and miserable, with an appointment the next day in New York! What will happen to me this time?

Even at home, in comfort, I am a restless sleeper. Sheep are boring, instead I count the beds I have slept in, in some forty-one countries (was my last count). Of course I can't remember them all, they have blurred with time. Scattered in universities and museums about the country are biologists I've shared quarters with. (Not intimately.) In tents, cottages, cabins, sheds. I count these companions too, wondering how their careers have worked out, what their wives are like, what their current ambitions are. In the Dry Tortugas we spread our sleeping sacks on the brick of sally ports. My first night I didn't know enough to anchor my clothing with these bricks (which had been expensively transported from Boston, by ship. Contractors were on the make in those days too.) Contentedly in the dark I listened to Sooty terns flying past the Fort through the soft night air. Fate was kind. In the morning my nylon underwear was fortunately not floating among barracudas in the moat below me but was found by an amused companion, blown out onto the parade ground. In Arizona mice stashed sunflower seed under my pillows as I slept. On migration I often stopped in a home on the Delaware dunes. This winter I was sent a tape of a song made to the sound of waves breaking on the beach beyond those dunes. Each beach has its own sound. When I play this tape I see blue curtains blowing in the ocean wind. Loud in my ears are the waves pulling across the gravel, I smell bacon grilling. Wherever you have slept, however briefly, whether in bedrolls or under goosedown quilts, there are many choices to remember. I fall asleep, smiling, reaching for the man so long ago by my side.

June 1986

I am sorting slides for a seminar at the annual Vermont Bird
Conference. I've talked there several years, I don't really know
why. My friendship with the Director of the Vermont Institute of Natural Sciences, which runs this Conference, goes back
to a day twenty years ago when, with an amazing amount of
blond hair casually pinned against her neck, she had stopped
with her husband at my Florida banding station. When I first
hunted out the Institute in Woodstock, Vermont, it was little
bigger than its august name, in a shop off the main street.
Now, thanks to her vision, determined efforts, the fine staff
she has gathered, it is an important presence in the state's
conservation picture, housed in a handsome rural building. If
I can in any way contribute to the work she directs I am glad
to. I've nothing new to say and as usual am not sure what I
am getting into, or where. Arrangements are different each
year.

One year I talked in a small, hot university classroom, giving one program on the heels of another. If we opened the
door papers blew all over the room; if we closed the door we

stifled. I'd had a radio interview just before, and had performed poorly. It had been hot, in a small office. I'd eaten too much lunch, having had an early breakfast on the other side of the state. I wasn't feeling spirited and alert, as my interviewer advertised me. I was asked back, though, so maybe my performance wasn't too bad. Hard to know. The woman who asked hadn't heard me.

Another year, at Bennington College, I arrived late, disordered and definitely unacademic; again in June heat. The lecture room was locked so I started addressing my victims on a porch. When the key, and a projector, were found I had tripped and spilled my box of slides all over the floor. Dismayed hands helped gather these up. I kept on talking, casually sorting the little squares, running them through the projector as they came to hand. The audience took it in stride. Later a delighted letter from two novice birders thanked me for such a human interlude in what, to them, had been a series of overscientific speeches. I carried their letter next to my heart all week. I should have it with me today.

A seminar, in my glossary, is where I don't have many people and they may know as much or more than I. We have a question and answer discussion, I learn as much as they do. The trouble with a group is that some of them know nothing of our subject, every word I utter evidently glitters to them like gold, while at the same time I must satisfy those at the other end of the scale to whom these same words are dross. It's hard to strike a balance.

A talk is another category. A talk is where I sit on the edge of a table, tell stories, get my message across (I have to hope) but none of us are very serious. People interrupt, I get off my subject, must ask where I was. They steer me back, we laugh and have a fine time. From my point of view anyway.

A lecture is formal. It is supposed to be formal, mine may disintegrate. I am put behind a lectern, supplied with a glass of water, cider, or, rarely, wine. I am given a microphone and a pointer, am expected to have my slides in order, none of them upside down. For lectures I am paid. For the others sometimes I am paid but I may not take it, or accept instead a check for the Nature Conservancy or our Museum. How can I take money when nature centers, hospitals, civic groups are always short of funds, the work they do is so important? I am paid in friendship. It's a fine life, the most rewarding volunteer work I've ever done (except being blown in a small plane over the Everglades, over the pellucid Florida Bay). I do it on my own terms, on my own time. Some friendly hostess cooks my dinner, washes the dishes, has made my bed, sets out a good book for me to read before I sleep, sometimes even a glass of sherry if she is worried that her bed may be uncomfortable. (I'm too tired to notice.) All I have to do is be driven to the hall where I will talk, and get my ego stroked. I get tired, I grumble, but I love it.

Next Day

My destination is near Rutland, I'll use the map they sent me when I get there. I take the scenic route to Williamstown over the Mohawk Trail instead of a straight state highway that would also connect me to Route 7. I have a friend in Williamstown. She lives in a country barn with cats, sheep gamboling her yard, a welcoming dog. Her kitchen door is always open. There will be fruit on a counter, nuts, cookies, a cool drink in the fridge. If she isn't there a list of numbers by her telephone will reach her. We go freely into each other's homes.

The trail twists and rises through woods with now and again

a Scenic View opening onto wide valleys. I drove this road far back in my past, taking our two small boys—four and five?—from one set of grandparents in Boston to another in Vermont. I was not an experienced driver, our borrowed car ran out of water. The steam rising from the hood terrified me, enchanted the children. In those days midweek the Trail was lonely, no Good Samaritan came to our rescue. Improvising small water carriers from our lunchbox, in our best clothes we slid down and climbed up, back and forth to a small stream until weary small legs rebelled. The boys gulped the milk in our thermos, then watched me until our vehicle was appeased. An incident that would be ordinary now, someone in the constant traffic stopping to help, had been so traumatic then that when today I pass that small stream still burbling down its hillside, I recognize it, see our young selves, muddy, anxious, finally victorious, down the telescope of time.

Next Day

Leaving Williamstown I pass the race track by the state line. I thought of my father and mother on their honeymoon driving this same road, dusty then, in a horse and buggy. I wonder where the small inn was where they had conceived, my mother once told me, blushing, my sister. Inns are common now.

North of Bennington I swing off the broad modern highway that runs between cloud-shadowed mountains rubbed smooth by time. Route 7, before the ski industry and influx of vacation homes changed Vermont, used to be the main road north and south. Smugglers' Highway we called it in Prohibition days, at night hearing the trucks pounding south from Canada with their illicit loads. This old valley road, curved by millponds, through woods, over streams that yearly washed out in spring floods. Modern technology and concrete have taken care of these latter, although there is little traffic now. A few road-side stands hang on selling cheese, maple syrup and souvenirs. Their buildings are familiar to me. The opening at Arlington is still shaded, old-fashioned, the stones of its ancient cemetery still askew. I can't find the great pine once used for the Seal of Vermont; storm or age has removed it. A few miles further north I take a back road that parallels Route 7 south of Man-chester and pause before the small Sunderland church, where Grandfather Bradley, for whom my husband, our son and two of his great-grandchildren are named, was a lay preacher a century and more ago. This back road crosses the Battenkill back and forth on small bridges, and over railroad tracks where Grandfather, in the early days of automobiles, always insisted one of us get out to make sure no lethal train was snorting around a curve on its way from New York to Canada, looking for human sacrifice.

"But the train whistles, Grandfather," we would protest each time, mindful of the long-drawn, mournful hootings that sounded through our dreams at the Farm. Grandfather ignored us, sure that someday an engineer would forget, or be weary of pulling his cord so constantly. A mile further we must get out again.

Grandfather escaped to New York as a youth, returned to buy the land he had worked on as a lad in his first job, and the wooded ridges and valley about it. Across the road once named for him, beyond his stone wall capped with marble, the fields where Jersey cows used to file through deep grass in summer twilights, ran the Battenkill. Grandfather often fished in its trout pools but bade me not swim in the cool, clear water because of a hog farm upstream. Hogs, I used to wonder, affect only people, not trout?

I want to see how the present owners of the Farm are maintaining our land, if wild strawberries still grow in the hollow behind white birches planted in 1920. The house needs paint. No one is there. The strawberries are plentiful and sweet. I follow a path through a tangle of bushes to a small plank bridge that crosses the river—actually here only a stream. Horses come snuffling along a fence to inspect me. Our small children and I had spent many happy summer weeks on that bridge, watching the trout and leaves that floated below it. Not always happy—we were restive under Grandmother's rigid rules. The barn was fragrant with hay and droppings. The boys helped the hired man bring in pails of fresh milk for our suppers. Next morning it would be my job to skim off the heavy cream for our breakfast, churn what was left into butter. The tempo was peaceful. The children snapped beans at the kitchen table watching the country cook drop doughnuts into a bubbling kettle. Table leavings went to the barn instead of a town dump. Climbing the pig pen railing the children would give names to their crinkle-tailed occupants, not yet aware of where their breakfast bacon came from. There was no constant jumping into a car to Go Somewhere. No jumping to answer an irritable telephone. The clock struck through the lazy afternoons, ticking our hours away. It warned us of bedtimes, held our world steady if we woke in the night.

Last year our families gathered to place a son's ashes in the old cemetery where his ancestors lie. I had asked the current owners of the Farm if we might use that bridge over the Battenkill for a picnic, out of sight and sound of the house. Just as well! In reaction to the burial service first the grandchildren, then their cousins and friends of various ages jumped into the cool water, some in underwear, some with wide skirts floating about them; splashing, ducking, teasing each other. It was joyous, a fine end to emotional tensions, lasting until someone suggested we adjourn to the village for ice cream cones.

Today I sit in the June sun on this small bridge. I should visit the cemetery to make sure the generations are still sleeping quietly. I should lay meadow daisies on the orderly stones, see if a song sparrow is trilling from viburnums I had planted there to relieve the barrenness. A song sparrow on a bush here cocks his head, accepts me, trills. I continue sitting, lulled by its song, by water purling beneath me, remembering. Years of remembering. Hearing my children's voices. Standing with their father in starlight, his arm warm about me, his head bent to mine.

Then I leave my past, drive on to the excellent Northshire Bookshop in Manchester Center, where I am welcomed, recognized in my professional persona. I drive on north to the bird conference that is my goal, to join friends, check my slides. I have commitments.

July 1986

"The first time I saw you," says a pleasant-faced woman in New Hampshire, "you were giving a program titled 'From Town Dump to the Taj Mahal.' I've no idea what you said but I've never forgotten that title. . . . The second time you were brandishing a fish net, with blood streaming down your arms and legs."

I looked at her in bewilderment.

"You were wearing a dress, too," she adds, pleased by my mystification, "which my sister told me was definitely not your usual summer morning costume." She smiles again. "My sister lives next door to you, we were having breakfast on her porch. You stopped by to report that a Bald eagle had been captured in the marsh by your son's boatyard. It is now in a cage at the Vermont Institute of Natural Sciences Raptor Center, named for you. I saw it last week."

I suppose if you plan the happenings in your life they come back to you in recognizable packages but my life isn't like that. I have to fish about in my memory for this eagle.

I see myself running down our dirt road on a hot July morning with a long-handled fish net I had hurriedly snatched up, in my hand. Yes, I was wearing a dress. I had been about to set off for town. It had been too hot for slacks and you don't wear shorts when your legs have become octogenarian, so I was tidily arrayed. Out of breath as I ran down the road I called to a woman in a doorway—

"Do you have an old blanket you can bring?"

It was her husband who telephoned me. For a week or more, no one had informed me (but I go away a lot, maybe they had tried) an injured immature eagle had been about our salt pond, resting on the railing of a small disused dock, supervising boatyard activities from a perch on the hoist, sunning on the back of an overturned red dory, watching the children's daily sailing class from the peak of a boathouse. Because it was the immature dark chocolate brown, no white head or tail, no fierce presence as in representations of our proud national emblem, no one had paid much attention to it, only the man who had called me. He had been photographing it, noting a white patch under one eye that perhaps troubled its vision.

The woman who owned the small dock brought fish heads and set these out on the railing, only she didn't know that an eagle plucks its prey from the surface and had bought deep-water fish. In my absence the Massachusetts Audubon local personnel who capture turtles, push beached whales back into the sea, respond to calls on foxes and poaching, who are generalists of much expertise, had arrived quietly in canoes and kayaks to capture this bird. With no success. Men from the U.S. Fish and Wildlife Service Boston office had come down with traps but, sniffed my informant, they hadn't asked questions about its habits of people at the boatyard and set their traps in the wrong places. No one had asked me. What good does it do to be the Local Bird Lady? Spreading a sheaf of fine photographs out on his table the man had chuckled with me.

Together we monitored our eagle. Some days it seemed stronger. One day it was joined by another juvenile that encouraged it to soar, they had sailed down river on the noon thermals but after a few hours it returned alone.

The morning my woman in New Hampshire refers to, it had flown into a utility wire, hurt a wing, landed in the road vulnerable to the first car that might come around the curve. By the time I reached the spot its protector had herded it off, into the pines. I called to him to steer it into the long grass of the marsh where I might drop my net over it but he misunderstood. The eagle flapped into a thick tangle of wild rose and poison ivy. Thorn branches tore my legs. I am highly allergic to poison ivy but which is more important to catch—that or an eagle? I had pushed through the tangles, managed finally to pin down this powerful, flailing creature. The blanket arrived. A man with a scythe clipped branches valiantly, made a path to us. Massachusetts Audubon arrived, not in the person of the brawny man I work with and expected, but of his assistant, a small woman I know as more used to dealing with robins and house finches than with the lethal talons of an eagle. I've handled hawks, and once in Florida an eagle, but I was happy to keep this bird pinned and let her get the glory of the capture and any torn ligaments—as she seemed willing to do. Together we lifted our catch into a carton, placed that inside another and off the bird went—first to Tufts University's Bird Rehabilitation Center, ultimately to the Vermont Institute. It arrived there wearing my name because Mark Pokras, the Rehabilitation Center's Director, is a joker, and a long-time friend.

Returning home I had stopped at a neighbor's—the wife of our local paper's editor—to report it would be all right for him to run a story on the eagle now that we no longer need fear the traffic and harassment (both of the bird and the boatyard) publicity would have brought. I had coffee with her and her sister, then went home to wash off my scratches, scrub my legs with cleanser against the poison ivy oil, and had proceeded to town on my errands. I had forgotten the incident.

In my mail is an exciting invitation to the Fiftieth Anniversary of National Audubon's Maine Camp. There will be boat rides on Muscongus Bay to the puffin island and to cormorant colonies; a lobster cookout on the beach but most of all—the reason I'll go—a chance to meet again those foregathered from many states, many periods in my life.

I've stayed often at that Camp. It's name changes, its Directors, but its conservation purpose has been steadfast. Since 1962 I've been there as student, Board member, bird bander, visitor, lecturer; fogbound on its Bay, lost in the night on its trails without a flashlight; always happy. I was there for the celebration of the eightieth birthday of Millicent Todd Bingham, the generous donor of that spruce-thick, fern-meadowed, sea-girt stretch of granite with the unattractive name of Hog Island. Imagine being eighty I had thought, in ignorance of my future. Often since I've wondered if she could have envisioned the effect her gift would have upon environmental thinking in this country—land saved, college courses sprung up, research done by campers and kitchen staff graduated from that small, enduring Camp. Go to a meeting of conservationists anywhere, run your eye down any list of government wildlife men, and you will find the owner of a Maine Camp tee-shirt, however faded and ragged.

My first stay I knew little of what was to become my vocation. I was a zombie, lost in the shadowed valley of Brad's death—reaching for a compass by which to chart some new course but equally eyeing, each afternoon, the tide that sucked on the rocky shore where a mattress of obscuring seaweed would carry me, if I were to stretch in its embrace, out to where I need not return.

Most of my fellow students were teachers, men and women bent on serious education but I was not the only zombie. In our dormitory cottage was a woman who curled her eyelashes every night by flashlight, thinking us asleep; a woman who went to town whenever the boat did, returning with a small satchel of candy and crackers. She didn't share these, she absorbed them in privacy, greedily; hoarding them under her cot where red squirrels and mice joyfully found them. A third woman disappeared briefly before supper every night. I came across her once, hidden in a thicket, taking a bottle of wine from her knapsack.

"It's the only way," she told me, shyly but without apology, "I can make it to bedtime, that I can face all those people." She offered me her cup. "I don't drink out of the bottle and there is rarely time for more than one, we are kept so busy." Her eyes begged me for understanding.

I understood. I also was going to classes without hearing what was said, putting in time until I could function again. I did learn something of the scientific attitude, new to me, I couldn't avoid that. I remember—although not his name. Yes. Dr. Borror—a duck of an old professor who carefully cut a branch holding a tent caterpillar colony from an apple tree. He instructed us in this aspect of nature's checks and balances, then as carefully restored the branch to its tree. To my expressed horror. I had expected him to put it on our campfire. He eyed me with amusement, he had been through this many times before.

"It belongs here, on this island," he told us, "as much as you do. In ways these insects are harmful, yes. But in ways are not you?" His arm swept our group—feet that pounded down the soil; appetites that demanded chicken, milk, fish; wheat, rippling to the horizon across states where bison used to roam; firewood; wine from grapes coating the tamed California hills. He smiled at me. It was he who occasionally, kindly, rowed the boat that must accompany me when I asked to swim in the icy cove. He must have been through grief himself. I wish he could know where his teaching took me.

I became a teacher of sorts there myself. We didn't get the

exercise my body craved, we were too much in class or boats, hurried too fast along the paths to meals or appointments, explored too deliberately rocky pools and the ocean's edge. I am a bender and stretcher. Shortly, morning and night in my red flannel nightshirt I was leading a class in our dormitory, reaching for the rafters, grunting as they tried for their toes—One Two Three Four—my Scout training to the fore.

A Week Later

I can't go to Maine. I stare forlornly at rain outside my window, watching a woodpecker teach its young to master the suet feeder. Weeks ago I promised to give a program this Friday night, thirty miles in the wrong direction. It will be a small group, meeting in a church, but I promised. The woman who called had had a colleague listening on the line with her. When I assented—they didn't seem to expect I would—to celebrate, she said, they would pour themselves a glass of sherry. Would I also pour one for myself, drink as they drank, a toast over the miles? They had read *Peacocks* so they knew I was fond of sherry, when I am in need of comfort, am really tired, from a glass that was my father's: when I have friends for dinner from wine glasses that were an aunt's both better quality, I fear, than the wine poured into them. I can't rudely, ethically, cancel this program at this date.

On the other hand . . . I think. Usually I lighten my trips with visits, adventures on back roads. This keeps friendships green, I see more country. But if for once I make a straight shot on Turnpikes, if I get up early enough I could reach Camp Saturday afternoon in time for the cocktail hour. Someone will see me standing on the mainland dock, send a boat to fetch me. My eyes dance again.

The telephone rings. A friend has been trying to arrange a meeting between me and the founders of the *Bird Watchers Digest*. This is a small magazine for nonprofessional birders which Bill and Elsa Thompson started with its layout sheets spread on the counterpane of their bedroom. It has become enormously successful even with the difficulties of the owners living in Ohio, the editor in Maryland. Now here are the Thompsons on my telephone, asking me for lunch in Boston. Boston! You can't park in Boston even if I could find my way through its narrow cluttered streets. But they will be, I learn, weekending in Rockport, on the North Shore. Halfway between Rockport and Route 93 where I will be racing north in the small village of Rowley. Surely there is an ice cream store in Rowley? I'll be needing sustenance by then, a break from driving. We agree to meet at a dairy store they've been told about with a cow on its roof, surely we can both find that. The Thompsons sound nice, I am eager to meet them.

My program Friday night goes well (I have to hope. How do I know?). I get to climb the stairs in the church steeple too, ring the bell on its heavy rope. Next morning I leave home early enough but my half-hour pause with the Thompsons stretches to an hour, I am having too good a time with them to leave. In the heat my ice cream cone drips on the blue linen dress I have worn for the occasion. Bill finds an outside faucet and sponges me off. We plan for them to come to the Cape.

Back on the turnpike I make good time, no patrol officers in sight. I get lost on the back roads that take me to the shore but at the dock is a boat that ferries me, my nightgown and toothbrush across the cove, I hear familiar voices at the top of the hill, find a crowd I rejoice to join. Sandy Sprunt announces my arrival—The Eagle Woman! Word has spread fast, that was only a few days ago.

"Pretty good," says Sandy, hugging me, "for an octogenarian." Sandy has taught me far more than he knows over our years in Florida, at meetings. The amused welcome in his eyes is worth all those miles of driving.

I gave my promised program. I rang a church bell. I met the Thompsons. I reached Camp in time for the lobster cookout. It's crazy trying to fit so many things into twenty-four hours, but why not? I can rest next week, I haven't much on my calendar. Until the telephone rings. Besides, I can rest in my grave.

On my last visit to the Maine Camp I stayed for ten days redolent of salt spray and fog, of seaweed and mosquito repellent. The skies were drenched with stars at night. I wrote much of *The Bird with the Silver Bracelet* in the camp library, thieving the office typewriter as I could. I gave two seminars and went out again to the puffin island (Eastern Egg Rock), a two-acre uplift lost in fog five miles offshore. With international permission, minimum funding, a boat, a tent (in early days) and a handful of eager young assistants, Steve Kress has successfully restored these small seabirds with ridiculous bills to former breeding grounds.

Steve was—is—a curly-haired fellow with an infectious grin, thoughtful intelligence, highly imaginative handwriting: a solid scientist. I have known him for years. He was hoping I might stay a few days on his puffin rock to get firsthand background for the journals his students had been keeping, that I could turn these into a book to interest my publisher, bring in donations. The idea attracted me. How we all grab at the possibility of being useful! Alas, his faith was misplaced. I found the journals enthusiastic but repetitious, only skimming the surface of what must have been deeply emotional experiences. I could have written a book on the hazards of landing my octogenarian bones on those seaweed-slick rocks. At night I listened to stories of smugglers, of poachers' bodies floating in on the tide. If I'd stayed long enough I could have had material for that whodunit I keep putting off.

Again I walked the trails, sat on rocky peninsulas in the noon sun, watched again the tides pull in and out below the mats of seaweed with their hidden depths. Wind still carried flotsam out into the fog that lurks behind the islands but that year, and this, there is too much in my future for me to grieve the past. I wonder what happened to the woman with wine in her knapsack? If she managed to make it to some *terra firma,* to rebuild her life? If her professor's smile gave her something to cling to? If along her way she has been as lucky as I?

Labor Day, 1986

What delightfully crazy people the world is full of!

I am lying in bed on the holiday weekend lacking strength

to go up attic and see what animal is there, rustling among boxes, empty suitcases, Christmas ornaments; pushing discarded furniture around. The telephone rings. Fumbling through the Kleenex, cough syrup, a glass of honey lemonade, and books I brought up to read while I outlive a throat infection, I pick up the receiver. An enthusiastic young woman in California has been told I give an offbeat program and have California relatives I might visit. Would I be willing to talk to her wildlife organization in Los Angeles next January?

Fly to California from Cape Cod to talk for an hour?

I give programs so my books produce royalties for conservation organizations. They will live longer than I will and with this throat I may well be dead by the end of the week, or in a hospital which to me is worse. I cheerfully drive any reasonable distance to give a program, it keeps me in touch with friends, adds depth and sparkle to my life. But tonight, supine and miserable, from Cape Cod to Los Angeles seems a bit much, particularly in January as she suggests. In January, I tell this eager voice, if it has snowed I may not even be able to get down my drive. One year I had to, using my suitcase as a sled, to the amusement of the airport taxi driver. Last January a program chairman in New Hampshire had snorted at my wimpiness. She had said she would drive south to fetch me, then thought for a moment—She would have to bring me back, too. How about next summer?

I thank this voice from across the continent. Yes, I would enjoy meeting her, I would enjoy the tour of her neighboring mountains she offers as bait, but I must regret.

I can't laugh when I hang up, it would bring on a spasm of coughing. Yesterday I was plastered against a wall and x-rayed for pneumonia. No. Now I have an array of pills and bottles, each one warning that its contents may cause drowsiness, which they have. I've slept all day. Fortunately, as obviously with whatever home construction is going on above my head among the Christmas ornaments I will not rest easily tonight. I'm too deaf to hear a mouse, this must be a raccoon? I trapped a baby skunk in my cellar this spring, maybe it had staked out a future path through the beams? I wrap up, trudge to the cellar, open the garage door, then climb to the attic, trying with a powerful flashlight to urge my unwanted visitor to leave. I am too frail to do more, or even to worry. All over the world people live with animals, I comfort myself. It is only us cleanly Americans who lock them out.

On the edge of sleep I remember another woman who had called me last spring, asking me to speak to an environmental group in Maine. Maine! In summer traffic? Six hours?

I have friends in Maine, though. So while she charmingly detailed her invitation—I would of course stay with her and her husband, there would of course be an honorarium; perhaps sailing the next day, a trip to a nearby wildlife area—I outlined this journey in my mind. I could stay a night outside Boston with Jeannette, we always have lots to talk about. After a leisurely breakfast of her special omelet, good coffee with real cream, I could go on to Kennebunk to lunch with other goods friends, then continue to Brunswick and overnight with Mrs. R, whose warmth glows too rarely in my life. We could pick vegetables from her well-kept garden, eat blueberries she would have stored in her freezer. Blueberries would be ripe by then? Maybe pick more in a coastal pasture the next morning before I set out on the last leg of my journey? Coming home I could reverse these stops, even incorporate a day at the Maine Audubon Camp. Its new manager doesn't know me but I've been there so often in official capacities that he couldn't turn me away.

Emerging from these plans I caught the voice on the telephone saying she had just remembered—there would be a second speaker so I needn't give an hour's program, just twenty minutes. A six-hour drive for twenty minutes? I've never talked only twenty minutes. I ramble on and on, more than the allotted hour if my audience is receptive, if I am enjoying myself. But by now I have laid out a joyous vacation, even decided what hostess presents to carry. I stifle my laughter. We would confirm this in writing, the voice finished happily. She was so pleased to have me consent.

Alas for my fantasy trip. Save the Date, I had immediately written my prospective hostesses. Before my letters had reached them the Maine lady called again. She wasn't the program chairman, she admitted most apologetically. She hadn't known that another speaker had already been engaged. She was *so* sorry.

Oh well—my life is full of soap bubble dreams. Besides, I was needed here, in August, we get more visitors, more children at my banding demonstrations than than in other months, I oughtn't to leave.

Sucking on a teaspoon of brown cough medicine, traveling in my mind on that aborted Maine excursion, laughing I drift off to sleep.

November 1986

The dentist has cleaned my teeth, the eye doctor given me thumbs up; the doctor has assured me that while my tired heart may quit any day probably I will last another year. What shall I get into next? Where can I be useful now that my bird-banding demonstrations have drawn to a chilly close? My zest is in a lull. Or am I just putting off the vacuum cleaner? Before I haul it out I had better summon the chimney sweep. November chores.

I wander outside to pick a few zinnias and find that last night's gale dropped a dead pine tree, fortunately small, across my path. I'd save it for woodpeckers and chickadees to nest in. I set to work with my handy Swedish handsaw, flaking off bark, leaving a feast for flickers and nuthatches. An electric chain saw would do the job in only a few minutes but then how would I get my exercise? Birds have been stuffing themselves at the feeders all morning, another front must be coming through. Aware of ominous creakings and groanings as gusts of wind roar overhead I decide I'll be safer indoors. Pines must be deep-rooted, only two have blown down in the years I've lived here. If a big one should snap—there would go my roof, the side of the house. Oh well, I say as always, I'll be dead by then. My successor probably will take down the trees anyway, to get more light for a garden, a better view of the neighbors. She won't wait to see where jonquils and wildflowers come up in the spring. He will clear and till and put in a big grass lawn which then he will have to mow.

December 1986

I am old. Does it matter? Sitting at my table, looking at the reflections of a fire dying I consider.

When I was widowed it never occurred to me I would live beyond sixty. I gave away possessions, cleared my decks; lived full tilt each day because it didn't matter. All these years whenever I've been asked for a commitment I've said, and meant it—"If I'm still alive." Periodically I set my affairs in order, list what might go to grandchildren to prove I've loved them. All wasted time. Their circumstances change. Mine too.

"Will I be able to do this project three months from now?" I ask my doctor, anxious about something I hesitate to take on because it involves other people, their money.

"Do whatever you want," he answers, jotting on my sheet. "You're going to drop dead some time, everybody does. So don't limit yourself." He eyes me over his glasses. "Use common sense, though."

I've had angina for several years. My father had it for fifteen. My gimpy hip is worse some days than others but I accommodate, if I keep too busy to notice it. When I can't open a jar top someone else does it for me, looking surprised (particularly if it is a wine bottle). If I can no longer live in tents in the tropics with young researchers I can give them my enthusiasm and my backing. Actually I don't want to sleep in a tent, I'm very comfortable, thank you, here under an electric blanket. No lumps, no bugs, no snakes. A hot shower and soap versus a stream with nibbling fish. Instead of hacking my way through thickets of scrub vegetation I can sit in a busy schoolroom, help some small person hack his way through the thickets of reading, of lack of confidence. You adjust, you accommodate. It's important, though, that you don't think about it.

My window reflects embers from the fire. The thought of that electric blanket surfaces but it isn't so late that I can't take time for a glass of wine and the final chapter of Gail Markham's *West with the Night.* Only if I forget to blow out the big new Christmas candle burning on the piano I won't live to fulfill the promises I keep making.

As snow threatening to blank out the Atlantic coast begins to fall I drive out for my mail, lay in a supply of milk and lettuce. I can live from cans and the many containers of leftovers in my freezer but milk and lettuce are essential. I retrieve my warm snow-shovelling pants from the cleaner and settle at the table by my front window to enjoy a postcard blizzard.

My project while housebound is to go through the fan letters that have come to me. This might be a task except it proves so interesting. I find they have come from old and young of many conditions—from a city attorney in California, a famous entertainer in New York, a famous industrialist in Delaware; from a Texan priest, a woman my niece nursed in a Chicago hospital bringing her my *Peacocks* to take with her pills; from Ph.D.s and college freshmen, refuge managers, factory superintendents; birders, biologists, botanists both hopeful and professional; writers and would-be writers; armchair adventurers housebound by illness, the demands of family. The stamps read England, France, Spain, Peru, Alaska, Mexico, Zambia, Australia. One woman writes of how she and her husband successfully extricated a robin tangled in their badminton net thanks to my instruction. A man upbraids me for the candor with which I reveal my inner life. That's why I read journals, I had answered him, to learn of other peoples' inner lives. I pause now to wonder if this is a difference between men and women, men reading for exploits of outer lives, women wanting to see inward?

When I was a young mother books were windows on a wider living than home and small children afforded. At Christmas I would send a card of thanks to authors whose work I had particularly enjoyed. I might receive a brief, pleasant note in return, or not. One came from Brooks Atkinson, a drama critic and former book review editor of the *New York Times*. Brad went often to New York on business, I yearned to know more about this glamorous metropolis. *Once Around the Sun* painted its scenes for me. Mt. Atkinson must have had a fabulous memory. Years later he and Brad met in an elevator at the Harvard Club.

"I had a very nice letter from your wife once," Mr. A said. "Please remember me to her."

How I wish I had a memory like that! Often I meet someone who says he (or she) wrote me, don't I remember? I am embarrassed. I have the same problem with those who have come to my banding demonstrations. For years I have given maybe thirty of these a season, each attended by ten to forty people.

"Perhaps you remember me," someone will say, meeting me at a party, at the market, in another town. "You had me release a catbird one day."

I let as many people release catbirds as my nets provide the birds. It gives them, however momentarily, participation in the life of a fellow creature that, as Henry Beston wrote in his *Outermost House* "is gifted with extensions of the senses we have lost or never attained, living by voices we shall never hear . . . caught with ourselves in the net of life and time."

I see these people and their faces across my banding table but my attention is on the delicate feathered few ounces I am handling. Besides, I am notorious for my poor memory. I once introduced a woman to her husband at the British Embassy in Washington. We were eating strawberries and cream on the lawn in honor of the Queen's Birthday. I was proud of remembering this man's name as she joined our group of dignitaries.

"It wouldn't have been so bad," sighed Brad with resignation as we drove home, "if you hadn't had her for dinner a couple of weeks ago." I pointed out indignantly that she hadn't worn a hat at dinner and I had been busy seeing she was fed, sat by a man she might like to talk with. I hated those diplomatic dinners. The Good Fairy at Brad's birth had given him total recall. She must have been off picking forget-me-nots for herself in the ditches of Nova Scotia the day I was born there.

These fan letters I am rereading, sorting, restoring to their file box, offer a quilt to warm my spirit when I remember depressing incidents like this. Only they were not written to the woman reflected in windows by this table, by my desk, my kitchen. The woman who wrote my books has become a wraith, only appearing sometimes when I must drive a distance to lecture, or at midnight when the moon lays a path across my bed. I need her but I can't lay hand on her. Bereft . . .

"I am thinking of getting a cat," I tell Mrs. R, stroking the soft throat of hers, holding its purring comfort in my lap. "Maybe two. They won't come when I want them either but at least they will be there, they will be company."

Mrs. R has two cats. She leads a warm, well-organized, useful life, it makes me wish I did. She laughs, reminds me that I am a bird lady. And if I had two cats how could I rush about giving programs, selling books for my organizations, getting my ego stroked?

My friends don't believe me when I tell them I am two women, one desperately lonely for the other.

Christmas Week 1986

On the railing of a dock across our pond someone has placed a small pine tree. Spindly, scraggly, probably cut from his hillside, by day it is inconspicuous unless a gull perches on it. At night its lights dance, reflecting in the water, wishing Christmas Joy to all who see it from their windows. On our side of the pond a fat juniper growing through my son's deck twinkles, speaking similarly of the love inside his home. The young men at the boatyard have outlined the rigging of a sailboat with green, gold, scarlet, crystal.

I refuse to look at these objectively; self-discipline goes only so far. Then I regard the basket of cards that have come in my mail carrying warmth, time and stamps. Can't I see these as an acceptable substitute for the former bursts of song and laughter at our door, for joyous children running to our bedside where I lay sleeping in my man's arms, snow falling silently beyond the open windows? How many women are lucky enough to have such a substitute, such memories?

Christmas is an annual struggle.

January 3, 1987

Today is perihelion, the earth nearer to the sun than it will be for another year. An iron sky, bitter cold do not reflect this. I wouldn't have known if I hadn't been idly marking my new year's calendar with the children's, grandchildren's birthdays. When you are busy indoors the large events of the planet that supports us go unnoticed. When you live in solitude, as that winter I spent in the shadow of a mountain peak sacred to the Papago Indians, you have time to notice. You pay attention, measure what is important, granite, against what is ephemeral, stardust. What did I write about perihelion that day in 1973?

I fetch my first book, so handsomely produced by my publisher, cradling it before I open its pages. In Arizona on perihelion there had been no sun either. I had misdated, making it January 4th. Dates have little meaning when you live alone, they are only arbitrary measures of time. I'm not much on time, on the changing zones across the continents and oceans. Our first grandchild has a double birthday—one in California where she emerged to life red and squalling, another in India, where Brad and I were notified as we dined in a New Delhi hotel with spotless linen and six white-clad, brass-buttoned men serving us—one only with silver, one only with water, one only with fruit, and so forth. She keeps trying to persuade me that this means two birthday gifts each year.

I read a few pages in my book, marveling that these had come from my pen, marveling that on perihelion I had lived so happily beneath the rock of Baboquivari, seventy miles from friends. The Papago gods had watched over me, I had had no need of dates.

Today it is a marvel that I manage my car across the ice of my driveway, over the frozen humps at the post office to collect my mail. I exchange greetings with other bundled figures at a counter where we sort junk mail from letters, toss pounds of catalogues into a trash can. We are supposed to recycle paper in our town, our dump overflows. I wonder, and ask my companions if this unwanted poundage we daily discard is taken for recycling? No one knows. Some day, shockingly, we will find our dump unable to accommodate the newspapers, plastics, glass and other refuse of our throwaway society, will rebel against the double and triple wrappings our purchases are purveyed in, become willing to sort and stack, compost. It had better be soon.

In my mail, acknowledging my Christmas greeting, is a letter from a California artist. He wrote a fan letter last year, sent a mutual friend to me. Now he invites me to an exhibition of his desert paintings to be held in San Diego, 3,000 miles away! A woman I had thought dead writes, very much alive, wanting me to go to China with her. A professor in Miami who years ago taught me to skin birds for museum specimens asks if this winter I plan to return to South Florida, he can keep me busy? Across the post office counter I had exchanged a pink package slip for a holiday box of oranges.

Inside a note reads—"the vitamin C is to keep up your strength so you will write another book for us." This man wants me at my desk.

At tea time I carry a steaming mug of tea to the telephone. A man is calling from another state. I had thought how he might be dead, had sent him a Christmas card on chance because I knew how hard the death of his wife had hit him.

"No, not dead," he assures me cheerfully, "just full of the usual disabilities of our ages." He describes a recent storm that ravaged his woods, how clearing them had beggared him. Both of us, needing company, talk about the years we used to visit his country home. If he and Helen were not there to greet us I would run down their wildflowered slope to swim in a natural pool sheltered by those trees now felled, Helen had loved that pool, those wildflowers. Hearing the sadness in his voice as we reminisce I clumsily try to cheer him by saying that at least he must have plenty of firewood. His voice blurs. Without Helen, he says, he no longer lights a fire in their living room curtained against the night, where the two of them had been enclosed in contentment.

"It is too much trouble," he confesses, "just for me alone."

Men don't seem able to sit alone through evenings the way women can, stroking a cat, writing letters, playing a musical instrument. Men must be occupied, have some hobby or study. Lacking this they go out with friends, sit and talk by someone else's fire. An empty room to them is airless. I am surprised Harvey hasn't remarried, shaken off his grief after three years.

Then he tells me, he must apologize for cutting our conversation short (after twenty-five minutes!) because he is taking a woman for dinner. If he keeps her waiting any longer she will get too hungry, he can't afford this.

He joins in my laughter. I won't live till the day Harvey

can't afford to eat out. This cookbook you've said you are writing, he asks. Will it have recipes simple enough for a widower to follow, or am I just writing about cooking birds? Will I put in it a recipe for Starling pie? He is infested with starlings. What was good enough for a King of England will be good enough for him. We hang up, neither of us for the moment lonely.

Whatever I was thinking this morning on perihelion has been wiped right out of my mind—the small events of a day, as I said, obscuring the larger rhythms of our universe.

Ten-degree windless air has frozen our tidal salt pond. Yesterday I saw fishermen chopping holes in the ice, then prodding with long flexible poles for eels in the mud below. This morning as I walk along the road before breakfast an eel man parks his truck and starts out from shore, slipping and sliding in his high boots. We wave good morning to each other. After a minute, curious, I turn back and follow him, slipping and sliding also as I make my away about the frozen hummocks of yesterday's holes. By the time I reach him he is swinging an axe, cutting a circle two feet wide. He shows me the spearing rake at the end of his long pole, then thrusts it down to the pond bottom, working it in different directions until he brings up an eel. He shakes this off the sharp tines of the rake, leaves it wriggling and bleeding on the ice while he prods for another. He knows from experience, he tells me, the springs where eels congregate. Sometimes he quickly gets a bucketful but this is a poor eel year. He works three holes while I watch. Not too good a day, he says, but a man has to make a living somehow, even at seven o'clock on a bitter morning. He looked well bundled against the cold but the work is hard, he says, shortly he will be sweating. Yesterday he had fallen heavily, had had to lie on the ice for a bit, but he had been warm. Today he is back, careful as he steps in his rubber boots. Eels are a delicacy with some ethnic groups. If he sells them at a distance he gets $3.00 a pound but it is easier to let a local friend have them for $2.00.

I slither back to shore, to my warm home and a hot breakfast. I hadn't thought to ask if he wears orange-glow gloves so he would be easier to find if the ice broke under him. He is big, he wouldn't be easy to fish out. I trace him through the morning by his bright emerald bucket, the gloves. Two other men join him, working companionably in the same areas; one has a chain saw to cut his holes. I like to swing an axe, I'd like to prod for eels. For a little time, maybe. Instead I am working on the manuscript of *The Birdwatcher's Cookbook,* which, if successful, may raise enough funds to send other people out to swing axes, research wildlife. Secondhand living, but better than none.

Because we have been shut in by winter storms the women at today's luncheon are eager to talk. I listen, curious about their days as compared with mine.

"It was a dull trip," reports Natalie, our most fashionable member, just returned from New York. But who did she sit beside in the plane? Where did she eat, with whom, what were the small events and joys of her trip? She had looked forward to an Exhibit Opening—how had its reality been? Were the people thronging the rooms glamorous in importance and clothing? What did they discuss, standing about a controversial sculpture, a painting? She doesn't tell us this, she paints only the broad picture, the difficulties of obtaining taxis, the expense of her hotel. She opens a window on herself but the Exhibit, in which we are genuinely interested, remains shadowy.

My life is full of people I want to get inside of, behind their armor. Sometimes—too rarely—if they are beset by emotion, they have been drinking, gone out of control—but how often does that happen? Otherwise for my writing I have to make people up, and am not satisfied. If you write commercial fiction this doesn't matter. Switch bone structures, occupations, moral attitudes, change a previous plot a bit and there you are. (At least that's the way a lot of it reads to me.) If you write interviews you place a background—real or guessed at—around your subject, ask personal questions not even a friend would dare, build something (for good or ill) from the stuttered responses. I've read interviews with myself that stunned me—some with their sensitive awareness, others—well, let's be polite and say I find their woman hard to recognize.

My group realizes I am studying them.

"What are you working on now?" they ask. I don't need to answer—those who know about the cookbook tell the others, laughing.

"But that's not your style." Natalie's bracelets jingle as she takes a chocolate mint, pushes them across the table to me.

"What about those years you went to countries that were still exotic, before commercial tours started herding people into buses and boats, arranging travels for us from Alaska and China to the Straits of Magellan? Your bird trips to primitive villages in Central America? You must know Trinidad as well as you know Cape Cod. You have a dozen books in you."

I shake my head. "How was I to know I'd end up here with one foot in the grave, the other under a typewriter table? I didn't keep diaries. In India it was so hot, my experiences were so overwhelming. I did do a series of articles for the *Buffalo Evening News*. They are still in my attic feeding silverfish but that was too long ago, the memories are faded. It's the small daily incidents, the details of weather, the voices of people you eat with and what you eat that bring a book to life. It's what goes on inside your head at the time, and in your heart. I've lost that. Besides, my days weren't all that glamorous. When I traveled with Brad we lived in cities, my job was to be there when he brought men to the hotel for lunch or dinner, to be a hostess. I couldn't take excursions into the country by myself. Besides, I was a scaredy cat, the model of the conventional female needing a man to take care of her, buy her tickets. Don't laugh—in those days I was."

I still am, I think to myself. I just pretend.

"How about the homes you've been in when you were off lecturing?" Ellen suggests. Ellen is sensible. She dresses in sweaters and flannel skirts, pulls her hair back into a neat coil. She is our librarian. "They must have been very different. A maid to turn down your bed in one home, a cot in the husband's study in another; tropical birds pecking on the kitchen counter while you squeeze your own orange juice. That man who treated you like a queen, carrying your equipment, putting you in and out of your car, not because his mother had trained him to such manners but because he was Program Chairman, he said, he would have done the same if you had been a man?"

Remembering that earnest young fellow squiring me on a rainy night I chuckle but again shake my head.

"I can't use people who have been kind any more than I could use you, at this table." My eyes flick over Natalie, repairing her lipstick line. "There's a story in each of you, if only I could pry it out. You say I'm brave to have lived alone on my mountain but here is Alice, who cared for her parents for so many years, only now free to do as she wants; Beth returning to college at fifty, going for an advanced degree; Marge marrying a man with five children—in my book *that's* bravery. I've gone through life on a velvet pillow.

"I see marvelous journals in the lives of biologists I've been fond of, came to know well. They scale cliffs, track animals, live in uncomfortable quarters with companions they may violently dislike. They dive on reefs, spend weary, humid days in jungle tree houses, parch in desert blinds. Too busy living to write about what they do, when I ask to they willingly will detail physical events, results but, darn it, their inner responses, their emotional calendars and blowups, the small philosophical decisions that guide and control them—hands off, Mrs. Fisk. Maybe it's the difference between men and women? Men talk and write about where they've been, what they've done and seen. Women's interest is more in the patterns of our interior worlds, in what moves us from one bus stop to another on our journey."

The group agrees with me, or if they don't they are too busy picking up handbags, pushing back their chairs, to argue.

On the way home I scold myself for talking too much, being

too serious but Emily reassures me. Emily is gentle, plump, relaxing to be with. When I'm down she pulls me out of my shell, sees I get places on time.

"Remember Sunday?" she says. "The lecture at the Library?"

We had sat beside an older couple just returned from New York City—a major event in their lives. The man had talked about where they had stayed, what they had seen, how long the trip had been. The woman in three casual sentences unconsciously painted a picture of the tensions between them, the forbearance and iron control that lay hidden beneath her seemingly placid, housewifely exterior.

"Yes," I counter. "but I'm not necessarily right. I don't really know how men think. I'm reading a journal by a cripple whose windows overlook the Pacific. His pages are loud with surf, bright with flowers, painful with the screaming of a neighbor's chain saw. There is nothing unusual in what he depicts—the interest lies in his attitudes, his crochets, the ways, sometimes quiet, sometimes stormy, with which he deals with his handicap. The way men think is different from how women do. I said that in my last program. In the question period a man asked, rather disagreeably, 'What is the difference?'

"How do I know? All I could answer was that if he were to ask any woman in the audience I'd bet she would back me up. This was a smashing and unexpected success. I have a lot of fun at my programs." I stop my car at her small gate.

"We still want you to write more about what you have done," she says, resting her hand on mine. "Think about it."

I do, a little, but when I walk in my door there lie those darned cookbook sheets all over my table, awaiting attention.

February 1987

If I am in the basement I don't hear the telephone ring, just sense a vibration. If I run I may reach my desk in time to interrupt my answering machine. Both of us talking at once is always good for a laugh (or a polite hesitancy) on the other end. This time it is a laugh from one of two sisters who run a local bookstore.

"If we arrange another Book Tea," asks May, "would you be willing to speak for us again? Winter is such a slack time we need to drum up trade."

"But I spoke for you in the fall," I protest. "You can't want me again, your customers have heard me. Besides, I did a poor job for you, I was out of adrenaline that day. If it hadn't been for the poet who talked first your afternoon would have fizzled. I didn't even know how to start when you introduced me, it was dismaying."

May laughs again. "You know how you did start? Flat out, no introductory remarks, you said—I wrote my first book when I was seventy-five. By the time it was in the book stores I was on an expedition in Central America, and working on my second. I wish you had seen those ladies munching tea cakes, putting two spoonfuls of sugar in their tea, sit up. You didn't have to say anything else. You jolted them. We want you to come do it again, there is so much work that needs doing in our town. Our customers are mostly older; they live vicariously, read about life in books. We want to see more of them living firsthand, volunteering. You could motivate them, assure them as you did that day, that even if they don't know how to handle a job there will be someone there to help them, to teach them, it will give them more reason for being. They've asked us about the third book you referred to, that you are working on now. A cookbook, that is boring you to death? How can *you* be writing a cookbook! But talking about it would be good for a few minutes, wouldn't it? You can tell them why you started lecturing, your adventures lecturing. Remember how everyone laughed about your Chinese luncheon?

May is astute enough—bookstore proprietors are good psychologists—to know that if she can make me laugh I'll say yes. I was laughing now, remembering a morning I had been lost in a maze of narrow downtown Boston streets, hunting Tufts Veterinary College. Being asked to talk to their classes at lunch time was comical enough to have made me consent. Trekking through dingy corridors, searching the office of a Dean I'd never met, I wondered what of import I could say to college students? That education never stops? That one thing leads to another? That if you go through one door a second will open before you? (I say this to all my audiences.) That if they think it is ridiculous for me to be on the stage of their auditorium so do I. A young man now high in the Tufts administration had come to me once for information. I had given him what I could, pretending to know far more than I did. And now look at where he is, and where I am because over the years he has taught me too?

The students munched their sandwiches, spooned yogurt. Lunchless I had envied them. They deal with animals, I deal with birds, turtles and armadillos, we spoke the same language.

The Dean took me to lunch at a nearby Chinese restaurant. On one side of the street was Boston, on the other Chinatown. As we settled at a window table outside a formally dressed Chinese band paraded by, playing top decibel. What a sight and sound! I beamed at the Dean. My talks had resulted in many interesting experiences, I said, but a band was a new and splendid gesture of appreciation. The Dean beamed back, said he was happy to provide this gift. He twinkled, being more aware of Chinese customs. Behind the band slowly filed two columns of men in full dress, stepping through a street being strewn with flowers, carrying—a coffin!

"All right," I tell May. "You're crazy but it's your money, your risk. You might ask the kitchen help to put a bit of rum in my tea, though, I'll talk better."

I didn't want to write a cookbook, I'm no cook! My young editor suggested it, persuasively—a project for the long gray days of winter. Because I haven't all that much to do, no goal I'm striving for, no routine to my weeks I am always taking on a project some man suggests. I've been doing this for years, it gives me a fine life. Usually it's a man I don't know, who makes me laugh with a telephone call, with a letter.

"Come to Arizona and live on a mountain alone, making a bird survey," said one. So I did. No heat, no light, no communication, no one to tell me what I was doing wrong. It was joyful.

"Come to Mexico, work with us in a rain forest," wrote another. That proved not joyful, but interesting.

"Stay in Trinidad and net birds for me to paint alive," asked the famous tropical bird artist and raconteur Don Eckelberry. I went to Trinidad fourteen times.

"Come across to Tobago," suggested a cocktail acquaintance. "Your Trinidad ticket is good for that. I've a good friend who wants to turn her Estate into a wildlife preserve:" I was there seven times.

"Come to south Florida. . . . I lived there twelve winters, at first as a volunteer at Everglades National Park, flying in a small plane making surveys, slogging through the Everglades among the mosquitos and alligators, then running my own banding station. I gave programs to schoolchildren—hundreds of schoolchildren and many of their elders before finally I abandoned Florida.

"As you drive north in May," requested an unknown official of the U.S. Fish and Wildlife Service, "could you check the breeding colonies of Least tern?" I did that for five Mays, searching every beach on the Atlantic coast I could get to, by car or by foot.

Writing a cookbook is not this adventurous. It is dull, demanding a precision I hate. To amuse myself I scatter people I have known and eaten with among the cups and teaspoons of ingredients. Bored with writing I gaze out at snow bending branches, at ice glittering around the edges of our salt pond; at gulls grouping together in islands, at ducks and the big Canada geese dipping for food at the inlet, drifting as I drift dipping into memories. This is fun. When I am tired of sitting, of measures, I stir up a recipe I'm unsure of, that sounds interesting; take the results to my friends or family. That is fun, too.

But you don't just *write* a book. There is the proofreading, the explanations to a copy editor whose mental outlook, generational language and ways are different from yours. Proofreading again. And again. The glum fear that my book is no good, there is no way it can fulfill the expectations of that man in my publisher's office, sitting at a desk, juggling a half dozen other books with no time to pay attention to my complaints and demands.

I am in New York, having dinner with a friend dear to me. We have worked together a period of years, seeing each other sometimes often, sometimes not.

"You love him," had teased a young woman involved in one of our projects. (These days my working friends seem all to be young.) "He's nowhere near your age, isn't that indecent?" She was driving me to the airport.

"Certainly not," I had answered tartly. "There are many kinds of love. At your age you equate male friendship with sex, as a pleasant adjunct to a dinner date, as far as I can see. Probably at your age I did too, but differently, we didn't have birth control pills. My co-workers of any age lengthen my stride as Psalmist 18 wrote in praise of the One who was his mainstay. I don't like the new biblical versions that destroy the music of my familiar King James, but this particular phrase comes better in translation."

"Lengthen my stride," she mused, easing our way through traffic. "I like that." But I could see her mind was really on the man she would be having dinner with.

I look now across his living room at the man *I* have had dinner with. His hair is grayer, the line has deepened between his eyes. We haven't met for months, I wonder what changes he sees in me? Better not to ask! We sip our wine, regard each other. The tensions, the living on a knife edge of happiness that first year when he was setting me off into a new career have eroded, but our friendship is solid. We cover the usual subjects of his business, our work, the people who are closest to us, the dreams that beckon in our different futures.

"I am weary," I say at last. "My world has changed around me. I have had to adapt to a kind of living I find difficult. Do you suppose I could go back—if I came over there, sat beside you, you held my hand, let me rest against your shoulder—do you suppose we could go back to what used to be? I was so— so innocent in those days, so joyful. An Alice in Wonderland you were leading through the hedges of a world new to me, full of Mad Hatters and Noisy Queens. I don't like the woman I've become, I want to go back."

He drops his arm about me, rubs my thumb with his. Outside traffic roars, sirens scream in rage, buildings dramatically pattern the skyline as when first I had come there. We sit quietly but I soon return to my corner.

"You can't go back in life, can you?" I watch him fill our wine glasses. "However much you'd like to. Time moves in."

Not speaking we toasted what had been, what is now, a future that—with luck—would still hold both of us. Differently.

"What are you thinking?" he asks as I remain silent.

"I am listening," I answer. "Instead of that unholy racket

down on your avenue I am hearing camel bells in Karachi, a flute in India; a merle—that's a bird—singing in a Paris garden; the beat of a steel band one night in the Caribbean when I was wearing a blue dress. Parts of my life I can't go back to either. It's like looking through a photograph album—the features, the tilt of heads are the same but the informing spirits have gone. You have to wonder where."

I smile at him. "Don't you go. I need you." But there is knowledge in our eyes as again we raise our glasses. Time will move in.

The barmaid of the Eastern Airlines shuttle is so stunned by my request for a glass of milk that, rummaging around in a refrigerator under the counter, she gives me a large one free. Sipping this, nibbling on a peanut butter sandwich I made while my host cooked breakfast, reading a book he had thoughtfully provided, I darn near miss my plane. Then, as we fly, instead of the usual peanuts and offer of a martini, Eastern feeds me a good sandwich, a pack of raisins and another glass of milk. Pretty good for senior citizen half-fare!

Again I sit at my table looking out at Winter. Snow again bends the pine boughs and bushes; lies thick on the pond. Ice glitters and clinks along the edges of the tide, gulls float in arcs of white, half seen through a veil of snow.

I am still working on the *Birdwatcher's Cookbook,* and the idea still bores me, why did I get talked into this? The only benefit is that I have winnowed down two boxes of recipes gathered over years, that I rarely use. Some of them are in cookbooks anyway, indexed, far easier to find. To avoid dealing with my own smudged cards over the past two weeks I have written records for U.S. Fish and Wildlife, weeded my files, located tern reports I've been asked for, put together IRS figures, answered Christmas mail. Now I shuffle the pages of an ornithological article I started in October, set aside. And I will set it aside today because what I really want to do is work on a novel I have been rewriting for two years. Its characters have become so familiar, so dear to me that I would recognize them anywhere—in a restaurant, walking a street, a beach, standing in line at the bank—which is more than I can say for most of the people I know. I hum with happiness as I type its paragraphs.

My first book had been an unplanned pregnancy, seeded by a mountain wind. It had swelled and thrashed inside me, demanding birth; grown, like all babies, into an astonishing life of its own. It changed my life, won a minor award. A year later I wrote a second book. This had been rather like adopting a child. Reviewers had outlined specifications, a copy editor would demand disciplined sentences, my editor insist on sturdiness of structure, on character. I wanted a cheerful disposition, an openness to love. Again my pages had refused to follow prescribed patterns; had made their own life, gone off in ways I had not planned. Like children nourished by the same mother, clothed by the same publisher, these two books bore only a family resemblance. The third book—it was really just an essay, I certainly didn't plan its future, was on bird banding, written for a nonprofit organization. I had it paperbacked (it was my editor's suggestion, he has more imagination and derringdo than I) to give to the natural history organizations I have worked with or lectured to, to sell for their own benefit. I never should have. "I'm no businesswoman. I've had to keep files, write hundreds of letters, I've packaged and mailed thousands of them (because they were given, they were *free*). I keep meaning to tack a map on my kitchen wall, stick pins in it to show the towns they have gone to. I'd enjoy that. Bird banding was little known to the general public when I first started in 1950, now it is a common component of research studies, as is the tagging of turtles, fish, reptiles, many animals. My booklet explains the purposes and benefits, its interest to the general public.

A fourth child of mine is still sleeping in its cradle, inked thumb in mouth, its own inner demands and consciousness wrinkling its face. Who knows how it is going to turn out? It is a love child, conceived in joy, come like the babes of fairy tales from under a rose bush, under the stars. Already I am hugging it to my heart, stand ready to defend it to my last breath. Like the others it will have a mind of its own, a character I don't plan. It may grow to be a fairy princess, a magician, a witch, a crippled king—who knows? Probably just a country woman scattering corn for hens.

Reluctantly I return to the cookbook pages spread about my table. I test recipes until my family and friends must wince to see me come up their walks with yet one more dish wrapped in a towel.

Fish—I have now reached. I wonder what imaginative illustration Lisa will sketch for that?

April 1987

It is Spring Festival in one of our small towns. Apple blossoms are pink on trees along the roadside, forsythia vivid yellow by doorsteps. Green and yellow balloons will tug in the wind, daffodils dance in sunlight along the grassy verges, cluster about gateposts. Bright-colored skirts will swirl on tourists as they push happily into art shows, pottery fairs, seafood cooking fests. I have been asked to sign my book for a small shop, sitting out in the sun at a table with my pen and a pitcher of lemonade.

Alas. The weather is discouragingly chill, gloomy. The balloons tugging on their strings are ineffectual, the hoped for gaiety hidden by winter's fading garb.

Never mind. I am welcomed, my table set inside, near enough the counter so the owner and I can talk. A woman filling her shopping bag with purchases lays four books in front of me to autograph. Her husband talks sociably as she goes off to prowl the children's section, buy a kite. Another woman shyly produces a book from under her arm. She had bought it elsewhere but would I be willing to sign it, would the proprietor not mind? A second woman follows on the same errand. I look inquiringly at Jane, she nods. A young photographer inquires permission before she raises her camera. She thanks me prettily, does not assume as so many do that it is her right to capture me. My dislike of being photographed is genuine but I am also influenced by experiences in countries where a camera is believed to capture the spirit, depletes a person. I've seen travelers happily focusing attacked by angry subjects.

The first time I was photographed as an author, I balked, I may even have been surly. I was giving my usual Saturday bird-banding demonstration. An elderly man waited patiently until I had finished, then explained that the paper he worked for was running a story on my book and needed an accompanying photograph. He had photographed five Presidents of the United States, he soothed me, I shouldn't be nervous. He gave me a fatherly lecture as I posed, on public relations, on the need to cooperate with the media if I wanted my book publicized. I was anxious for that book to sell—I had given the royalties to the Nature Conservancy—they would live longer than I would. I wanted to thank them for sending me up on my mountain.

So I listened, and have many times been grateful to that man for what he gently taught me, although I wince each time I see myself looking out from a page with an obedient smile.

The wind is chilling. I gather an armful of dry branches for a fire. I will sit by it with a book tonight, greeting the season. But first there is lunch—cold chicken and a bowl of the applesauce Lisa has brought me. Painstakingly strained so it is a lovely pink color. When I make applesauce I cook the peeled pieces in a sugar syrup made with lemon peel and candied ginger. It is lumpy.

I buy apples at the market and fill her pretty bowl with a sample of my lumpy product. I set chicken bones to simmer for broth, as necessary in my larder as orange juice. Like bread it gives off fragrance. What I really want for my lunch are the leftover beans and sausage I baked yesterday in a sturdy clay bean pot a friend made me but I'll be hungry again by suppertime. As you may see in these pages I live from meal to meal.

A TV station experimenting with interviews done in the Hyannis Mall had sent for me. A stage masked with green plants, a camera crew sets up lights, their cables snaking across the corridor attract customers. A fast-food chain has supplied coffee and sweet rolls, this attracts passersby too. My interviewer, Nancy, and I have worked together before, I like her a lot.

At her request I had opened a bird trap before breakfast and taken a glossy purple-green grackle quite well able to sustain the trip and public display. At first our audience is small; mostly, I decide, friends of the young girl who is to play a harp, but as I hold up my big bird, explain the purposes of bird banding, carefully affix the shiny, numbered government band on its leg, the chairs fill. The bird bites my finger, which pleases everyone but me. I tell why I must return it to where it and I live, where it knows the locations of food supplies and roosts. I return it to the cage and cover it.

Then Nancy skillfully leads me into chatter about the teaching I do, my books, the new career I have moved into. Nancy is attractive, efficient, expert in keeping me on track in our allotted time; pulling from me what she knows will appeal to her public. I enjoy her so much I forget I am on camera, that my voice goes out over the air waves. I'd like to take Nancy to

lunch some day, explore what is behind her cheery facade. I
tell her this during the commercial. She winces, saying I'd be
sorry.

The young harpist succeeds me. Her music silences the corridor, fills the commercial Mall with beauty.

Not until today when the telephone rings, there is a fan
letter in my mailbox, do I realize I hadn't just been renewing
a pleasant acquaintance with Nancy, enjoying our talk. We
don't *know* what we do, when an action or word of ours is
going to turn for—or against—us. Life is full of surprises. I
guess that's why I get up in the morning.

My tape will go on circuit, Nancy told me, be used by
stations on Nantucket and Martha's Vineyard as well as on the
Cape. She still uses, from time to time, the one we did on
Peacocks two years ago. Think of yourself being played over and
over like that, like an old phonograph record!

May 1987

A man I had thought a staunch friend has told me I am a
fraud. This hurts, I respect his opinions. I've been trying to
think why he would say that. Driving this past week I've had
time to think, to try to look at myself with someone else's
eyes.

I see myself as basically a housewife, happy to be stirring

something in the kitchen that I'll then burn because I've returned to my desk, or am laughing on the telephone. Happy to dig an ineffective garden, to maintain a home for people to come to. A pseudo-ornithologist no longer earning even that title; a Board member who falls asleep during fund-raising discussions. (As all my organizations talk mostly about raising money their meetings are restful.) I am a writer by accident, not a professional. A woman lonely, full of daily failings.

I grant that there is that other woman who sails grandly out my door in a hat—the great pontificator, a falsie. When this friend says I'm a fraud does this mean I have gradually covered myself over with a bright patchwork garment in which I am not comfortable, that I am well aware doesn't button properly, hangs askew? Does she represent how other people now see me? Have I shrugged myself into this fashionable Joseph's coat so often, pretended for so long that I have become this woman? Must I accept her, acknowledge her? I don't even *like* her! Which is reality? Shedding my domestic cocoon have I really become a butterfly sailing the wind on multicolored wings? Well, if I have it won't last long. You know what happens to butterflies—one season of sipping nectar, perhaps laying a few eggs under sheltering leaves and their wings grow ragged, they are gone. I'll be reverted to my honest self. Dull but honest.

I need to cook chocolate sauce to take to Emily's for dinner.

June 1987

I woke promptly at six as my inner clock bids me. It is one of those drizzly mornings when I can't tell if ten miles on the other side of the Cape it will be fair or raining. I can't handle birds when it is wet, their feathers come off in my hands.

I am weary from driving home from Connecticut yesterday in sluicing rain, trucks throwing sheets of water onto my windshield. I had given talks to Brownies in the afternoon, to an Audubon group at night whose business meeting droned on until I was asleep before I began; to a school class this morning—nice kids, really interested, so I had stayed later with them than I had intended. Finally home, dry, warmed with a cup of tea, I leafed through the mail left on my desk courtesy of my daughter-in-law. I listed the messages on my telephone answering machine, listed names to call today, listed those I must write to thank for hospitality, ate a second banana and went to bed.

Lying there I contemplate my weariness. When I turn over my gimpy hip will hurt. When I stand it will hurt more until I walk a bit about the room, the bones settle into position. Half an hour from now it won't hurt at all, I can go about my business.

My business today as soon as I eat and get my reluctant body down the road is—if the weather there is suitable—to give my usual bird-banding demonstration at Massachusett's Audubon Society's Wellfleet Bay Sanctuary. I give these twice weekly and more as school classes and touring natural history groups are scheduled. I've been doing this for years, it's as routine as tying my sneaker laces. Sometimes I have half a dozen people to instruct, sometimes forty or more. Sometimes I may have only one chickadee or blue jay to work with, sometimes—with luck—a score of different species. This year I have an assistant, Aurele, who monitors the mist nets placed inconspicuously about the property. It's important I train someone who can take over my work, carry it on when I am gone. Aurele takes the birds from the nets, brings them to me. That's the part *I* like to do—seeing a bird in a net at a distance, extricating it. Sun glints on the pond nearby, leaves are budding on shrubs, frogs croak, a turtle splashes from a log: birds carol spring songs, chasing rivals from their territories. I may bring back warblers, orioles, flycatchers, perhaps the phoebe that is building her nest in the barn eaves. But these days my hip limits me to talking, to instruction, while over the heads of my audience swallows curve against the sky, a hawk hangs, beating its wings over a meadow.

I lie a bit longer in my blanket's warmth, snarling at Age, then get up, go through the morning motions, arrive at the Sanctuary, carry out my materials. It is not drizzly. I pull my table out of the wind, perch on my stool.

A journalist called from the Midwest last week to ask if she might spend a few days following me about. She has contracted with the glossy *Cape Cod Compass* to write an article on the purposes and results of the fieldwork that has occupied me this last score of years. She wants to see how I live, hear me talk to schoolchildren, to a group at the Sanctuary; to follow me through a typical day.

"I don't *have* a typical day," I had told her crossly. I am really fond of Judy but I had hoped to spend this weekend peacefully working about my home. "What happens depends on the weather, my disposition, my audience. I'll be just back from Connecticut, there'll be no food, I'll be tired. My car needs servicing. But come, I'd love to see you. Stay with me, we always have a lot to talk about. I've a manuscript I'd like your opinion on, and I want to see some of the short stories you've been writing. Be sure to bring them."

What I didn't know when we talked was that my CPA, who inconveniently lives in Miami, whose photograph is in my Rogue's Gallery, had also planned to spend this weekend with me. With or without his college student son, who will have a healthy appetite and possibly a girl in tow. Chuck is coming north to buy a catboat from my son's boatyard down the lane. Why a man in Miami with its thousand marinas should feel the need to buy a boat on Cape Cod I can't fathom except that my son makes fine ones. I won't have to provide anything but beds, dinners, breakfasts (I hope). If his son's girl comes she can sleep on the couch, it's often used for this. When I'll do the necessary marketing . . . I won't think about that. One thing at a time.

So today here comes Judy, zipping her jacket against the cold, unzipping her camera bag. We give each other enthusiastic hugs, we talk nonstop.

"You are thinking," I warn her finally, "of how you saw me last summer—a crowd about my table, the sun warm, baby swallows chirping in the barn behind us. We won't have any of that today, it's too early in the season, and cold. You'll be disappointed. There may be only two or three people."

And that's all there were to begin with, though a few more drifted up to see what was going on. I took a chickadee—at least we had a bird—from the holding box and launched into my explanation of how birds are indicators of the environment, responding far faster than humans to the poisonous chemicals we use to kill the insects they feed on. I explain how and why we age and sex the different species, if this is possible; why we study plumages, migrations, habitat needs, life histories. Aurele arrives, smiling, with more birds. The Sanctuary naturalist arrives, smiling, with a barn swallow he has caught against a window.

Concentrating on a bird in my hand I become aware that a microphone has been thrust up to my face. I bristle. No one had warned me of this! If I am going to be broadcast I want to *know*. Startled, I look up to see a young woman who had interviewed me last year, sitting on the grass handling baby screech owls—adorable creatures. This had made a good program for the network, good publicity for the Sanctuary, which is part of my job. She smiles placatingly at me, I grimace back, affix a government band to my bird, release it.

As suddenly I find I am being photographed. A young man, I know him too, is taking a closeup of my face, then of the catbird in my hand. Again I bristle. No one had asked my permission for this either! I hate to be photographed, remembering how I used to look, avoiding mirrors that show me now. (Next day both photographs were on the front page of our local paper. Large. The paper must have been out of news.)

If I had been warned I would have worn a tidier jacket, at least combed my hair. I grumble mightily to myself, then start to chuckle. Judy will think this a typical day, that the media hounds me every week! I continue more cheerfully.

I am banding an oriole. A couple who often bring guests to hear me walk up with a short black man who sparkles with interest. Finding he is unacquainted with Northern orioles (Baltimore, they used to be called for their black and orange feathers, the colors of colonial Lord Baltimore). I go into details, show the ragged, last year's tail feathers that contradict statements in books that orioles assume their brilliant breeding plumage in the tropics before they fly north to nest. One of the values of banding is the establishment of facts. All my spring orioles—and I have handled many—arrive with ragged tails, only occasionally with one or two handsome new rectrices. I published an article on this once. A bander in Minnesota responded, also in print, that her orioles arrived with their tails bright and new, but with ragged wings. We struck up a fine, informative correspondence.

The next bird Aurele hands me is four and a half inches of spring beauty—a golden head, its white throat and underparts outlined with chestnut, its outer tail feathers white. I am enchanted, I haven't had a Chestnut-sided warbler in years. When it has been carefully banded, measured, examined, photographed, exclaimed over I ask our African visitor if he would care to release it to continue its journey to breeding territory. Not often am I privileged to give the pleasure I see on his face. Starting to deliver my usual instructions on care—not to sprain the wings, not to squeeze the lungs, to hold the bird firmly but knowledgeably, something stops me. ESP?

"Have you ever handled a bird?" I inquire.

His hosts erupt in laughter. "Jonnie, when Roger Tory

Peterson goes to Africa this man is his guide. You can trust him."

Serenely Alois Kabue Githiaka cups the bird in one hand, briefly runs his other over its back. The bird remains on his palm, not at all apprehensive, observing us as we observe it. I have seen this done with thrush, but they must be held belly up. In Arizona hummingbirds might not fly immediately, enjoying the warmth of my hand, but in thirty-five years I have never known a warbler to act like this. There is complete rapport and trust between this man and a wild, tiny, feathered creature. I draw a deep breath.

Roger Peterson and I have been on Boards together, we are friends, we trade our books, so while this bright bird lies, quietly photographed again and again—the bird, the bird and Alois, the bird and Alois and me, we talk about Roger. Judy has laid aside her camera, scribbles frantically in her notebook. I shake my head in hilarious disbelief, remembering my reluctance to get out of bed. TV, the newspaper, Alois.

"It isn't like this every program" in honesty I tell her. She laughs at me.

"Tomorrow at the Museum for a children's class?" she asks. "Same time? I'll be there."

I come home to an unmade bed, breakfast dishes in the sink, slides to sort for a program in Maine next week. A message on my machine says Chuck is canceling. (Hurrah) I leave messages for Judy all about town saying, Come, Come. *Mi casa es su casa.* Hurry.

I'll have three hostesses along my way to Maine. I should take each one a loaf of Peasant Bread, they are too busy to bake. While I wait for Judy I line up jars of grain, molasses, yeast, trying to ignore the mail on my desk. If I don't pay the electric bill I'll be in trouble. I was away when last month's came in, too. Reality, that's what I come home to. Every day. This at least is typical.

Judy has left. I mop the kitchen floor. We were only three for dinner last night, how could we have spilled so much? True, I had sipped a glass of wine while I was cooking but I've been doing that for years, ever since Brad and the children learned that dinner arrived more amiably if a loving cup was provided to encourage me. Our daughter kept a small pottery jug labeled Cook's Nips on the kitchen windowsill in case of emergency, if no one was home while I stirred and steamed. Rum it was in those days. Now that I am an old lady I stick decorously to wine, usually.

A telephone call advises me that a package from UPS is at the boatyard. I abandon the mop and stroll down the dirt lane where roses my son planted along the way are fragrant. I collect the package, chat a bit with the workers at the boatyard, have started home when an anxious call turns me. The men point in dismay—a bird is trapped in their salesroom. They are two big men with big, skillful hands but they are fearful of cornering a small bird against a windowpane! Last year it was an eagle I caught for them, this year it is a song sparrow; banded. We write down its number. I had banded it eight years ago, in my nearby yard. I give them a few minutes of my $100 lecture on birds and banding, again start home. A second call again stops me. At the end of one of their docks a bird is nesting in the furled sail of a boat. They lead me there, point to strands of grass hanging out. Carefully I ease my hand into the opening where the sail lies against the mast. A House finch darts out, flies to a telephone wire in an obvious state of indignation. My fingers count five eggs. We hope the weather will be poor, the boat owner won't want to sail for a couple of weeks.

I reach home well satisfied at what I have received in trade for the cookies I had taken with me in thanks for package service.

The package is from W. W. Norton. To my dismay it contains the copy-edited proofs of the cookbook I reluctantly wrote for them this winter. A note asks me to check and return these "As Soon As Possible." I should have set this package aside unopened, not humored my curiosity! I haven't *time* to deal with this, I am going to Vermont. The authors I know hate copy editors (however grateful we may be to them). They uncover our smallest weaknesses, they demand improved spelling and grammar, perfection. (Or at least effort.) This is their job, nothing personal in their criticisms but who wants, has time to deal with, again to annotate three hundred pages?

Now I ask you. Also in this package, carefully wrapped so as not to leak on the manuscript, is a jar each of chutney and marmalade, a gift from this unknown woman, I have been rude about, my copy editor! Stirred in her small apartment kitchen, she tells me. Ignoring the manuscript I open the jars and spoon into each. Wonder, as I carry mop and pail to the cellar how often she has had to mop her floor, after stirring *her* kettles? If her husband encourages her with a strengthening glass of wine? She has a nine-to-five job she must commute to, a husband waiting for her at home, dinner to get. Judy is a professional writer with two children and a husband. She is taking courses at a university to get an advanced degree. Where does she find the time? How can she also teach? I have another friend her age with two adopted small Salvadorean children. She and her husband sometimes show up with them to pick my brains on a subject she is writing on. What right have I, retired, no obligations, to complain that I lack time to do the little I do?

Talking with friends in the sun outside the post office I slit open a letter from Hong Kong, where, as far as I know, I have no connections. It is an amusing missive from Skip Lazell, a herpetologist who works on reptiles and amphibians, at the moment, according to a newspaper article in the envelope, in Hong Kong. For several summers, he writes, he has been researching the wildlife on Guana Island in the British Virgins. (If you call reptiles and bugs wildlife; I think more in terms of coyotes and mountain lions, Piping plover and terns.) He needs to know more about the birds there, he says, wants them netted for study. Last year he had a Chinese ornithologist working with him, would I be willing to replace him? Next month?

For ten years before Brad's death we had vacationed each winter on this small dot of land in the Caribbean. In 1952 the San Juan airport was a large empty hangar, a shelter from sluicing rain with one ticket desk. For a quarter a day you checked your northern overshoes and coats; they would be waiting for you on your return. The hangar in St. Thomas was smaller, equally empty, visitors so rare that we were greeted and dispatched with champagne brought on a tray by the one, smiling ticket clerk. Long ago!

The Island then—and now—had water for only twenty. The help rowed five miles daily from Tortola with supplies, rowed back again at night. Tortola was wholly undeveloped. One long rickety dock accommodated boats and fishermen's rude craft with their colorful catch in baskets. Meat for visiting yachtsmen hung from hooks under a ragged thatched roof. A single road edged the coast for a few miles to another primitive village with a boatyard that built from local trees. On my living room wall here hangs a painting of a shanty home on that road which would surely, now that tourism has so transformed the islands, be of value to the Tortola Historical Society. I wrote a paper for the Society once on Tortola and the islands as I had known them in the 1950s. Once a week the Guana Island boat would pick up Club guests in St. Thomas and woe to anyone who was not there by noon on Fridays! The only other transport for a week would be by native sloop, complete with goats, hens, a heavy low boom that could knock an unsuspecting greenhorn (like me; we once had to sail that way) into the water.

As civilization spread a small plane could land on a bumpy pasture in Tortola where occasionally an attendant in shockingly ragged shorts sat under a thatch, pleased to accept $2.00 American. There was a fine shallow pond by this pasture with shorebirds in it. When guests to the Island were met or dispatched I would stow away on the boat, if there was room among the luggage, to study birds feeding there, always wanting more time than I was given.

However amateur, I became the Island's first ornithologist. For ten years I prowled and climbed, making a lengthening list, identifying what I saw from Bond's *Birds of the West Indies*. I noted dates and habitats; watched Great Blue herons pick off tiny turtle hatchlings struggling over the rocky north shore to the dubious safety of the sea; pelican riding the air currents. I hunted booby nests on the cliffs, lay on my stomach under a lime tree to check out wintering warblers that came to a small seep, reported to Mr. Bond a couple of species he didn't have for the Island. These made their way into a supplement to his book. My list made its way to the British Commissioner, then in 1956, when St. John's Park was created, to the U.S. biologist there. My work at Everglades National Park resulted from that list after Brad's death, leading me through door after door to wherever I am now. (Wherever that is.)

Hong Kong Skip has found my original notes and my annotated Bond, spotted but still legible, in the Guana Club library. He wants me to return and update them. No details.

I met Skip one summer, over a chili supper with Cape Cod biologists. He had asked if I would like to help him on Sandy Neck, a long barrier island (where later I was to study plover and tern) on the Bay side of the Cape. I would have to live in a tent, he warned, survive on Spam and peanut butter, avoid the plentiful poison ivy, but he could promise me interesting work. My eyes had lit up, but I made the mistake of disappearing to the bathroom. When I returned Skip had also disappeared. This is the first I have heard from him since. Before I check my snorkeling equipment, try on last year's bathing suit I will wait until I hear from him again.

My mail is a daily Christmas stocking, I never know what it will bring.

Another Day

I'm not sure I want to go back to our beloved Guana Island. It will be full of memories, of bird calls, of sunsets over Jost van Dyck. My gimpy hip won't let me climb the steep, brushy mountains, work my way out onto cliffs. In a surge of grief will I hurl myself into the waves crashing and foaming below our small cottage there or will the years have dulled the loneliness that will flood over me? The thought of swimming again with pelicans diving into silvery schools of minnows, of lying in the shade of rustling sea grapes that edge that curving white beach, of learning again the botanical names of flowering trees entices me.

If I go for the mail there may be another letter from Skip, so I decide not to go. Better to pay bills, pay attention to mundane matters. Also the logistics of leaving dismays me. What will I do about my garden, my telephone, requests for programs? My gutters need cleaning, the plumber plans to inspect my heating system. Should I stay home, as anyone sensible would, see my friends, attend meetings? Be available with beds and meals for those coming to the Cape expecting these services? I'm put on Boards, I'm told, for my judgment but oh, dear. How can I decide?

Skip telephones—from Rhode Island, not Hong Kong, in a cheery, macho voice that wipes aside obstacles. He is especially interested, he says, in the DNA of hummingbirds. He is anxious for me to net hummingbirds. I'm not sure what DNA is, exactly, but I love men who take me in hand like this, tease me into activities I would never otherwise attempt. He details plans, schedules, assurance of help—whatever I need he'll take care of.

Of course wild horses won't keep me from this fling while my joints still function! On quiet evenings maybe I can start the mystery Norton keeps urging. I'll return with new stories, new photographs for programs. Maybe I'll come back in a box. So what? I've always wanted to die with my sneakers on. I start listing what I'll need—sunhat, sun lotion, sandals, notebooks. I've lots of scruffy shirts and shorts. A haircut. Adrenalin pours through me.

July 1987

"You're not eating my good pasta salad," says Catherine severely, watching me push the helping she has served around on my plate. "What's the trouble? It's all we're having but cookies and coffee."

"I'm not hungry," I answer feebly but they all know my appetite, tease me about it. So I plunge.

"I can't eat pasta. It's emotional. Our daughter was in a motorcycle accident on the Brenner Pass in Italy when she was a teen-ager. The air force pilot she was with must have turned his head to speak to her, they hit a roadside marker. For six weeks Brad and I tended her in a Verona hospital. We had no Italian and only her doctor had English. The nuns gave us a room next to hers, were grateful for our help. We took complete care of her. It was pretty awful.

"On doctor's orders I went walking every afternoon for a respite, or took the bus to town. I had only American hot weather dresses, sleeveless. On my first trip the nuns gave the bus driver orders to protect me until I could buy a shawl—being sleeveless was the sign of a prostitute. I used to bring back an armful of flowers from the market stalls to set before a statue of the Virgin down our corridor. A nun often sat by them, resting while she beat an egg with a fork for an eggnog for us to spoon into our child. The nuns had taken me into the kitchen to instruct them in these eggnogs we requested. Should the egg be fresh, they asked, or one used for cooking? Vanilla to them was a bean, not an absorbable liquid. Sugar, but not too much. Fresh milk. All this again beaten with a fork. Worrying about me, sometimes they would concoct an eggnog for me too, not knowing that I would slip a spot of rum in it to keep me going. Noon and night a heaping plate of pasta was our meal with a tablespoon of sauce—not nearly enough—pooled in its center. They gave us peaches, green, hard. The ones I saw at market were ripe and luscious so I brought them back until, coming out of my daze, I noticed how pigeons also walked through the fruit stalls but on the shelves, doing what pigeons do. One day, too, there was a peasant snoring among the fruit, his dirty boots sticking up through the peaches. The ground ran rivulets of waste water. After each excursion I would have to clean my sandals, wash my feet before placing my offering of flowers before Mary, the compassionate comforter.

"I know pasta is healthy, and I'm sure it is delicious the way you have fixed it but I've never been able to choke it down since. Never mind—I had a sturdy breakfast. I'll fill up on cookies."

I smile at Catherine but my mind is far away in that quiet hospital room, waiting with Brad for our child to stir from her coma, to speak to us.

August 1987

"Fashions," my urban daughter tells me over the phone, laughing to learn that I am sewing ruffles of lace on a petticoat "have changed. They've swung back to miniskirts, tightly sheathed about the hips."

"You're a bit old for that," I rebuke her, knowing she will buy one. She is slender, with lovely legs—a fashion model, a tennis player, nothing to indicate her years but a dusting of gray in her hair, and a discerning eye.

Sewing ruffles is a ridiculous occupation for a woman with a sheaf of mail to answer, a home that needs tidying after weekend guests. A sea change has come over me, I have returned to being domestic.

Ruffles to me are a statement of femininity, more effective than lipstick and jewelry. I love to watch a woman show a froth of lace as she settles into a chair. No matter how executive and cool her surface, here is a clue to her personality. When someone—so rarely that I tack their comment to my wall, sleep with it under my pillow—calls me feminine I am taken aback. Childhood photographs show my hair pulled taut, surmounted by an outsized bow. There is a sash about my middle, I have an anxious look. In school days my party dresses were hand-me-downs from a sister whose tastes were not mine, or creations of my mother's dressmaker, a tightly corsetted woman with a mouth always full of pins. These dresses covered my budding body to my mother's satisfaction but didn't feed my soul.

As a young matron I ran to tailored suits and sweeping pirate hats although I remember clearly and with love a deep rose taffeta ball gown, wide-skirted, tiered and ruffled, that I bought with the first—and only—$100 bill I have ever handled, a gift from my beloved father-in-law to wear at my first appearance ever as a Speaker (little knowing what my future held). I was on stage at a benefit for some Buffalo community organization—a hospital? the Symphony? I don't remember. What I do remember is the smell of that dusty stage, the whispering of my ruffled skirt as I stepped to the footlights, the frightening silence in the auditorium as I began to speak with my only backing the heavy folds of the theater curtains, and my Dad's love.

I remodel this petticoat that I made several years ago for a dinner here on the Cape given for the Honorable Nathaniel P. Reed, whom I had known in Florida. In his honor I had stitched a long, sea blue skirt, embroidered it with a flight of the Least tern that were our mutual interest. My figure having grown unfortunately—uh, robust—this skirt no longer can be worn but by shortening its petticoat, adding two wide rows of lace, I will have a garment to comfort me under a black woollen skirt I plan to wear this winter at Book Luncheons and Signings publicizing my *Cookbook*. The lacy froth will give me courage, belie the image of a little old lady birdwatcher. Nat will be there in spirit, laughing at me.

As I will be stashed behind lecterns it's really my hair I

should be concerned about. I'm not at ease at these events, people regarding me as if an author were something from a kind of zoo. I'm grateful for friends who show up to cheer me on. For courage I sip the wine I may be offered, knowing that later some critical woman—or man—will describe me as "that old woman who is always drinking." I bet they'd sip wine too, if they were in my slippers!

On my desk I find a yellow sheet with a scrawled message in my own writing. It has a telephone number and "Ernest— nasty and obnoxious." I wonder what residue from an overbusy day *that* is?

September 1987

Emily stops by to find me potting a parsley seedling from my garden to winter on my sunny kitchen shelf.

"Parsley," she muses. "Is it really as good for us as they say?" Emily is a practical woman, wanting proof before she accepts something.

"Who knows?" I answer. "A woman I knew claimed an infusion of it cured a dog her vet had given only a day to live. I grow it, and dill for swallowtail butterflies. Butterflies are not for sale. Greeks crowned heros with it, Romans wore garlands made from it to dinners." I am reading from a notebook I have plucked from a shelf. "It alleviates drunkenness, is good for prostrate trouble, night blindness, loose teeth. You can't eat enough of it, in soups, salads, sprinkled on eggs, fish, in casseroles. (Not on icecream, though.) It also allays 'torments of the thoughts.' I should take a mug of parsley tea to bed with me nights."

Emily is delighted. "Wait," I say. "I gave a program at a posh retirement home in Delaware last year. Three of us had lunch at Longwood Gardens. I used their soup in my *Cookbook* it was so delicious. Afterward, while my companions browsed through the gift shop I browsed through cookbooks and found an enchanting volume on the folklore of herbs. I propped the book open on the counter and scribbled, copying.

"Dill is important. It sprouts easily in a sunny winter window. Like coriander it has a reputation for whatever may ail you—love sickness, wounds, casting spells, calming colicky babies; for curing hiccups, for growing hair and fingernails. A small sack of it worn over the heart will keep you from being hexed. I could use that. It's also good in cocktail dips, if you wish to be more practical. Or in mayonnaise.

"If you put poppy seed in your shoes you become invisible to creditors. I think I used that in my *Cookbook* too, and wondered if it affected the market.

"Bayleaf in the Middle Ages had a reputation for inducing abortions. It's a narcotic so should be used sparingly and *do not* substitute the bayberry leaves here on the Cape, they're poisonous. I didn't know that, I wonder how many guests I've poisoned?"

"Go on," says Emily, fascinated. "I'll ask a Wampoag friend in Mashpee if Native Americans use all this. What else?"

"I put caraway seeds in my dark bread. Folk history—I've browsed on a lot of books—claims it helps if you have been bitten by a venomous beast. Also it restores hair to the bald, is a cure for fickleness, was fed to pigeons to prevent their straying. As a child I used to spend my weekly nickel allowance on sugar-coated, colored ones. Whether or not these cured my cuts, helped when I was scratched by cats or prevented our neighbor's homing pigeons from straying out of territory I couldn't now say. I buy sesame seeds at the health food store and toast them to a delicate brown. If I don't forget and burn them. They make a fine topping for nearly anything. Peel an avocado, coat it with mayonnaise, sprinkle sesame seeds on it—it's great. My editor in New York taught me that one.

"I credit my good health to onions, garlic and dark rum when people ask me how I've lived so long, though I don't advertise the rum as freely. None of these, or cheeses for some reason, were served in my parents' home. I've been restoring the balance ever since. Workmen building the Egyptian pyramids considered onions a staple so why not I, digging in my garden, cleaning my gutters? Mustard—that's in my *Cookbook* too, I learned it from someone in Florida, is good for arthritis, pneumonia and scorpion bites. None of these is good in desserts. Except the rum.

"Fennel is the best, though. Another cure-all, it was used in witchcraft. Do you know that if you put a flower of it in your bedroom keyhole nothing—or no one—can disturb your sleep? I instruct my granddaughters in this when they leave for party weekends. After you take it out of the keyhole put it in your linen closet to repel insects. It slims down fat people, too."

"Mice," says Emily thoughtfully. "Are mice insects? I've used the Longwood Gardens' soup. If I make it again will you come for lunch? I'll ask Catherine, she's an herb gardener. We can see if she knows all this."

October 1987

Charlie and I are sitting in his living room, at a table, marking
locations on a map. Naturally you can't do that without sitting
close, leaning across each other, rubbing elbows. Halfway
through I begin to laugh.

Charlie raises an eyebrow, reaches for the cider jug. "What's
so funny? I find this a dull task, I'm grateful you are helping
me."

Charlie and I are good friends. He kisses me when we meet,
sees I get fed at parties, occasionally brings me flowers from
his bank. I keep on laughing, drink his good cider.

"After Brad died a Club he had belonged to approached me
about setting up a memorial fund for him. (Actually, I discovered, their House Committee wanted to buy a painting and

hoped, by pegging it on him, to raise enough money for the purchase.) One of their members came by late one afternoon with their membership list. It had been a business club, I knew few of them and I was too fresh a widow to cope with this, it embarrassed me.

"After a bit I found I was embarrassed in another way, too. You can't very well go over lists without sitting close, your heads and pencils bent together, can you? The way you and I are? I noticed this man kept edging away from me on the couch and couldn't figure out why. He was a neighbor, we had been in his home a couple of times, he and his wife in ours, but he was nothing to me. Definitely, though, he kept moving away—and suddenly I realized why. His name was Charlie too," I tease, leaning close to this Charlie, rubbing against his arm.

"If it had been now I would have said, 'You blithering idiot!' Only I would now use more pungent words my grandchildren and their friends have taught me. 'Do you think because I'm a new widow I'm on the make? How in hell can we work on this list without sitting close?' But then I didn't know how to handle the situation. Sexual harassment, in reverse. Turned me into an instant feminist."

Charlie chuckles. "Hard to imagine you as a helpless female. What did you do? Stupid fellow."

"Told him to leave his darned list with me, I'd go over it alone; that it was getting on toward dinner time, his wife would be wondering where he was, I didn't want suspicious black looks from her. The next year when I was back in the District I took time to go to the Club and hunt up this memorial. I was sorry Brad's ghost wasn't along, its subject was so comically foreign to any of his interests. I used to run into other situations like that—men who seem to think that because you're a widow you are on the prowl, anxious to curl up beside them on a couch, or in bed. Men!"

I laugh again. "I knocked one of them down at a party in his own house once. I didn't mean to, he had cornered me behind a door, he must have been off balance. The women were delighted, evidently I wasn't his first victim." I flex my muscles.

Charlie reaches across me for another map. "Good thing I put cider instead of a whiskey jug out," he grunts, going back to work.

The dentist is rebuilding my mouth. My hip hurts and is untrustworthy. My throat is sore, which is why I am sitting in Dr. Robert's office.

"I haven't any right coming here to sprinkle germs on those elderly people in your waiting room," I tell him, forgetting that I am mighty elderly myself. "I'm tired of living, Dr. Bob. I'd hang myself from a rafter in my living room only that would be rough on whoever finds me. Besides, it would devalue my home, and the children need the money. I can't turn on the motor in my car either, a delivery man or a nosy neighbor would surely hear it. Or it would run out of gas. My grand-daughter needs a car badly but she would never be willing to use it with my ghost in the driver's seat." I look at him despondently.

He smiles at me, reaching for his stethoscope, knowing as I do that in another week I will have recovered my spirits, be out talking to a businessmen's Pancake Breakfast.

Today I step backward into a life I'd thought behind me. I've stopped lecturing. I'm sick to death of talking about myself and the unexpected, joyful events that brought me to where I am. Today's engagement was arranged months ago, I had forgotten it. Well, not entirely forgotten, I had just put off thinking about it. Yesterday the program chairman called to remind me, and to ask if I was bringing slides. Oof, I had forgotten those, too. I can show the series I keep on my winter on Baboquivari. These make my programs easy—I love to talk about Arizona. I can weave in my stories of field work, of where I've lived and why in the last twenty years; of how I came to write my books. I show photographs of birds and of the road leading to my lonely mountain cabin. This always startles them.

But first, in my professional suit and professional hat (the only time I wear a hat) I must go to an elementary school where I help small pupils with reading disabilities. I know by heart, as they must, the book they will choose, on how a monkey tricks a hungry crocodile, but they enjoy the repetition. A new girl, older, selects a stunningly illustrated book on American Indians. This proves not too successful. Tepees and rain dances are far from her Cape Cod experience, and I have my eye on the clock. I am due at noon, somewhere off the main road to Worcester, in unknown territory. But I have gasoline, a sandwich, it won't matter if I am a little late.

Ladies Aid ladies bring lunch to lectures. They are nice, I like talking with them, we can be housewives together. They really want to know how I happened to write a book, how long it took, the practical details of decisions on print, colors, binding, illustrations. I tell them about other Cape authors I know. The ladies share their apples and sandwiches when I forget mine. They have vases of wildflowers, or china birds on our tables, in honor of the Bird Lady. I come away warmed by their friendship.

I can't tell until I see my audience what I am going to say, how I will begin. The group today is either a church group or a Ladies Aid, I don't seem to have paid much attention to it. I drive eighty miles north to a small town I have trouble finding, to a big church I have trouble locating. A small, brisk woman arriving on foot helps carry in my heavy projector and the carton of books I lug, hoping to raise royalties for my organizations. Sometimes I sell two, sometimes twenty, so I take too many. Books are heavy! This woman, I learn as we hang up our coats, is a world traveler with fifteen lectures at her finger—tongue—tips. Under her questions my amateur status becomes apparent. If this club is accustomed to speakers of her caliber I am in trouble.

Arizona is a never-never land to coastal women not lucky enough to travel. To encourage them, to prove you can face challenges no matter what your age, as I talk I show slides of the vast emptiness of the mountain terrain that had surrounded my ranch, the creek bed that had been my road, the one-room homestead cabin where I had lived all by myself.

As I finished answering questions, autographing, three sweet old ladies came up, worrying. "You aren't going to drive all the way back to Cape Cod at this hour *all by yourself,* are you?" they asked.

A lecturer should never take herself seriously, think her sentences are listened to!

I miss a turn and become mired in the 4 P.M. business traffic of a factory town. I missed it because I was remembering a big luncheon in Washington, D.C., where I had talked when I was inexperienced and nervous. My daughter was an officer of the club and had introduced me—a sentimental touch which had thrown me completely off balance but softened up my audience. Telling them how ill at ease I felt, an amateur addressing such a prestigious group of activists, I had said that in this new career I was running the gamut from their type to—to—I grabbed wildly and came up with the East Dennis Ladies Aid (not knowing if there was such). As they started to laugh a hand shot up in the back of the room, a voice carried firmly over heads: *"Now wait a minute. I belong to the East Dennis Ladies Aid!"* Then they had really laughed, setting us all at ease. I laugh again now, remembering that room full of fashionable women and two lone men who had come from the Nature Conservancy to scout out this bird lady who had worked on three of their Arizona ranches.

Extricating myself from the small-town business streets I decide if I continue far enough down this back road I can reach Bob Hale's Westwinds Bookshop in Duxbury before it closes, where I can have a warm welcome, a warm mug of coffee and a chat with Mark if Bob himself isn't there to greet me with a warm hug. Bob moved into new quarters in the spring, glorying in the extra space this gave him. But as in his former shop this space has become a maze of stacks. Today books are piled even on the floor. Neatly, but on the floor! Mark fetches me coffee, I chat with his customers about the books they buy, Bob returns from a program *he* has been giving, it is a fine, friendly end to a busy day. Well, not quite the end—I have sixty miles yet to drive, nibbling on the peanuts I carry in the car for emergency.

My telephone light is flashing red. My Cambridge granddaughter has been taken to the hospital for an emergency operation. This dealt with I must figure out from scribbled notes and cash in my handbag how many of which books I sold at that program, now receded into the past. But I am home. I can light a fire. I can put some rum in my tea—or tea in my rum is better at this point, I think; I can make a spinach omelet, eat an apple, finish a story by Edith Wharton before I go late to bed.

I am on my way to Falmouth, to speak at a Book Breakfast for Caroline and Bill Banks of the Market Bookshop. They are friends, I must do a good job for them, but though I am to speak on my *Birdwatcher's Cookbook I haven't even seen it yet!* Because of printing delays their boxes of copies didn't arrive until late yesterday, to our mutual considerable relief, I may say.

As I drive I try to remember why I wrote this book, it was Norton's idea. My illustrator encouraged me, my friends thought it hilarious. I had recipes I'd gathered over the years because they sounded interesting or had odd names. Most of them I'd never even cooked. Now I did, inflicting them on skeptical friends. This was rather fun. Detailing precise instructions bored me, so between listing cups of this, teaspoons of that, I amused myself writing how and where I had encountered some of these dishes—in Ecuador, Trinidad, Mexico, Arizona, Maine. This was rather fun too. Waiting on this book to appear I have been wondering where I might be going next, if anywhere. This is what worries me—*am* I going anywhere?

Now, this morning, properly lipsticked and combed I stand before an anticipatory audience who have paid to get more than cinnamon buns and coffee.

"But what," I ask as they push aside their cups, settle to listen, "can I say for twenty minutes about a *cookbook?* Particularly when I only saw it, held this child of mine in my hands ten minutes ago? I've not had time to open it, I am in too much of a daze seeing it. I left home too early to eat a proper breakfast, my fingers are sticky from these good cinnamon buns. I haven't yet seen where the designer placed Lisa Russell's illustrations, what the pages, the binding, the jacket look like. I do know that I omitted flour from the Chewy Molasses cookies on page 215 and shortening in my bread on page 153. I heard about these too late to fix it. Proofreading is a hateful chore. I did it three times, a very thorough copy editor went over it twice, somehow we both missed this."

The speaker on my left chuckles. His name on the jacket of one of his books had been misspelled, he comforted me later, and in the one he is presenting today Tip O'Neill's name has two different versions. Don't be dismayed, he soothed me.

I need to fill out my time before this roomful of faces so I talk about the process of publishing as seen by a nonprofessional. The silences, the delays, the pleasant relationships you develop with people at the other end. Of how my editor had become a friendly, father figure as for months we conferred over the telephone, the shock it had been finally to meet a man in jeans and sneakers, younger than my children. I had thought publishers read proof but I had had to do this in haste between trips to Belize and Arizona, making so many mistakes in my first book that it had cost me a small fortune. I tell them about my friend Sewall Pettingill, who proofs his texts by reading each sentence backward. He had set weekend visitors at this chore once. In print the only typo had been in the name of the man who had proofed that section. I prattle glibly on, eyeing my book on the table before me, wondering what is inside its jacket. I yield with gracious relief to the speaker who follows me.

He is a man who has seen much of life and come to terms with it; a really nice man, not much younger than I. It isn't what authors say at these programs, it's what comes through of the character behind. The comforter on my left had had to leave his wife at a hospital on his way. He speaks smoothly, making us laugh again and again but I notice his fingers rub together in a nervous life of their own. I know him best as a man who has been doggedly fighting city hall in our small town. When he sketchily refers to these engagements our audience murmurs with sympathy. The towns of Cape Cod are still mostly run by part-time, community-minded selectmen unprepared for the explosions of population, development, traffic and conservation problems suddenly besetting us. Our water, our laws and land protection are inadequate.

I am too interested in listening to these men, then kept too occupied signing my book to more than let its copies pass through my hands, although I shamelessly eavesdrop on two men examining it.

"Handsome," says one. He takes the jacket off, inspects the binding, details. "Well done."

"Norton is known for that," says the other, riffling the pages. *Without reading a word* they set their copies down and move away! When *I* riffled I didn't really see anything, I was too distracted. Perhaps a copy of my own will arrive in tomorrow's mail, I'll be able to study its pages in quiet. In amazement. I'll bet it won't come inscribed by that man who teased it out of me, though.

A columnist who interviewed me after *Parrots' Wood* has called to ask if she might do another on the *Cookbook,* and bring her photographer husband with her? Three years ago I would have been excited. Now—although I still feel a stir of incredulity that I am thought subject for an interview, I take such a request calmly, look to see where she can be fitted into my schedule.

Interviewers don't send you copies of what they write, or the photographs they take, in spite of their promises. They are busy, off pinning down their next victim. Friends aren't much better. "That was a fine piece about you in our paper," they will write, even if their paper was the *New York Times* or the *Washington Post* (they should have sent these in silver frames). I thought publishers kept track of such material, had a clipping service on their authors, but they are busy too. Usually the ones they send me are xeroxes of ones I had boastfully sent to my editor to impress him.

Excited by my first book I kept a scrapbook with copies of everything—posters, news stories, notices in ornithological journals, letters from prestigious friends. The second scrapbook was less bulky. I haven't bought one for my third. Who is going to look at them? People are busy with their own lives, busy putting together scrapbooks of their own. Families don't have big attics anymore. Why should I complain? I've met a lot of nice people, maybe this woman today will prove to be among them.

A photographer. What a bore. What will I wear? I used to take my body for granted, used it hard. It was neither servant nor master, just there. Regrettably it has changed over the years. When I glimpse it reflected in windows, in an unexpected mirror I give it ugly looks. Remorseful ones, anyway. Somewhere inside it the schoolgirl, the college athlete, the mother must live, slender, strong. I don't want to slough off the years, just the pounds. A container in my freezer is labeled

Cooky Dough. If this is correct—it may as easily be mush-rooms—I'll bake my inquisitor and her husband some cookies. (Alas, it turns out to be barley soup.)

At the Book Tea today I talked in a bar. (There has to be a first time for everything.) I was tired and increasingly nervous as middle-aged ladies, and a few men, filled the chairs. *Paying to enter.* Longingly I looked at the gleaming row of bottles only a few feet away behind a cheery young bartender waiting to serve us tea and cakes. A short rum sour would loosen me up, I thought wistfully, but common sense prevailed, I was on display. I had no idea what I was going to say to this group. What *can* you say about a cookbook?

My co-speaker solved the problem. She has written three successful mysteries, the latest slated for the movies for a sum that widened her eyes just to speak about. On the proceeds of her second she had learned to fly. She barely mentioned her third, just out, but talked instead about the process of writ-ing, of how creativity flows through her mind like a magic—like the magic she feels is all that keeps an airplane aloft. As I also often do she explained how making a book is similar to making a baby—it comes to life deep within you, proceeds through similar periods of uncertainty, of pain, of waiting; ending in triumphant excitement with the ministrations of editors and a publisher replacing nurses and a physician. Amid champagne and flowers it starts off on a life of its own.

She told how she enjoys laying a base through research, talking to people of many types until she can write from a thoroughly knowledgeable background. She was slender, with dark hair, brown eyes, wearing a rose- and flame-colored sweater. Was she pretty? Homely? I have no idea. Spirit and intelligence animated her face, I found her enchanting. Her professional experiences of the publishing process were so different from mine that I was shaken but she had given me the clue I needed, so when it came my turn I could recount mine.

I told of the accidental writing of my first book, the amusing history that led to its final publication; of writing the second because I was so enjoying the new world I had been pitched into in my dotage.

"And your third?" piped a voice from the back. I'd been so in love with that third manuscript, so sure it was better than either of my others that stupidly I had talked about it, word had gotten around.

"Everyone fails," I answered shortly. That failure is a knife twisting through my every day, I can't talk about it. It was a novel, the love story of a woman who, idly rubbing a small dusty lamp in her family's attic, had summoned up a genie.

I couldn't urge our audience to buy my *Cookbook,* I said. This might disappoint the bookshop proprietors sitting across the room, but I had to be honest. Our audience laughed, bought it anyway, brought their purchases to the table where Anne LeClaire and I had to interrupt our eager interest in each other to sign them. They bought more of hers than mine but, as I pointed out severely, hers was a paperback and less expensive. Unfair competition.

As we ate teacakes, autographed our books, Anne and I spoke on how at these events our ego expands, we grow in stature—in our own eyes—find the attention thoroughly enjoyable. Then—I don't know about her, she has a husband with whom she can decompress as they drive home—by the time I reach my driveway the glow has ebbed. The praise I have been given is like Christmas tinsel—a little of it still glittered on evergreens along my way but most of it hung bedraggled, tattered, on branches of misshapen saplings.

I go out in the dark to gather laundry on the line. Across the white sheets, light from a window throws a pattern of bare winter branches, of stark tree trunks: like a black and white painting, lovely. Tonight those patterns will be what I remember most vividly from my day—those and my young co-speaker, talking from a depth most lecturers gloss over, giving each of us a gift.

When I redeemed Brad's big punchbowl this morning from a party it had serviced there had been a jar of eggnog in it along with the ladle. Instead of working tonight I'll build a fire and read Anne's mystery.

November 1987

Last week I had taken a platter of muffins made from a recipe in my *Birdwatcher's Cookbook* to a signing at Bob Hale's Westwinds Bookshop in Duxbury. They were miniatures, baked in little cups of crinkled paper so fingers needn't be licked.

Today I am returning from a luncheon at the Chilton Club in Boston (aah, what delicious food they serve!). I had spent the night in Cambridge with a granddaughter, breakfasted with a friend in Weston, stopped at Wellesley College to see another granddaughter. The campus is large and lovely although security at colleges these days is frightening, police cars marred the landscape. My directions were hazy but I finally find her dormitory, manage to park, manage to locate an information desk, Granddaughter is not in her room. I try to cram all I can into my driving; I had also called on the book buyer at the Harvard Coop, a very pleasant, helpful man never too busy to advise me. Now I am detouring to Duxbury to put my head in at Westwinds for a cup of coffee, to catch up on their news. A woman planning a trip to Belize is at the counter, come to buy my *Parrots' Wood,* which is based in Belize. Well, more or less, it wanders, but I don't tell her that as we talk. Another woman enters in an obvious hurry, pushes between us, demands of Mark a copy of *The Bird Woman's Muffin Book.* Though we all look momentarily blank booksellers are used to this. Mark lifts a copy of my *Cookbook* from a stack by the cash register and indicates me.

"Would you like the Muffin Lady to sign it? She is right beside you."

Of such are the grace notes of my travels. Worth every minute I had spent baking those muffins.

At home is a package from W. W. Norton. "Ah," I say happily. "Instead of dealing with catalogues and bills I'll build a fire, pour a sherry and cozy down with the whodunit my editor said last week he would send me." But when I open the package it is only a book *I* sent *him* a year ago. No fire. No sherry. Just bills dutifully paid. Grace notes come on a sliding scale.

I am grown old. Or is it that I'm tired, have lost my sense of adventure? Or that I have reached the end of a cycle, I need something new? Or is it just because it's November?

This morning a man calls from New Haven, asking me to drive there to hear a mutual friend lecture, and to see a conservation program he has built up for schoolchildren. It is a long way from the elbow of Cape Cod to New Haven. I have friends along the route but—No, I tell him. I've done so much driving this year I can't face any more. I am pleased, flattered that you should want me, I would enjoy seeing all of you, but No.

Last year I did drive to New Haven to speak at an Annual Meeting, talking to a Brownie group on my way. Dinner was late, the business affairs lengthy, it was nearly ten o'clock before I was introduced. Ten o'clock is my bedtime! The next morning I'd talked at a school. Perhaps the weariness of that evening has me refuse another such trip?

At teatime I am still depressed, waiting for the kettle to hum, reading a book before stirring up supper. I have no interest in supper. What is wrong with me?

"Full moon," says Lisa, calling to check on me. "Of course you can go to Connecticut, you haven't been there since spring. What else do you have to do?"

They won't let me quit, sit peacefully in front of a fire, reading, these so-called friends of mine. They won't let me hang up my muddy boots, my stylish, professional hat.

"How are you doing on revising that whodunit?" asked my young editor cheerily, only yesterday. I'd written one as a joke, to stop him badgering me. "Fine," he had reported. "Only it needs to be twice as long, with another murder. What else do you have to do?"

I don't want to write a whodunit!

A Cape Cod Journal

Gray and Dreary

The year is drawing to its close. The visitors and tasks of summer are past, my home's oriented toward winter. And like the season I am colorless. I have come to a wall I cannot surmount. It is built of failure, of friendship and confidence eroded, it blocks my horizon. I find no handhold on it, no vine spreading tendrils across its surface, no clear song, no lad whistling on his morning way to tell me of life on its other side. I, who have always sprung out of bed eager for what the day may bring now lie passively looking at the ceiling, noting with distaste an inconspicuous hole a painter left there. I haven't enough spirit even to be angry with myself.

The novel I had thought better than either of my other books has again been rejected, so often now that finally I must admit failure. How long in happiness did it take me to write, to type and retype its pages, to set these on a shelf to ripen, then to revise, type again, revise once more? The gestation of a book is an investment not only of time but of spirit, of joy. A stillborn child is not your fault. A book rejected is. Similar to rejection by a spouse it leaves you deformed.

Stop sniveling, my logical self scolds as I take an egg from the fridge for my breakfast, chop parsley. You have been riding high for too long, being flattered, fussed over, now you are paying for it.

A well that runs dry fills again, a deeper self reminds me, water seeping slowly into it. Perhaps creativity is like that. Perhaps over time the tide governing my inner core will rise as imperceptibly as the tides rise through dead clumps and reaches of the brown marsh grass of the pond until again a shining mirror reflects the life around it, the blue sky.

At the moment I don't seem strong enough to handle this.

Midmorning a man stops me at the post office. "I've wanted to thank you," he says. "My wife and I have enjoyed your books. I hope you are writing another?"

I can't cry. I can't let him see behind my thanks.

"A cookbook doesn't seem your style," he continues, "but we've put an order in for it."

I shake my head at him, thank him again. Why isn't this enough for me? It's far more than I deserve, far more than I could have imagined a few years ago. Back home I go upstairs for something. I still haven't made my bed, hung up my nightgown. I don't care. My mirror tells me I need a haircut. I don't care. A friend calls to ask if she may visit. I lie to her. "No," I say, "I'm busy that weekend." The goblins'll git you, my Sensible Self warns me. I don't care.

"But you don't just quit," I tell myself. "Cry into your tea, sit on a couch reading magazines and mysteries. No one gets their own way, dances on a tightrope of happiness all the time. Shape up! What is it you tell the groups you talk to? That if one door doesn't open you try another?"

"It isn't me saying that!" I argue despondently. "That's that other woman in a rose suit with a silver Pegasus on its lapel. She hasn't anything to do with me. It's time she dropped dead anyway, all that vigorous optimism, false courage. What right does she have to talk the way she does?" My two selves seesaw back and forth.

You can't talk your way out of depression, you have to wait for life to pick you up by the scruff of the neck and, for better or worse, set you on a new path. I can't let anyone know I feel like this, I have to work it out by myself.

I decide I will go through the papers and letters on my desk; clean out old magazines piled "to read again someday," stack them for the recycling bin at the dump. While I'm about it I might start on organizing the photographs and letters in the mahogany chest my mother carved for me, for my families to put in their mahogany chests. I might even clean my basement.

While I contemplate these unattractive activities the doorbell rings. A lad with a shy, eager look wants to know if I can tell him what is the skull he cradles carefully in his hands? I don't know anything about skulls! But I have a car, I can take him to the Museum, where he can look at full trays of them, his eyes widening with delight, with the chance to learn. He doesn't know about, and I forget that rejected manuscript lying on my table.

This morning I am still sniveling. Stop it! says my Logical Self. Everyone gets tired, has failures. Stop it! There's a full moon behind those clouds, in a few days you will be energized again. In the meantime there is work on your desk, firewood to stack, enough buttermilk left in the fridge to make those good bran muffins you like. You can take some to Emily for lunch.

Logic is a cold bedfellow with cold feet, a raspy chin. Disregarding the buttermilk I put a slice of bread in the toaster, crack an egg into a pan. The toaster pops. I eat the egg, put in a second slice of bread.

"You could write a book called *Scrapheap*," a cynical friend tries to cheer me. "Scrapheaps are fun—bedsprings and bones, boxes of old papers, boathooks, buttons—all sorts of interesting objects poke up between the plastic cups and trash. Birds pry into them, find nourishment, why not you? Hang in there."

"I'm not interested in bits and pieces of the past," I answer grumpily. "It's a future I want—fruit on a tropical tree, no matter how far out of my reach." The second piece of toast was burned, I hadn't heard the timer.

My calendar bids that I am to give a program this morning, join friends for lunch. I perform adequately but underneath my surface gaiety lies that weight of depression. I am not willing to impose it on my friends (and be told to write a *Scrapheap*.) It would be ridiculous to go to a psychiatrist. My doctor would only take my blood pressure, always excellent; tell me not to eat so many peanuts, get more exercise. Walking, that's his idea of exercise!

Well, you've been through this before I tell myself, only differently. Nothing stays the same. This is the season when life withdraws, plants and animals go underground to rest, conserve energy for another year, for growth. Why not you, also an animal? You tell people in your lectures to put one foot in front of another, practice what you preach.

I contemplate my feet. (I am home now.) My shoes are shabby; comfortable, which the fashionable ones I wore this morning weren't. I kick them off and lie flat on the couch. Afternoon shadows cross the rafters over my head, throw into relief the decoys standing there. One I whittled in Quebec, keeping Brad company while he fished—that's a yellowlegs. Another I whittled as a plover, also at our camp in Quebec. The plover isn't stocky enough but sentimentally it pleases me. Another I bought years ago in Maryland. Driving home from a fishing weekend we had passed a roadside home with decoys patterning its modest windows. "Stop," I had asked.

I am not a fisherwoman. I had spent that afternoon in the boat with binoculars letting our companions twitch their lines, bring in the catch we shiveringly grilled later for supper outside our cabin, under a Hunter's Moon. As we chugged home at sunset through a narrow channel in the coastal marsh I had been puzzled by a boat ahead of us where men steadily chopped on a board, throwing over some unwanted residue.

"Rails," explained our captain. "This is prime rail country. When the tide is extra high as it is today the birds move to the top of the grasses and are easy to shoot."

He had dipped a net overboard and brought up two heads for me, floating on the still water. Those lovely, long-legged birds with their clattering calls, their camouflaged dun bodies slipping through the marsh—the men had shot scores of them, the heads floated now all around us. I smoothed the soft feathers, studied the long bills, the distinguishing white line by the eye. No worse, I tried to comfort myself, than our catching a creel of fish we would eat for supper. The shorebird in the decoy shop changed hands for $15.00. I look at it now, still unsure which species it is. Remembering that weekend, sunset gold on the marsh, the smell of fish frying over a fire in the evening chill as a white moon rose, the comfort of my man waiting patiently in the car for me.

Those birds must be dusty, casting their shadows across my ceiling. I should fetch a ladder, climb up and dust them. Some other afternoon.

Still November

I have regained my energy and balance although it's taken a while. It's a matter of philosophy. Do you try to control the world or do you take what comes? I've always taken what came so why should I change now?

Again I was asked today at a book talk where I was gratefully only in the audience "Are you writing another book? We like to walk around with you, your days are so different. There must be much you haven't told us."

I shook my head. "I don't see my days that way. Like most women I wash dishes and floors, feed friends and family, fall in love and out of love, go to bed in tears or content. I do what a day brings whether it is shoveling snow or planting pansies, having learned along my lonely road that if I just set one foot in front of the other, no goal in mind, not looking where I am going, a door opens before me.

" 'Never mind if you don't know what's on the far side of that door,' " I tell my audiences. I say this in each of my programs, urging people to get more involved in life. Why— I don't ask this but surely it's implicit—why are they wasting their time, spending money to listen to me when they could be out working for their community; Learning. Growing.

" 'Take the risk,' I admonish them, 'it's how you learn. Someone will be there to teach you, pick you up if you fall on your face. It's how you stay alive.'

I don't tell them how hard this sometimes is for me to do.

"I've gone back to doing volunteer work," I tell my questioner. "I guess I'm used up. Maybe this year, next year something will trigger me. But I thank you for your encouragement."

December 1987

A carton of promotional postcards advertising my *Cookbook* arrived today. A month late but I am a minor figure in the corridors of W. W. Norton, whose business is textbooks, historians, artists. On one side of the card is a reproduction of Lisa's jacket—very handsome, eye-catching. The other has room, if I write small, for an address, a Season's Greetings (in case they don't arrive until New Year's) and as much message as probably I would write on a formal Christmas card. I hadn't planned to send cards this year except to friends in special need of support but these are attractive even if commercial. (I'll hear about that.) They'll explain what I've been up to, why I haven't written as often as I might these last few months. I'll say I am really sending my affection, not urging them to rush out and buy my book, although if they do it will drop shekels into the coffers of the Cornell Laboratory of Ornithology, to which I have given my royalties; where once I worked at the front desk, where I have been on the Board of Directors.

While I consider this project I watch a cardinal prospecting for seeds where house finches have scattered their leftovers. House finches are like children, willing to eat at any time of day, untidy. The female cardinal waits on one side for her master to have his fill, then comes for leavings. Like the women of many cultures, of our own frontier, who feed men, be they ranch hands, guests or passing Indians, they wait until the men have finished.

If I am going to send out these cards I must hurry, it will take many hours I hadn't planned on so near Christmas. Well, I don't really need to give an Eggnog, I can substitute a Holiday Mop Up in January. I've done this before. Or I can wait for Valentine's Day. Making an eggnog is a major effort, and messy. (I think this is what really decides me.) I uncap a red pen, reach for my address file. If Norton had provided these cards a month ago my friends might have bought copies for gifts. Only then I would have had to go through my list twice, writing, licking all these stamps. Life is a series of trade-offs.

What I enjoy in the Christmas cards I am already receiving are glimpses of the people behind the holiday wish—a scrawl, sometimes hasty, sometimes detailed, on what is important to their current lives. My friends are scattered about the country, I like to know what they are doing. One, having retired, has gone back to a part-time job that exhausts her but keeps her spirit alive; another keeps traveling—China, Alaska, Mexico, anywhere in the effort to adjust to widowhood. One is building pens for a rare species of pheasant he raises, that his local foxes enjoy. Some write about grandbabies, some have become photographers. Their card is a landscape, a bird, a grouping of family members. One has written a book, can I help her find a publisher? Many are inarticulate, say little: I value their senders for other qualities. The most meaningful are put on my mantelpiece among the greens there. The rest go in a box I will return to, reread next month, enjoying again the warmth of friendship this season brings.

I am beginning to get acknowledgments of copies of the *Cookbook* I sent to those whose recipes I pilfered.

"Oh! Oh!" writes one in dismay. "I didn't tell you to use a full cup of burgundy in my stew! And it should be served over wild rice. I said pasta by mistake."

"You omitted a line," says another sternly. "Mushroom quiche has to have a crust, you mixed up my instructions. Can this be changed in the next printing?" What an optimist, talking about a second printing!

"Don't you need shortening in your Five Grain Bread on page 153?" worries another, "or flour in the Molasses Cookies on page 215?"

Painstakingly I correct these omissions in books I personally sign, if there is time, though I am deciding no one really uses cookbooks, they just get lined up on a shelf. No one seems to have noticed the above omissions. Sometimes I write the corrections on the title page under my name instead of on the applicable page. With people standing about talking, laughing, dictating names it is easy to get confused. For me to get confused.

Signings are like people—the same basic structure but each one different. There is food—cheese and crackers, cookies; drink—cider, punch, sometimes wine. I sit at a table with a

THE CAPE COD MUSEUM OF NATURAL HISTORY

stack of books, a pen and am left to my own devices. Some customers stop out of curiosity, to see an author in the flesh. I feel they are disappointed. An author after all is just a person, like your piano tuner, your butcher, your sister-in-law. Some are embarrassed to inspect a book they may not want. I try to avoid eye contact, busy myself writing my name in copies that may be put on the shelf to be sold another week, or be returned to the publisher. Occasionally I come across one I have already signed and wonder which shop I was in, in what state. Signings don't necessarily fatten the ego, just the figure.

Today I signed at our Museum, where I am a Trustee. The two hours were a pleasure. This is my home town, friends came to support me. Lisa Russell, also allied with the Museum, came to keep me company and write her name as illustrator, small and neat in the proper place. A brown-eyed man leaned, laughing, across our table. He had promised a mutual friend in New York, he said, to deliver a kiss and did so, full on the mouth. My status rose considerably. Bob Finch is a nationally known writer, a prominent local conservationist, far better known than I am. He signed one of *his* books for me. I forgot to pay for it, but I will, I will. It was a festive party.

It isn't always that way. The other night my daughter telephoned from Washington. "How was your Signing?" she asked. "Didn't you have one this week?"

"Dull," I answered. "I just sat at a table looking out at rain. Only three books sold. No one had interest in me."

"Oh, Mother," she had laughed. "How jaded you have become. Two years ago you would have been beside yourself with excitement. Did Lisa join you? Didn't you come away with any funny stories?"

I had thought ruefully how we change with living. A year, a month, even a day makes a difference.

"Yes. It was Homecoming Day for the High School. A parade had been advertised which would provide excitement, bring shoppers along Main Street.

" 'Here they come,' someone cried. I went to the window expecting a band, decorated vehicles, flags. What passed was a pickup truck with kids in jeans, waving and hollering. Not even singing.

" 'That's my niece,' said a customer proudly. 'The one in the red sweater.' The truck went down the street, circled the rotary, returned. Big deal. Give me Washington, Fort Lauderdale, Phoenix anytime."

"Well, you don't have to live in the boondocks of Cape Cod," my daughter said.

But I do. This sunny, wide-windowed house has become my home place. Perhaps it is the dents in the woodwork; or a mouse hole in the pine wall I have hidden with a painting; or the plantings outside that have grown slowly, along with my relationships inside with plumbers and carpenters, but now here, I am sustained by a contentment finally achieved.

I look about as we continue talking—at furniture and rugs accumulated over the years; at the paintings, the crowded bookcases, the wholly unsuitable Italian chandelier we all love; a piano I keep saying I am going back to playing, but don't. Music reaches to too deep a level, disturbs what I still have to cover over if I am to maintain my serenity. I run chords on it, fool around with kindergarten Bach, I love to look at its warm walnut wood, but my typewriter has replaced it at another window which keeps me looking out, prevents too much looking in.

"You come here," I tell my child. "The airlines lose my suitcase. On my last trip I had to ask the man who was putting me up if he had a hairbrush I could borrow, and did he keep a lady's nightgown in his bottom bureau drawer? Besides, I'm too comfortable to go anywhere."

"Mother!" she laughs, "is this *you*? Not wanting to travel? Finding Signings dull? Don't you remember the Bishop?"

After we hung up I made a small fire and sat by it with a mug of hot chocolate in my hand, remembering.

Every day in those first weeks after *Peacocks* was published had been like Christmas. Norton had provided attractive advertising cards for me to mail to my friends. The day they came I had taken a handful to a bookstore for their sales counter and had stood talking to the proprietor. A young lad regarded me round-eyed.

"Geeze," he had asked, "would you autograph one of those for me?"

In one day my mail held a letter from a travel agent I'd not dealt with in years. She wanted to put *Peacocks* in her mail order list but was it an adventure story, a personal journal or a bird book? There were invitations to speak in Buffalo, to a Rotary Club in California. Crazy! I didn't want to travel, I wanted to sit right here, sending out those cards. I figure if I were to write ten letters a day to go with them—who has time to write ten letters a day?—it would take only twenty-five days to cover my list. Except that every day the list grew longer. It was intoxicating.

Recently I attended a dinner dance at the Chatham Bars Inn, an old and lovely seaside hostelry that in another generation had cared for both my mother and mother-in-law, one coming for bridge on the verandah, one to play in golf tournaments. A dinner dance isn't my usual habitat but this had been organized by a friend for a cause I am glad to support.

I say attended because I didn't dance, and not being hungry didn't heap a plate from the magnificent buffet set out among ice sculptures and flowers. I sat in the lee of the head table quietly sipping wine, observing. Mostly, as the crowd settled to eat, observing a table next to us. My eyes had locked in disbelieving astonishment on a man there—a man come to life from the pages of the novel I have been writing. A man I have invented, cooked for, slept with, not ten feet from me, laughing down at the woman beside him—the quick smile curving the generous mouth I have run my fingers across; with the dark eyes, the thick unruly hair, broad shoulders I have given him, the square hands of a sailor. As in my book I would need to stand on tiptoe to kiss him. I watched this real man rise courteously for his mother's friends, follow a younger woman with his eyes. I couldn't take my own off him. Aware of my scrutiny he smiled at me, raised an eyebrow I have often smoothed. I had to decide—for my own protection—that he was too attractive, too much the focus for too many other women. My fictional man is quiet, not glamorous.

A few nights later I met this prototype in a friend's living room. Certainly he was handsome; impeccably dressed, magnetic. But his dark hair like his beard was bushier, in need of a haircut. He was heavy in body, self-assured. Sitting on a couch with him, nibbling crackers I found he roused no spark in me. Disappointing. I laugh at how we deceive ourselves, how my days—anyone's days—are a succession of fantasies, of bubbles burst, songs half heard, people invented out of our needs. I didn't mind leaving him in the kitchen with a pretty young woman, chopping vegetables for salad.

Having munched all the hors d'oeuvres I decently could I left to sign books at a local shop open on this Saturday night for the holiday trade, for Christmas revelers coming down streets bright with tinsel and lighted trees. For an hour or two I talked with customers who picked my books up, set them down, occasionally bought one. I drank festive champagne with them, tried to see through their surfaces real persons that someday I might incorporate into another book. A male quartet came in and sang to us, enjoying their performance as much as we did. They were comfortable, nice men in their fifties whose equally nice, comfortable wives would be shopping along the street. As I watched them I had to wonder what sets off a fantasy, what leads you or me—one, I suppose is the grammatical word—to respond to one person only in a crowded room; to go out with him for dinner or a drink, hope he will kiss you goodnight on your doorstep? Age doesn't affect this, it's chemistry—a glance across a room, an unexpected locking of eyes—a magic that suddenly lights your placid existence. Do men wonder like this, or only women? How old do I have to be to learn how men think?

Last night my Look-alike Man asked me, "Why do you always laugh when we meet?" We have both been at the same holiday parties, have become friendly, mostly I suspect, because I keep arriving at his elbow to listen to him talk, to find out what he is like behind that extraordinarily familiar facade.

I laughed again. "Because I wrote you into a book. I've been in love with you, we've been in the Bahamas together. Illicitly. I was shocked to find you at the Ball—well known, prominent locally. I was afraid people would think it was you I was writing about, that I am just another of the women who trail you around. I went back to my manuscript, shaved off your neat beard, changed your walk, your eyebrows, your hands. It was a lot of trouble and for nothing, probably no publisher will like either of us. I killed you off at the end. Nobody will like that either. I laugh at us all the time because you are so different from my fantasy lover but I have to keep myself from lifting my mouth to kiss you goodnight, from wanting to go home with you. Which"—I ended severely, assessing the twinkle in his eyes—"I don't. There are plenty of other women here hoping for that privilege."

He kissed me anyway. "I'd like to read your book," he said before we were interrupted, those other women claimed him.

What a way to end the year! An errant jetstream that fortunately swept the worst of a serious storm out to sea has dropped its fringe on us.

"The Cape is closed," advises the radio I brought from the attic to replace my silent TV. "Nothing will be open. Schools, post offices, markets, banks. Do not try to travel."

My son calls. "Do you have batteries for your radio? Do you need a better radio?"

I laugh. When the power goes out not only do I have no radio—unless I find batteries in the back of the fridge—but no heat, no light, no water. "I'm fine," I assure him. "I've firewood, lots of food and Christmas letters to acknowledge. I won't need to go anywhere for days."

It snows all day. I go out half a dozen times to my birdfeeders, trampling down a path, constructing a shelter for ground birds. I break the crust from a mince pie I've been given for the half dozen crows that keep an alert eye on my yard, and put water from a hoarded supply in the cellar, in a shallow bowl by my garden steps. To the delight of a starling. I hope he singes his feathers on the electric element in it, starlings are not my favorite birds. In breeding season I have watched them oust too many of our native birds from their nest holes, tossing out eggs and young, eating these. Then I remember the element isn't working. I go to the door and chase the dirty black creature away with snowballs.

I sweeten the breakfast rice cakes taught me by a grandmother with Christmas elderberry jelly sent from Florida. I wipe my oven of its Thanksgiving turkey splatter. I mop, and dust. I'll set French bread to rise. I bought myself the proper tins as a Christmas gift and want to practice with different recipes. The birds can have one loaf, I'll have the other with soup for lunch. French bread isn't anything but water and flour, a spoonful of yeast, of sugar, of oil.

"And *time*," says my college grandson coming over in the afternoon to check on me. He helps pull the double tin from the oven, breaks off the tip of one loaf to sample.

"I don't count *time* except when I'm pushing a vacuum sweeper," I tell him, "or chipping ice in the driveway as I did this morning while you were sleeping. If this hasn't turned out well the birds won't mind. It's cheaper than stale loaves I buy for them on sale in the market." I break off a piece for myself.

He flips through the newspaper he has brought me, shows me an advertisement offering English Muffins Free. "I guess you can't beat that," he says. He breaks off another piece, tucks the second loaf, still hot, under his arm to take to his mother for supper (if it lasts that long) kisses me and is off, his long legs loping through the snow.

I assess my fridge. I have milk, eggs, spinach and frozen chicken (still frozen). I have fruit cakes I made to give away but haven't yet. I am ready for the New Year. If my grand-daughter and her friends should make it down from Boston later in the week, they can shovel the driveway for me. They are young and energetic.

"You were on TV this morning," Emily calls to tell me. "Did you know? You're historical. Nancy Lancaster was doing a wrap-up of the year and used part of the interview you did last spring at the Hyannis Mall. The part where you said one way to live is to stay wrapped in your warm cocoon, comfortable, content, doing what you know how to do."

The other way, I remember, wincing at how easily Nancy always manages to get me pontificating, is to open yourself to kinds of living you don't know how to handle, to take risks, to learn. I should start the New Year remembering this, pat-tern my own life on it; be grateful to Nancy for reminding me.

January 1988

"I'm tired of sitting in my living room waiting to die," I storm at my doctor. I am in his office to learn what damage I have done to a foot, skidding on pine needles. "I've spent all winter in the doldrums, not working at anything. So this week I have volunteered to go to the Adirondacks with an Audubon group. I'll gnash my teeth when I watch them going off in canoes, hiking when I can't, but I can run mist nets, show them migrant birds in the hand. I love those woods, those lakes. Then I've volunteered to go on an Earthwatch expedition to Panama. They'd be crazy to take me, an untrained grad student would be more useful to them than a woman my age. Massachusetts Audubon wants me on board a banding and snorkeling trip to Belize, in the Bay of Honduras, we're to live on a boat. The black flies in the Adirondacks in June are awful, They get behind my glasses, my eyelids swell so I can hardly see. The climate in Panama will be unendurable. I get seasick on boats. But I'm tired of living the way I am."

Dr. Robert considers me; he doesn't even take my blood pressure, which must momentarily be high, or thump my rib cage which is always all right.

"You're going to drop dead some day," he says cheerfully, "why not in Panama or Belize? I suppose if I suggest you rest your foot for a few days, don't walk on uneven ground . . . That would help your cold, too."

I shake my head. "I have to get our nets up at the Sanctuary this week, we've some school programs coming, and our banding demonstrations begin Saturday. My foot hurts but I'll try not to do more than I have to."

I like to visit Dr. Robert. He knows my insides from x-rays and tests, my outsides from my vain refusals to be weighed with heavy shoes on, from my monthly chattering, from my books which leave me as open as his x-rays. I don't have to pretend to be anything but what I am with him, it's restful. He doesn't restrict me, lets me make my own decisions. As usual—

"You might write another book," he suggests as he hands me his bill, walks me to the door. "That would help your foot too."

Write another book—that's what everyone says, pushing me.

"You could write one on places you've banded," suggests Liz, listening to me deplore my current inactivity.

Well, I suppose I could—each place was unique. A hundred snips and snards from them float in my mind. But it's the future I want to embrace, not my past. And what, except for the need of Kleenex and a fresh bandage on my foot, is in my future?

I finally sort the box of Christmas cards I have kept, rereading them, grateful for their messages, then tear off their backs for telephone notes and grocery lists. They trigger vignettes too. Why do I let these scenes from my past depress me, I should get enormous satisfaction from them, smile instead of sigh. I am put together wrong.

"You surely are." Liz knows my haphazard ways, is a friend in spite of them. "Have you forgotten you are speaking at a Bookshop Tea near here tomorrow? If you come over afterward I'll give you supper: if you aren't fussy what it is."

Well, there's my future, if only a crumb (though Liz doesn't serve crumbs, in spite of her warning). I'd forgotten about tomorrow, and I'll need more energy than today I can summon. Actually I needn't worry. Before an audience, whether sixth-grade schoolchildren eager for knowledge, or senior citizens hoping for entertainment, Myself, the woman I really am, disappears, I become vibrant, caring about what I say, anxious to reach my listeners. Myself stands in the wings in astonishment, eggs this other woman on. She is a woman I hadn't known existed. Has she been inside me all these years, no one knowing? I wonder if Brad knew, if that was whom he loved, so soon to be buried beneath the housewife, the diapers and dishes? It's a startling thought.

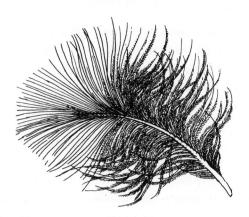

February 1988

A friend of many years stopped by today. Distance keeps us apart but when we meet we pick up from where we have left off, trading news, deaths, triumphs, losses, our enjoyment of each other as keen as always. He sits on a kitchen stool while I make lunch. He laughs at my unkept garden, so different from the orderly greens of his. We stroll down the lane by the water, watch men at the small marina tow boats out to their moorings. When he must leave—

"Thank you for coming," I say, my hands still in his. "You give me your time, your strength, you give me confidence. I don't know why I need confidence when I rush about the country so much, enjoying my new career, but I do." I smile up at him. "Is it because audiences are impersonal? I need someone closer, someone who knows and accepts the real me, who listens to my puzzlements and hesitations with attention? The way you do?"

"The way you do to me," he counters, kissing me.

I walk to his car with him, watch it pass around the curve.

I wonder if we will meet again. Of all the people I visit, enjoy, may have had long association with there are less than half a dozen who reach through the walls I have built around myself as if these didn't exist. Seeing his car disappear is a small death. I refuse to accept this. He will be back, I tell myself. You will be here.

Someone you have loved you never lose. Life will obscure or overlay those we have cherished, the happinesses may be buried deep but when you need them they will surface. This man will always be with me—on a trail, sprawled comfortably by a fire discussing our work with his students; in my kitchen, his living room, a car. He is woven into my life, a companion death will not eradicate. His values, his irritation when I have not performed to his standards, his belief in me, his affection—he won't have left me. And if I die first he will not have lost me. We carry our past always with us.

March 1988

Bob Hale called yesterday to ask if I would drive an author to one of his book programs in Duxbury—seventy miles north as her car is giving her trouble. I would do anything for Bob. Genial, outgoing, generous, he moves like a prince through the book world. Retired—his idea of retirement, not mine— he runs a bookshop, lectures, hosts TV programs and book shows out of town—and is available any time to his friends. He and Liddy live in a 1702 Colonial home on nineteen acres where she raises prize Pygmy goats, sheep, lovely flowers, the vegetables they serve at lunch.

"I'll bet you stacked that wood, too," I said one day as we passed a workmanlike pile on our way to her immaculate barn, a terrier, a cat or two accompanying us. I was correct about the woodpile but astonished to learn that she also has time to shear her sheep, card and use their wool. *I* lead a rich life, occasionally wielding a dust rag, writing letters?

The author I deliver, Joan Colebrook, is celebrating a book on her childhood in the outback of Australia. The few pages I had time to read yesterday, the passages she chooses to read to us today are written with a lucid descriptive touch, picturing a life more real, more interesting than that of many novels. Or is it just that, older, I prefer fact, real people to fiction? She has written many children's books from the base of a small, hidden home near Provincetown. And like my other Provincetown friends she is refreshingly unfashionable. She settles into my car with a handbag, a large, unwieldy sack whose purpose I never discern, and a basket with a thermos of tea and nourishing supplies—a necessity, I judge, if you drive an untrustworthy car and live on the Outer Cape where there is no public transportation.

When she reads the hand holding her book shakes but her voice is steady, its accent a pleasure. What she presents, simply, is herself, a woman who has lived in many places; a full life. I am grateful I have been asked to deliver her, to hear her, to hold the copy of her book Bob won't let me pay for.

The other speaker is Cleveland Amory, a large man, a polished entertainer who keeps the roomful of ladies laughing. While he mentions his efforts to protect the rights of animals for which he is famous, he does not push this. Quartering the country, lecturing to raise funds for his animal foundation, he is also selling his books. At his age this can't be an easy life. I notice how he carefully lowers and raises himself in his chair, takes a moment to get underway, as often now I must do.

Bob and Liddy take us home for a gourmet meal presented with a flourish by a smiling young caterer. The two authors are taped in the living room by a charming TV couple I recognize from my similar performance last year. Bob is a skilled interviewer, pulling out of his subjects what really matters, allaying their nervousness. As we depart I notice Mr. Amory pauses by the kitchen to thank the young caterer—an old-fashioned courtesy I don't often see these days.

I put my Australian passenger back in my car, drive home to an empty house, bring in the laundry, chortle over Mr. Amory's cat book as I eat a slimming supper of cheese and tomatoes. I read a little about Joan's Australian childhood, wonder what she is having for her supper; write a grandchild, take the pills that may keep my lazy heart going for another week and go to bed.

I suppose what seems normal, ordinary to each of us to someone else is not ordinary, is a subject for envy. Of course when I am flattered a little of it must rub off on me. I worry, as I consider my days, what I have been fortunate to participate in, that I may become arrogant, take compliments for granted.

May 1988

Myra asks me for dinner. She wants me to meet a man coming
down from Boston.

"All right," I laugh, "but I'm a little old for that, don't you
think?" I needn't have worried. Myra isn't a matchmaker, like
Emily. Myra doesn't share her men.

"He asked especially that you should be here," she says crisply,
a hint of surprise in her voice. "Ben and Carol can pick you
up, they're coming. My son and his wife will be here, too."

The man from Boston looks up quickly as we enter. His
eyes are intent, searching for something in mine as we are
introduced. He holds my hand longer than necessary. He has
white hair, a neat white mustache. He limps a little as he
crosses the room, leads me to a sofa, his eyes still searching.

"Who are you, really?" he asks abruptly, in a break in the
general social chatter.

"Personally or professionally?" I ask. Always answer a question with a question, it gives you time. How do I know who
I am?

Before I must reply Myra's undisciplined retriever switches
its tail too close to a low table, spilling glasses, peanuts and
cheese sticks onto the floor. By the time the confusion has
cleared we are summoned to dinner. Who am I really, I wonder, enjoying Myra's good food, admiring her elegant table
setting, her flowers. Talk is general and after dinner Ben and

the other men steer my inquisitor to the other side of the room, talking business. Those blue Boston eyes watch me but by the time he makes his way back the moment has passed. Or his curiosity has been satisfied.

Who am I really, I muse, going to bed, looking at myself in the bathroom mirror, slipping a ruffled pink nightgown over my head, renewing a bandaid on a wrist. I can't see that it matters. Why did that man want to know? If he reads my books I'm one person. If he sits beside me at dinner I'm another woman though somewhere below that polite conversation, so deep down that even she is unaware, is a kernel that is listening, looking, absorbing; a kernel that may some day swell, grow. I ought to be curious about who he is but I'm sleepy.

June 1988

I had managed to squeeze my VW Rabbit into a tree-shaded backyard in Cambridge while I flew to Ohio for a conference. This green oasis is host, I judged on my return, to all the well-fed, active house sparrows of Harvard Square. This morning I am out in my own yard washing off the droppings that abundantly decorate its windshield and pale blue body. The telephone rings. An unknown, unhappy real estate agent from the other end of the Cape has a problem. His office, he tells me, has a small evergreen on either side of its front door. A bird has built a nest in one of these. When anyone goes in or out the door the bird flies, startling, scaring them. This bird is bad for his business. He called the Association for the Preservation of Cape Cod, they referred him to me.

"How big a bird?" I ask.

Oh, small, but it is bad for his business, he repeats. Having a bird attack a client is bad for business. What can he do? No, the bird doesn't really attack. . . . No, he doesn't know what kind of bird, it flies too fast. Brown.

I try to soothe him. If the chicks have hatched—yes, he has heard peeping—it will not be long before they will fledge, fly away. I try to persuade him that not everyone is lucky enough to have a bird trustingly build by his door. I tell him that in these days of declining wildlife a bird's nest is something to be treasured. Probably it had been built over the long holiday weekend when his office was empty. The mother couldn't leave her precious eggs. Probably his tenant is a house finch. Finches build anywhere—in hanging baskets on porches, in the kitchens and bathrooms of houses that have no screens. They seem to like the company of humans.

I tell him about the vultures that roost on the white wedding cake tiers of Miami's City Hall each year, refusing to be dislodged. They have become a source of pride, like the swallows of Capistrano. How many major cities have vultures living on their City Hall? Isn't he in the real estate business? A nesting bird is an advertisement! He should brag about his bird nest.

I return to cleaning my car. Again the telephone summons. It is a voice at W. W. Norton. The Library of Congress wants to know my age.

Dinner candles reflect in the wide window looking out to the salt pond that connects eventually to the Atlantic Ocean.

"As we connect ultimately to something far larger," Arthur had mused earlier as dusk obscured the terrace where we sat. The flames of the candles waver, picking out the ruby and topaz of wine left in our glasses. My guests watch as I pour coffee into small Mexican mugs.

"Probably full of lead, only we didn't know about lead poisoning then," says Meg, who had brought them to me years ago from San Miguel d'Allende. We are enveloped in comfortable after-dinner well-being, in an affectionate relationship of many years. They are trying to plan my future.

"A future that holds nothing," I had been complaining. "I'm a has-been."

"If you consider having friends for dinner, taking in grandchildren, their dogs, cats, companions; volunteering, giving programs nothing," counters Arthur. He considers me through a haze of pipe smoke. "I suppose you are unhappy because your Earthwatch expedition to Panama has been canceled. With the political situation I should hope you wouldn't have been sent to run loose in the jungle. Why don't you use the time to write another book?" He is serious. Arthur is my severest critic, a professional whose opinion I respect.

"About what?" I grumble. "I've written two journals, what have I left to say? I tried a novel, it bombed. My editor blarneyed me into a whodunit, it was terrible. My last two trips to the Caribbean were fiascos, both dull. I'm not doing anything exciting."

Mary pours more coffee. "You don't have to go to a foreign country to write a book," she says. "You could write about what has happened here since you have been sleeping in a proper bed, living comfortably. How about the beds you've slept in in this country, the fan letters you get, the quirky people you've met?"

"But I can't use them to write a book," I object. "Like me they need help, are looking for some road to follow that isn't just haphazard."

"That's what I mean," Mary continues. "All of us here tonight, we live in twos. Our lives have responsibilities, can't be haphazard. What have you found to steer by? I'd like a book that tells us that." Arthur nods.

I look at them distractedly. "But I don't steer. I just put one foot in front of the other. Every day, without looking where I am going. I tell all my audiences that's the exciting part of living. A door will open, it always does. But this summer staying here, reading, cooking—I haven't done anything exciting, no door opens."

Still . . . Only yesterday Dr. Robert said, "I don't want you bouncing about in an exercise class, or driving a hundred miles to give a program and then home again." He had eyed me sternly. "You aren't the same woman who came to me ten years ago. Why don't you write a book about that, on what goes on inside your head instead of under your feet?"

Only yesterday too, from Alaska—"I read your books to find out what another woman does with her time. Are you working on something else for us?" She had sent me a recipe of her grandmother's for Russian Black Bread because I'd complained in my *Cookbook* that I couldn't make this to my satisfaction. A woman teaching in a remote Indian village! How I would like to know how she spends *her* time! I wonder if the caraway seeds I sent reached her, and how? By plane? Dogsled?

I look about the table at my friends, now deep in another discussion. The candles are guttering. I turn to Arthur.

"It's astonishing," I say in a low voice, "how with persistence and joy you can build a life you never dreamed of, that you don't realize until years later you have built. Why do I need more than all of you here tonight? I'll settle for this."

He puffs on his pipe, holding it as Brad did his so long ago. Is this one reason I am fond of him? He also is a rock in my life.

"No," he says, equally quietly and smiles at me. "We won't let you."

August 4, 1988: My Birthday

I didn't mean to grow this old! I don't *want* to be this old! I had thought sixty would be my life span, I was comfortable with that. Widowed, actually I didn't want to live at all, I was just going through the motions. The woman I had lived with all those years no longer existed, no one had stepped forward to take her place.

Now, I tell my audiences in a firm voice, push against the wall of the cocoon you are wrapped in, whether it is of grief or inertia. Don't look where you are going, just go.

It still hurts me to see a couple kissing, exchanging private glances across a restaurant table, a living room. Loneliness, a heart-stopping stab, can catch you in mid-sentence, will always be a subliminal ache. You tamp it down, learn to ignore it. Everyone is lonely. You must accept it as you accept the shape of your face, your changing body, whatever may be crippling you. We are all crippled in some way. It makes you watch people with a deeper sensitivity.

A full moon, huge, orange from some disturbance of dust in the air has woken me, laying a path across my bed. Just so it would those summers I was writing my books, scribbling page after page in its radiance. But this summer I am writing nothing. The happiness, the pulsing energy that welled through me are gone. I remember how I would turn on my lamp, write; settle for sleep, then prop myself up again to write another paragraph, another page. Slowly the earth would tip, darkness blot my windows, but the moon, my eagerness would return the next night.

My sturdier persona speaks up. You should know by now, she chides, that the lunar cycle is a meeting of two currents, as when the Gulf Stream collides with the deeper ocean. You've seen this off Florida, off New Jersey. The colors change, waters that have been smooth become roiled as cold welling from the depths brings in its turbulence all manner of hidden life as happiness, or as now your failures well up to excite or torment you. Clean your cupboards, balance your checkbook (ugh); type the report you promised on Guana Island, it is overdue. The peaches ripening on your kitchen windowsill will make fine chutney. Age really makes no difference. How do you know what tomorrow, a telephone call will bring?

I plump my pillows. Listening for an owl as the moonlight leaves my bed, the glowing circle passes behind trees, beyond sight, as I disregard my age, fall asleep.

My daughter is here, running errands, cooking, improving my garden. While my friends are stewing tomatoes and currant jelly in the 90° heat I am sitting, tongue in cheek, my daughter encouraging me, air rising from the pond to cool me at my window. I am trying to concoct a mystery. After all, I went on a recent trip with a crew of marine biologists plus two professors and a hateful woman. We were a disparate lot and when we were tired hostilities flared. The food was poor, too. I should be able to work into this scene at least one attempted murder, treasure in a cave and a love affair—perhaps my own unrequited desire for our chief coordinator, who somehow always managed to be unwrinkled in contrast to our grubbiness? I have dreamed up a title and an ending, just not what goes between. I laugh as I write. My pages are so sophomoric that no publisher in his senses would consider them. I won't be offended. It is rather fun working on it although I have no emotional investment. It will be anyway two months before I hear from that august, busy office. By then I'll be into something else. What name should I give my villain, I ask my daughter? He's not really evil, just greedy.

Last week at a Book Brunch I was asked, as usual, what I am working on now. I tell them of this schoolgirl effort. It wouldn't sell, I assure them. I won't use the four-letter words today considered so essential. I'm unwilling on page two to have my characters rolling around on beds or beaches in torrid embraces.

The speaker before me had left his book on the podium. I picked it up. "Let's see what Doug Hornig has to say, how he starts his mystery." The glance Doug had shot me was merry. "Page 1, line 1," I read. I couldn't believe it. "Priscilla and I were in bed together."

It brought down the house. No more questions. Doug and I have been friends ever since.

September 1988

Tonight I am to take a group at dusk to watch the evening flight of Black-crowned night herons going to roost. It won't be as spectacular as the flamingos I used to watch streaming against a flaming sunset, their silhouettes changing from rose to black as they left the salt pans of Aruba, but the herons will be handsome in their black and white, restrained New England way. Beyond the marsh as they fly a thousand or more terns, disturbed by a passing boat, will lift from a small island, their calls coming clear across the water.

Four of us are having lunch at the beach grill of Chatham Bars Inn before brisk fall winds drive us indoors. Hamburgers and hot dogs amuse us, none of us would serve either of these at home.

"Aren't you going to Arizona this winter?" Myra asks me. Myra is always on the go, her home seems to hold no contentment for her since Harry died. "I thought you went every year?"

I am startled. It's true I've been to Arizona since the early 1940s, when Scottsdale was just a dusty crossroad with a shabby gas station on one corner, a dusty gift shop on the other, but I have only gone when I had reason to. For a while my sister lived in Paradise Valley, the only light at night beyond her corral a twinkle from Frank Lloyd Wright's Taliesin forty miles across the empty desert. Once I accompanied my mother to a ranch where a palmist told me disagreeable truths about myself. More recently I've been there for meetings of National Audubon and the Nature Conservancy and many times to visit my friends the Spoffords, who retired from Ithaca to Portal. One year I worked for the Conservancy at Riggs Ranch in the shadow of Baboquivari, fifteen miles from the Mexican border. The next fall I studied migrants at Aravaipa Canyon; one spring I was at Muleshoe Ranch, again making a bird survey before this remote outpost was made comfortably habitable. Another year I made a promotional tour for the Conservancy. I'd go again to Arizona but not as a snow bunny to sit in the sun, drive about the desert admiring those wonderfully craggy mountains. All my toys are home, my mail and magazines would never catch up with me.

To deflect Myra, who evidently takes it for granted that anyone with the means would of course leave Cape Cod's gray winter for the Arizona Sunbelt, now that Florida and California have become so overcrowded, I ask—

Did I ever tell you about the Nature Conservancy meeting where I was asked to sit at the head table at their banquet? No? It was terrific. It was the year *Peacocks* was published. I'd arranged, with some difficulty, there was no precedent for this concept of fund raising, to give my royalties to the Conservancy. They would live longer than I would, they had sent me up my mountain, I owed them a debt. It took an appeal to the Chairman himself to straighten this out so I guess my name had stuck in their minds. Two months ahead of time they invited me to the Annual Conference, to be held in a lush hotel on the outskirts of Tucson, complete with field trips, barbecues, business meetings and at the end a Banquet for several hundred people. At least it had seemed like several hundred when I looked out from my elevated vantage point. I didn't have to go to the business meetings, I was really there to publicize and sell my book. When we weren't being fed, bussed about, taken to desert ranches I sat mostly, a timid new author, in the salesroom with binoculars, tee-shirts, attractive gift items and an equally attractive refreshment table in the rear to lure customers.

By the final afternoon, tired and dusty from a field trip, I had forgotten about that head table, was thinking only that if I sat in my sales corner through the last half hour before it closed we might sell a few more books. At the last moment the new Board Chairman hurried in, a short, brisk man, friendly.

"I guess I have to buy Jonnie Fisk's book," he said cheerily. "Is it too late?" He looked at me in my field clothes—tee-shirt, jeans, tousled hair; realized who I was. He consulted his watch, took the book gently from under my autographing pen.

"You haven't forgotten," he asked, a slight edge in his voice, "that in ten minutes you are due to be sitting at the Head Table with us?" The Capital Letters were implicit in his voice.

I didn't wait to hear more. I was out the door and running, dodging rough gardens, past the swimming pool. Showered, in a long dress, a corsage I had been sent—never mind by whom, Myra—pinned on my shoulder I was correctly in place as we dignitaries were seated behind the flowers and candles. I winked at the Chairman. Twinkled is maybe a better word, friends had arranged a long rum sour for me when they saw me dashing through the palm trees.

I felt properly honored, looking out over the room, although I couldn't take my authorship seriously. How did the Conservancy know there would *be* any royalties? The climax of the dinner, after the usual speeches, was the presentation of an Award (with more speeches) to the Honorable Nathaniel P. Reed, former Assistant Secretary of the Interior under two U.S. Presidents. I first met Nat in Florida when I was a lowly Audubon member from the Everglades selling tickets at some function. Nat never forgets anyone. We ran into each other occasionally, we were on the National Audubon Board together. The years I worked on Least tern, trying to get protection for them on Atlantic coastal beaches, I ended up reporting directly to him, going to his office at Interior as casually as I might have to Brad's in the Commerce Department. Brad was an Assistant Secretary too, so to me the occupants of these high offices are just men, I needn't genuflect.

It had been rumored that Nat wouldn't get to the banquet, he had been ill, but he was there. His Award was for what he had done so passionately, so effectively for conservation, for wildlife, for saving Alaskan wilderness. Standing at the far end of our long table he spoke briefly, graceful and humorous as always. When he had finished, brushing aside the men about

him, "I have something I want to do," he said. I don't think
he knew his voice went out over the microphone, over the big
room. Slowly he made his way along the back of our table;
past the Directors, past the Chairman, past the flowers to where
I sat; leaned over and kissed me. In front of all those people!
Nat! I was stunned. He was whisked away before I could speak.

Looking across Pleasant Bay to the barrier beach that pro-
tects our mainland I see again the gardens of that luxurious
hotel, its lobby jostling with people I didn't know; the crowded
cocktail terrace before the dinner, Nat very tall and angular
with his equally tall, handsome wife standing out above the
others. It had taken more than one rum sour to get me to that
Head Table. One of the chief ingredients bartenders sell is
courage.

I am kept alive by pills of various sizes, shapes and colors.
They strangle me. I hate them. The tiniest is the most expensive. I complain to Dr. Robert.

"You are still alive, aren't you?" he soothes, writing a pre-
scription for a new one.

"Aargh" I snarl. "Their instructions say some are to be taken
only with food, some never with food. Never with alcohol. I
take them all together, at breakfast, lunch and dinner. When

I go to bed I take them with the glass of wine I have to put me to sleep, give me dramatic dreams."

"You're still alive, aren't you?" he asks again, laughing. He writes down my blood pressure. "You pay rent for the roof that shelters you. Look at these pills as a roof over your life, sheltering it. Come back in a month."

"Aargh" I snarl at him again. "I have programs in New York, Ohio, Boston. And three book fairs. Besides you'll be on vacation on your island in the Caribbean, I'd die and you'd never know it."

"I have to keep you going to finish that book you're writing." He pats my shoulder. He knows I love him, trust him. I tell Dr. Robert things I don't tell other people, even my publisher, like about a book I am working on. I took most of it to the dump last week, but I am struggling with it again.

I go out for dinner, forgetting my pills.

October 1988

What are you *doing*, staying indoors on a day like this? I sputter at myself. It's been Indian Summer all week while you've crouched over this machine writing an article no one will care about five years from now—two years from now. Give those men driving down from Boston pot roast instead of fussing over the fancy Mexican dish it will take an hour to assemble. Go see the baby whale that washed ashore in Chatham. Lisa says it's lovely—mind-shaking as she walked its length, touched it. Stop being so earnest.

I reach for the telephone. Jean likes to go striding along beaches, through woods. She lives near where the whale beached, she'll know which cove it is in.

The afternoon is glorious—maples and scarlet oaks flame

against evergreens and blue sky as I drive along Pleasant Bay. The barrier beach on the far side is clear in the crisp air. Jean knows just where to go, whose backyard to trespass through to shorten our route. I glory in being outdoors.

Deep car track run between the tide and the marsh grass. Our whale is a disappointment. Perhaps if we had been able to get close to it, feel its skin as Lisa did, realize its size against our own—but it is obscured by a truck, a front end loader and a half dozen men, the area is roped off. Also as we approach the ground becomes wet, we hadn't thought to wear boots. The men are struggling to secure the dead gray oblong with chains. Each time they think they have succeeded, start slowly hoisting, the animal slips or a chain breaks. An excavation has been bulldozed for it at the town dump, a bystander tells us, and the whale will have to be removed before the tide comes in much further, while the vehicles can still drive through the sand. As we watch the carcass finally inch toward and by us our respect for the men handling it is as great as for the body of their charge. The cetacean is just a lump of flesh and blubber, nothing at all romantic about it.

"When you're dead you're dead," says Jean, a practical woman. "If you believe in reincarnation does this apply also to whales? To the skunks and raccoons, the squirrels we see run over on the roads? The dove that broke its neck against my picture window this morning? They are animated by spirit too. Do you see the air as full of ghosts?"

I look out over the Bay, sparkling in autumn light. It is empty. "Only when my stairs creak at night, something I can't identify wakes me," I answer. "We'd better be on our way before that loader drops the whale again, if it slides off on Route 28 there'll be no cars moving for an hour."

I'd thought there would be a flock of gulls following this creature like pall bearers, but there are just a dozen of us curious humans.

I've been away. Only to western Massachusetts but I made four stops to see friends so I am not yet settled back into myself. When I wake in gray light this morning the last thing I want to do is pull on jeans, eat a sketchy breakfast and drive ten miles to my last bird-banding session of the season. Aurele will be there, she is always on time, helpful, cheerful; she will have opened the nets, she doesn't mind if I am not awake enough to chat with her. This late in the season there won't be children, probably only a few adults. It's late for migrant birds, I'll have only chickadees and jays to work with. If them.

At the Sanctuary I set out pliers, bands and notebooks, go the round of the nets finding nothing. I move slowly, my hip hurts from sitting all yesterday in a car. I walk a trail to see if there may still be Yellowlegs in the tidal pools. This is a routine I've followed, with minor variations, for eight years here. Surprisingly, on my return I find an audience watching with interest as Aurele takes, from the cotton bags she carries them in, a jay and a cardinal, a house finch and a chickadee, putting these into our compartmented holding box. I suppose I say pretty much the same thing every time but it comes out always differently as questions send me off in unplanned directions. No one seems to mind that I leap from the shape of a bill to the destruction of tropical forests, from the purposes of banding to work I did in the Everglades, in Arizona. When we have no birds (or only a jay to work with for an hour!) I talk about my birding adventures and about my books, set out on the table. The Sanctuary makes $6.00 on every sale.

Today the group is interested and of an easy size to handle, in a few minutes I am enjoying myself. I take them down the hill to see our demonstration net in the woods, tell them how there may be two miles of nylon thread in it. Originally they were brought to this country by Dr. Oliver Austin, Jr., who with his father monitored more than five hundred tree swallows and bluebird houses scattered about the fields when they lived here working intensively on the terns of Cape Cod. Yellowed articles they published are on my shelves, much thumbed. I write Oliver, now in Florida, retired from a distinguished career, how the trees he and his father planted have grown, what goes on now in the way of educational programs, how swallows still nest in his barns, delighting visitors as they swoop in and out, cramming insects into the gaping red mouths of their young. My programs are supposed to run for an hour but often they are longer as newcomers arrive at our table, ask their questions.

At last today I carry our holding box and my stool back inside. I stand for a moment looking at the swallow nests, now empty, built on top of earlier ones on the rafters. I think of the many times I have stood on my stool, reaching for the half-grown chicks inside, bracing myself against a wall, handing them down to someone holding a hat for them. I have never had reports back on their bands so this year I didn't make the effort. Our curly-capped, blond Sanctuary manager appears while I am still standing in the barn. He is always full of bounce and vigor. While I was still curled under a blanket he will have been out chasing whales or turtles, organizing a hawk watch, doing whatever it is he does eighteen hours a day. I used to be like that too, it was marvelous. Not any more. He carries my table in. He is excited about something, it concerns me. What can it be? I am too tired to concentrate.

"Next spring," he starts. I interrupt him.

"No, Bob," I say firmly. "Next spring I'm not going to do this. Eight years are enough. I'm stale, I'm too old. You have a dozen other programs going now, you don't need me."

Unbelieving, he looks at me, speechless. Bob's being speechless is about as uncharacteristic as is my being speechless. He sees I mean what I have said.

After a minute, slowly, "Yesterday"—his blue eyes hold mine—"yesterday I received a grant from the State to bus the fifth and sixth grades of every school on the Cape here next spring. Aurele will go into the classes ahead of time, work with the teachers and the children. Then they will come to you for a hands-on session—to see the birds you hold to their ears to hear the incredibly rapid heartbeats, to learn the differences in bills and feet—all the stuff you teach. The classes will come right through the migration, May into June, and already we are getting requests from out-of-state groups, more even than we've had this year; for whale watching, trips to Monomoy, walks on Seashore dunes, workshops. You are on the programs for all of these."

I don't answer. His eyes question me.

"No," I say finally, picking up my car keys. "I've done this long enough, Bob. I'm sorry."

I cry all the way home. I'm old. I've paid my dues. If there is no one at the moment to replace me someone will come along. No one is irreplaceable.

I sleep all afternoon, then go out for dinner, sitting by a man not much younger than I. Retired, he is putting his lifetime of executive experience into community organizations. His wife volunteers effectively too. I tell him my problem.

"These young men I've worked with all these years who take me out in their boats and trucks (as if I knew more than they do!) who bring me into their programs, they all expect me to go on forever, full tilt. So I've had to. Because the work they do is valuable, because they are so sure I can help them, want to help them. I suppose"—I manage a laugh—"I'd rather die with my boots on, in a river, on a mountain, climbing a sand dune than in bed. Can you die sitting at a typewriter? I shouldn't think so. But I'm weary. I can't keep on."

"Is it the banding or the lecturing you want to stop?" asks Philip.

"The lecturing," I answer promptly. "I love banding. It keeps me outdoors, I can do it in Mexico or Ecuador, or stretch a net in my own yard. It's peaceful. I am always learning something. Maybe not something important, but enough to write an occasional paper that gets published. Summers, though I drive about New England talking, I am tied to the Sanctuary, must fit everything into their frame. Actually," I finish rebelliously, "I want to do *nothing*. Read. Prune my bushes. Lie in a hammock I bought years ago in Carolina and never get to use. Sleep."

"How many people come to your programs?" Philip asks.

"Oh—at demonstrations some days a dozen, in midsummer maybe forty. Two or three times a week. It's hard to count them. There are new faces when I'm halfway through, I have to repeat. At formal lectures maybe a hundred. Or sixteen."

"And how many programs do you give a year?"

I am too tired to see where he is leading me. "Fifty?" I hazard. "A hundred or more this past year, I don't keep track, it would scare me."

He slides a second piece of Eve's good chocolate pie that neither of us should indulge in onto my plate. He lays his hand gently on mine. "May I suggest, my dear, that throwing your nets over people is more valuable to the conservation you care

ERMA J. FISK

about than throwing them over birds? These schoolchildren
who will come to you . . ." He leaves it to me to finish his
sentence. As I do, driving home, crying again.

Today Aurele and I are taking down the last nets, putting
away poles and guy ropes. We sit on the steps, resting. She
says nothing, but looks at me, questioning.

"Children," I say at last. "If you go into the schools, prepare
them as Bob plans, you are doing two thirds of our work along
with all the other volunteer jobs you carry here and never complain about. If out of thirty children each time we reach five
. . . there are always a few who really listen, who may take
fire, go on into some field of biology, of conservation. More
learn a respect for the birds that fly through their yards, the
fox and heron and turtles who also belong on our earth. They
may take their new knowledge home to their parents, spill it
over on their friends." I spread my hands. "I guess there's no
way I can quit, is there? I have a bear by the tail—or it has
me." I sit silently, tie a shoe lace. "Maybe next spring I'll feel
stronger. Or"—I laugh—"I'll be dead. Then you'll have to do
it all."

Aurele laughs too. "Bob didn't dare tell you that what with
weather and school bus schedules you'd be on call five days a
week. But he knows you'll do it." There is still question in her
voice.

Without thinking—"There are holes in the nets that were
in the berry patch," I answer. "I can mend them next week"—
and realize I have answered her, committed myself.

Well, I ask myself on the drive home, what else do you
have to do? That you know how to do as well? That matters
as much as this does? The children you teach are going to have

to handle our planet, clean up the messes our generation has made. Tonight I call Bob.

"All right," I tell him reluctantly, "if you really want me, if I am still alive."

He laughs. "I thought you would," he says.

They won't let me quit, these young people I work with. I should be grateful to them.

"Do you like flying in small planes? Would you like me to fly you around Cape Cod when the weather clears?" This is Anne LeClaire on the telephone. I don't really know her, we spoke together at a Book Tea.

"Would I! Any day, any time," I answer in excitement.

Flying has always been an adventure, from the day when I was first taken barn-storming on a grassy field. Flying across the vast, varied expanse of our continent in the days when this took eleven hours if all went well; across the Alps in a storm, over the Andes, the seas of India, Japan, Indonesia, the Caribbean; checking eagle nests and the heronries of Everglades National Park, leaning out the window because, *faute de mieux,* I had become the Park photographer. Flying the coast of the Gulf of Mexico, the Bay of Honduras. Short hops to Boston, astonished at the number of small lakes on the way, the geography so different from that seen on the busy highways; along Long Island Sound to New York, flying low enough to recognize homes I had stayed in, beaches I had walked.

My most fun flight had been in the bucket seat of an ancient training plane from the Adirondacks to south Florida. On a fine day we flew over the sprawl of New York City, the hideous industrial highways of New Jersey I used to dread so, driving north and south each year. It had been a July 4th weekend, the coastal beaches I had tramped making bird surveys were crowded, the water dotted with miniature sailboats, the sand with miniature, bifurcated stick people in bright colors. We had passed over historical plantations, forts of past centuries. The plane had two seats only, one behind the other. Mine restricted movement. I knew enough not to put my feet on levers but when I grew restless I would rest my elbow on a convenient sort of ledge. That night, over dinner, Ralph, an old Navy pilot, told me this was a vital part of the mechanism. The first time I had put weight on it the plane nose-dived, in alarm he had searched for a meadow where he might land. Looking at my reflection in the windshield he had uncovered the problem, and allowed for it thereafter when he saw me shifting in my seat.

"Kept me on the alert," he said. "It gets pretty dull flying such long hours, cramped up." We were on the alert too when we flew over government installations. That air was forbidden, we weren't sure of the boundaries. The only map Ralph could find on our stops were of where we had been, not of where we were going. Fortunately it was the holiday, no one intercepted us.

We had put down every three hours for gas, a coke and a check-up. The plane's top speed was ninety miles an hour, by evening we were only halfway. Myrtle Beach, where we expected to overnight, was jammed not only with holiday crowds but by a convention. The airport clerk offered armchairs in his lobby for $10.00 apiece. Unbelieving Ralph telephoned motels until I plucked insistently at his sleeve.

"It's almost dark," I begged. "This man says Georgetown isn't much further, if we hurry we can still land there."

Georgetown's small grassy field was dark, no one in attendance. We took toothbrushes and pajamas from our luggage and started walking. An elderly man picked us up, listened with amusement to our story. Georgetown also had a convention, complete with parades and more visitors than the town could accommodate. He scratched an unshaven chin.

"Old Mamie Hopkins sometimes takes people in," he said. "She has two rooms on her third floor." He turned in his seat and looked us over. "She charges $5.00, you good for that?"

Thinking of what two rooms in Myrtle Beach would have cost us we assured him we were. He looked us over again, noting the disparity in our ages. "For Pete's sake don't let her know you ain't married," he cautioned. "She won't let you up the stairs. I better go in first, see as she'll take you."

Mrs. Hopkins not only would but the dear old lady was so flustered at the thought of unexpected money that we needn't sign the guest book on her table. She had only one room. It provided one chair, one chest and a narrow iron double bed. At the Dry Tortugas and elsewhere the quarters were unisex but biologists are impersonal. We each had our own sack, we rose before light, went to bed in the dark of a lantern or candle. Depositing our toothbrushes Ralph found us a restaurant which didn't serve liquor but had an open door leading into a bar. We were hot and tired, Ralph from flying, me from looking out the window, enjoying. He fetched us each a drink, then, studying me, suggested, "I think you'd better have a second."

I agreed. "I'm not as accustomed to sharing a bed as I expect you are. I'm glad you're thin, Do you kick, thrash or snore?"

"You'll find out," he said cheerfully. Clutching my edge of the mattress I slept poorly, heard another couple mount the stairs to the second bedroom, brush their teeth.

"I decided I couldn't make a funny story of this, tell my children," I say to Anne. "It would besmirch our family name.

This was before Women's Lib, before women kept their own names, casually shared beds with men. I certainly never had."

Anne laughs. "My front seat is comfortable, and I guess not much scares you. Meet me at the airport at nine o'clock, depending on the weather?"

When I am working on a book I pull off to the side of the road to sketch a paragraph. I wonder what Anne does, flying in a plane?

I used to look forward with eagerness to each excursion. But now—is it familiarity or the laziness of age that airplanes have become only crowded buses where I must fight for luggage space, for elbow room, be interminably delayed, lose my suitcase? Last year I was flying to New York to address a prestigious women's organization. Feeling I should appear in suitable sartorial elegance I had bought a new outfit, packed it with care. When our small Cape puddle jumper arrived in New York I had only my handbag. My host produced an ice-green Japanese robe far too elegant to sleep in and a limp hairbrush that had survived since his college days. A manuscript needed for a meeting the next morning was also in that vanished suitcase, which, without apology, was delivered to me eight days later. Coming back from my last trip to the Virgin Islands a duffel bag reached me nearly a month later, but as it held mostly dirty laundry, sneakers, a sleeping bag and bathing suit I didn't mind. It also had the pills I take four times a day, but I survived, I could buy more here.

So I don't fly as eagerly as I used to. To reach Boston, rather than chance summer fog or winter blizzards at the local small airport it is easier to drive my car to Barnstable, wait for the bus that will take me to Logan Airport (allowing plenty of extra time, like an hour, for traffic jams) then wait again for my next flight. I study the shoes of the passersby to occupy the time. Unless—one afternoon I was catching a small plane for Albany, to give an evening program. On arrival at Logan I found the gate had been moved.

"Run," bade the woman at the information booth. "The gate is now at the extreme end of the airport. No, there's not time for the shuttle bus. *Run.*"

I was lugging a heavy carton of books as well as a suitcase. I have a heart condition. I ran. The plane was being held for another passenger, a man panting equally. Sometimes too, at the other end a gate has been changed, as in Chicago where I was to be met by a stranger; as in Buffalo late one afternoon where the nature center that was my only contact had closed; as in Mexico one midnight, in torrential rain. . . . However deeply I bury the memory of that last it is always in my mind.

When finally I do arrive wherever, fortified by airplane peanuts and fruit juice, with luck by a short snooze, I usually am met and transported by strangers. which involves social chatter when what I need is peace. There will be a dinner with people I don't know who are expecting someone more glamorous, or intellectual, or humorous. I am on display.

Why do I do this, why am I here," I rebelliously asked the man beside me at dinner on my last such expedition. "I have to wonder what motivates me, why I subject myself to this." I emptied my wine glass at a gulp.

He considered me thoughtfully. He was the head of a corporation, his job was motivating people.

"Because you enjoy taking risks. However they turn out I expect you profit from them. It's why people come to listen to you. It motivates them to open out to life." He smiled. "Am I right?"

I considered him, and his words as thoughtfully, then nodded.

"There has to be someone above—St. Anthony, perhaps a Papago Indian god—someone has watched over me these past few years, who won't let me go until it is my time, until in His eyes I am no longer useful. It doesn't seem to be for me to say. It's hard for me to look at my work objectively. If you call this work." I looked about at the tables of diners, the friendly faces, the good dinner on our plates in an attractive room; at the stack of my books waiting to be autographed, the proceeds of which would further conservation causes I believe in. "I get more than I give from an evening like this."

He patted my arm, held my chair as I rose, held my eyes as we parted. Often since when I have been tired, when I have felt I have served my purpose in life and can honorably quit I see again his thoughtful gray eyes, the firm mouth above his firm chin. I don't believe in myself but if someone like him does . . .

"Yes," I answer a voice on the telephone requesting a program. "Only you had better arrange for a back-up speaker. I may be snowbound, or dead." They always laugh when I say this. They don't worry. Just me, I do.

November 1988

Languidly soothing a sore throat with lemon juice and honey I am languidly also trying to soothe my ego by considering the accomplishments of my last few years (in case I don't have any more). Ignoring the failures I concentrate instead on the pleasure of so many friends remet in my travels, the many interesting new ones even if I fail to recognize them when I meet them out of context, when I fail to remember their names. The nicer ones forgive me on the basis of my being a crone, saying they are forgetful too. In my dictionary a crone is "a withered old woman" but when I said that the other night a Native American reassured me. In his culture, he said firmly, "a crone is a woman wise, full of knowledge, of medicine powers; often of few words, but direct in speech. Revered." This presented a different picture, especially those "few words," and I'd translate "direct in speech" as "tactless," but I paused in front of the next mirror I passed to look for signs of the knowledge, the medicine power.

I told Dr. Robert this today as he thumped my chest and again he said, "You aren't the woman you were ten years ago. No worse," he added, seeing me bristle, "Different. You've done a lot of living these last few years." I wanted to discuss my medicine power, stack it up against his, but he was too busy.

Ten years ago, I think now, what excited me, what depressed me? It's hard to remember. I had sore throats then, I survived. What will I survive for this year? I have a psychic friend who wants to read my cards, maybe she can tell me. She claims I have a blue aura with purple bells about its edges. Blue is the color of serenity, she says, purple the color for royalty.

Serenity, like beauty, is only in the eye of the beholder, she should see what churns inside that calm face I present to her. I picture royalty as a woman in a full long skirt and jewels, erect in a velvet chair, with servants, not out in jeans raking leaves on a driveway. Still—on a recent trip to the Midwest, where I encountered no Native Americans, I was constantly, courteously put into cars, handed out of them. Not once did I carry my suitcase, refill my plate at buffets, have to stand in a coffee line. I was guided carefully down an unlit, uncertain path at night, a gesture I accepted although a year ago to have had my elbow held would have outraged me. Maybe I am learning to grow old gracefully? I'll have to read up on medicine power. I thought Native Americans put their crones out in the snow when they were no longer useful, or drew lots to see who should hit them over the head with a pipe. I'd better hunt around for some way to keep being useful, then I needn't worry yet.

December 1988

> The old year slips past
>   Unseen, the way a snake goes.
> Vanishes
>   and the grass closes behind it.

writes Donald Justice on the first page of *The Sunset Maker,* given me for Christmas. He must have been young when he wrote that, not yet having noted how the small events of a day or a year leave their mark under the changing light of sun and storm; how the grass never wholly closes, is always in motion from wind, the passage of a mouse, a feather settling from the air; from the path of a rabbit, a coyote, lovers. There are bright flashes of wildflowers, bare patches exposing soil, rocks, potholes that nourish unseen life. Or is it age that teaches us to look each day for the small happinesses that connect us to the universal web?

When I was young I also let the years slip past, too busy to record all but framework, or events that burst like rockets in beauty and fire, tearing the fabric of time. A need to savor each day, the benefits of motion in the grass came slowly to me, tempering loneliness and fear, sending me to bed each night in some measure accommodated to what the day might have brought me.

This journal has not been a daily recital. It is bits and pieces of what has surfaced in my days, has let my mind drift quietly into sleep at night. It is not even chronological, so that on the page of a day headed January on my desk calendar I am not here at my window on Cape Cod but am in another year, entering a hospital door carrying a small suitcase, a sack of books I won't read. Or on a May morning I may be out on a wide beach in Carolina, counting skimmers; studying terns from a truck. The years overlap. A child running across a field recalls another child running a generation ago. Never mind what medical men say, the heart beats irregularly.

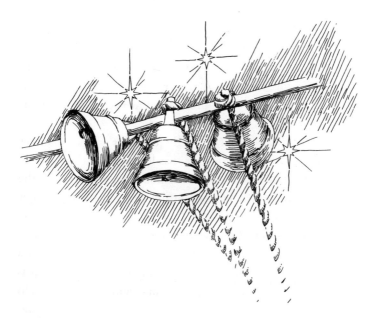

New Year's Eve 1988

My desk is cleared. I have paid the town tax bill that arrived
the day before Christmas, the plumber's bill that came the day
after; have wrapped for mailing a jacket left by a departed
grandchild. Over the last of the eggnog, by the embers of a
fire I have finished a Christmas book. A bowl of paperwhite
narcissus spreads its fragrance through the room.

Although it is not yet midnight I turn down the thermostat
and go upstairs. I close my bedroom door on the exuberance
of the holidays, the joys, the challenges, the failures of the
past year. On friends lost or gained; hopes fulfilled and hopes
unfulfilled; regrets and pain forgotten, or buried deep. All
sealed off into the past by the closing of my bedroom door.

I lean out a window into the dark, remembering the resonant voice of a desert friend quoting Emerson on another New Year's Eve.

> Ring out, wild bells, in the wild sky:
> The flying cloud, the frosty light.
> The year is dying in the night.
> Ring out, wild bells, and let him die.

No bells are ringing, the night is silent. Out there in the quiet awaits a new year. No horoscope, no palmist, no doctor can tell me what it will bring—what sorrows or joys, what measures of love. Below my hill the tide is rising. Above my trees the stars are bright. From far away I half hear, half sense a stirring in the air, a vibration. It is an owl hooting, calling in the future, marking a new calendar. Presaging what?